GW00374356

The Tenant's Tale

A Chronicle of life in rural Ireland during the 19th Century

Terence Casey

First published in 2013 by
Dolman Scott Ltd

The Tenant's Tale© 2013 by
Terence Casey

Cover design by
Terence Casey

ISBN 978-1-909204-18-8

Dolman Scott Ltd
www.dolmanscott.com

*This book is dedicated to my wife Margaret
who was my inspiration*

INTRODUCTION

In September eighteen ninety, I left my family home in Grafton Street in the fashionable part of Dublin and travelled by train to the rural town of Charleville, County Cork to take up the position as a trainee teacher at the local National School. As I had only recently passed my exams at college I was very apprehensive about this journey into the unknown. But on my arrival at Charleville station I was pleasantly surprised to be met by my future colleague another very young man named Joseph Connelly.

On the long walk into town I soon realised that I had a great deal in common with my new companion, as he also was from Dublin and like me was very keen on sporting pursuits. On reaching the town Joseph took me to my lodgings where he introduced me to the landlady Kitty Egan. Mrs Egan made me very welcome and after showing me to my room I was invited into her kitchen for a bite to eat. That afternoon I went with Joseph on a tour of the town and was also shown around the school.

The new term started on the following Monday and with Joseph's help I quickly settled in. Fortunately the pupils that I taught both boys and girls were all very industrious and eager to learn which obviously made my task a great deal easier.

But after living in a large city I found the pace of life in Charleville very slow and wondered if I had made the right decision. Luckily my colleague Joseph realising that I was homesick encouraged me to join the local Gaelic Association club. At college I had excelled at both hurling and football so I soon became an integral part of a successful Charleville team. Although the playing of Gaelic sports was its main aim, cultural activities were also encouraged. Joseph, who spoke fluently in the Irish language worked tirelessly during the evenings teaching and encouraging others to learn their native tongue. As I settled into my new life I gradually became aware that the Charleville area was a hot bed of radical thinking with a long tradition of supporting the Nationalist cause dating back to Daniel O'Connell's time.

As an ardent supporter of Home Rule, I quickly became actively involved in politics locally and was befriended by Jack Casey the editor of The Charleville Courier. Jack was always looking for ways to boost the circulation of his paper and when I suggested that I could interview some of the areas local Fenians and recount their stories, he jumped at the idea. Over the next few weeks he

I

drew up a list of all the old Republicans that I should visit. Many of these men had been arrested and imprisoned after the attack on Kilmallock barrack during the abortive uprising in March eighteen sixty-seven. Most of them told me about the long sentences they had served and the appalling treatment that they had received at the hands of the authorities. Mr Casey was pleased with my articles as people all over County Cork were, it seemed, very interested in them. At his insistence the last person I interviewed was his cousin Patrick Casey of Springfort. At the time I thought that this was a strange request but in retrospect I now know why it was because Patrick's memories of a bygone age were fascinating and needed to be told. At first I began by telling his story in a series of articles, but because this did not seem to do him justice I decided to write this book. This narrative spans virtually the whole of the nineteenth century, a century that has been the most traumatic in Ireland's long and troubled history. Patrick witnessed first hand many of the tragedies that befell our Nation and somehow managed to survive the Famine. Also he was privileged to hear Daniel O'Connell speak and also meet and converse with Archbishop Croke of Cashel, the most charismatic clergyman of his age. Lastly and most importantly he met and was befriended by his famous cousin the founder of the Fenians, James Stephens. He was very fortunate because with Stephens help he obtained work during the famine years. He would later repay the debt by giving Stephens and his friend Michael Doheny sanctuary whilst they were on the run after the abortive rising in eighteen forty-eight.

As we will see Patrick had a very humble upbringing as his parents were extremely poor. But somehow his mother managed to pay for him to be educated, a luxury she herself had been denied. All through his life he remembered the sacrifices she had made on his behalf and her determination for him to better himself. Ultimately this was to lead to him and his brother Owen leaving Ireland to seek their fortune.

Their travels took them to England where after working as farm labourers the two brothers eventually became navvies working firstly on canal building and subsequently working on the world's first passenger railroad that linked the two great cities of Liverpool and Manchester. This work although very arduous was extremely well paid and by both being frugal they managed to save sufficient funds to return home and get a tenancy on a small farm near Charleville. This was the opportunity Patrick and his brother had dreamed of and they immediately began to implement farming methods that they had witnessed on their travels. These changes would ultimately improve their yields in the preceding years. But unfortunately this brief interlude in Patrick's life was shattered when his brother was falsely accused and transported.

This barbaric act by the authorities totally altered Patrick's attitude and from that time onwards he realised that the corrupt administration that governed Ireland would stop at nothing in imposing its authority. Although he never became an active Fenian he gradually came to understand that Ireland sadly would never achieve independence without an armed uprising. Unfortunately the country was not ready each time a rising occurred during his lifetime and also government spies had always infiltrated the Irish patriot organisations with disastrous consequences.

Patrick was in essence a family man, whose only thought was to feed and keep a roof over the heads of his family during the dreadful years of the Famine. Luckily with his past experience he managed to find work on the railroads that were being constructed in Ireland during that period. He was also to witness the near miracle of his brother Owens return from Australia, unfortunately Owen could not settle in Ireland and returned to Australia, lured like thousands of others by rumours that immense amounts of gold had been found in that colony.

Patrick and his wife had three sons and he was somewhat fortunate because unlike most families in Ireland where every one of their youngsters had emigrated, he was only to lose his eldest son who went to America. Luckily he had persuaded his other two sons to stay in Ireland and with his financial help they were eventually to become successful dairy farmers.

What I found most revealing about his story was the burning desire he had to one day purchase his beloved Springfort, an ambition that was finally to come into fruition over sixty years after his signing his first tenancy agreement. But he also confided in me how angry and frustrated he was at the way he and his fellow Irishmen had been treated throughout his long lifetime. At our last meeting he expressed the hope that I would eventually see our proud nation take its place in the world free from all outside interference.

Most of what I have written came from his reminisces but many of his journals have survived and they were a tremendous help to me. My only hope is that I have written a book that gives a true reflection of the life and struggles of an ordinary Irish tenant farmer who lived through one of the most extraordinary centuries in the history of Ireland. Sadly when I visited Springfort in early January eighteen ninety-four, Patrick was very ill and we were never to meet again.

RIP Patrick William Casey.
Born 26/12/1804. Deceased 20/01/1894

Thomas Harrington
Charleville National School.
County Cork.
19/10/1897

CHAPTER ONE

I, Patrick John Casey, was born on St. Stephens Day, the twenty sixth of December eighteen hundred and four, in a tiny cabin on the road between Charleville and Buttevant in County Cork. My parents John and Mary Casey would only have one other child, my brother and life long friend Owen. The intriguing tale of how my parents met has always fascinated me, as they both came from totally different parts of Ireland. In the following narrative I recount how fate brought them together.

As I grew up, I knew my father as a gentle giant of a man who had sadly fallen on hard times and was now one of the many spalpeens or farm labourers who tramped the country hoping to find work. But in his youth he had been the County Cork Wrestling Champion, who before being badly injured had high hopes of one day becoming the All Ireland Champion. His family had always lived in the vicinity of Charleville and when his wrestling days finished he would eventually return there with his young wife.

As a wrestler, to earn a living, he had toured the fair grounds of the south west of Ireland during the summer months, issuing a challenge to anyone who thought they could beat him for a purse of one pound. In later years he would tell us that he had fought hundreds of men but had only ever lost on two occasions. His only regret, he said, was that he wished he had saved some of that hard earned money. Sadly he told us, the only time he managed to save any money was in the brief few months between meeting our mother and his tragic injury.

My mother Mary Casey, nee O'Sullivan, was originally from a tiny village called Dreenagh. This very remote village lies deep in the Macgillycudy's Reeks mountain range in County Kerry. The people who came from this area, because of its remoteness have always retained many of the old Celtic ways and customs. Also they still have their own unique language, much of which my mother taught me as a child. The nearest town of Killorglin is nearly twenty miles from Beerenaugh and mother and her family normally only made this long journey once a year. This annual visit was obviously the highlight of their year. Preparations for it, she later told us, would start weeks in advance, with any livestock they hoped to sell being specially fattened up for the occasion. This was vital for the family's survival in the harsh winter weather that they always encountered on their mountain farm. She told us that all the income her father received from the sale of their cattle would be spent on the supplies they needed for the coming year. If there was any surplus money he would always buy all the family a small present. He was unlike most of the other small farmers who after selling their cattle wasted most of their money on drink. She would always tell us that Patrick O'Sullivan her father was the kindest man she had ever known. Unfortunately we never met him because I was very young when he passed away.

Their yearly pilgrimage to town always coincided with the famous Puck Fair. This fair, was always the largest of its kind in Ireland and in those times would last for a whole week. It still traditionally takes place in early August, but because of its terrible reputation for riotous behaviour, it has now been shortened to three days.

Very early one August morning in the year eighteen hundred and one, all my mothers' family left Beerenaugh driving their small herd of cattle before them. Little did my mother know that when she left for Puck Fair that morning, as a young girl of eighteen, her life was about to change for ever. It was a long tiring walk to Killorglin, but being young and very excited mother and her two sisters Kitty and Bridget, raced along with both their parents struggling to keep up with them. By mid-morning they were in town watching their father sell his livestock. Fortunately she recalls, farm prices were very good that year and so after buying all the provisions they needed, her father gave his three daughters sixpence each. This was, my mother told us, the most money she had ever had in her life. As she walked through the Fair wondering how she would spend her windfall, she recalls being attracted by the cheering and shouting of a large crowd. For some strange reason she pushed her way to the front of the throng, just in time to see crowds of well-wishers lifting their hero up onto their shoulders before parading him around a makeshift ring. When she looked up at the happy smiling face of the victor, my mother always said in later years that it was love at first sight. But for our father this was his chance to issue a challenge to all comers, hoping that he would be able to quickly attract another opponent. As my mother stood there watching all this happening in front of her, the local blacksmith James Carney stepped into the ring and said he would accept my fathers challenge. The blacksmith was renowned for his amazing strength and my mother recalls shaking with fear when my father accepted his challenge for a purse of four pounds. When the fight started, she soon realised that although

John Carney was enormously strong he was no match for my father. Father she recalls was too quick for his opponent in thought and deed and each time the blacksmith thought he had my father cornered he slipped through his grasp. As each round ended, my mother's earlier fears for her new hero quickly vanished, as she could see that his opponent was rapidly tiring. The end when it came was both brutal and savage, John Carney's supporters realising that their man was very tired were now urging him to make one final attempt to finish the fight. In his desperation he rushed blindly at my father who had been patiently waiting for this opportunity. My mother said that she had never seen anyone move so fast, as the blacksmith rushed towards him my father used the momentum of his opponent to throw him high into the air; there was then a deathly hush as the blacksmith went crashing to the ground. Sadly my father was to find out later that both of Carney's legs had been broken in the fall. But for a brief few minutes my father was once again the hero and he was jubilant when he collected the four pounds for his endeavours.

The news of his victory against the local champion quickly spread around the town of Killorglin and although he was to spend the next hour issuing his challenge to all comers, nobody came forward. Within thirty minutes everyone had left the scene of my fathers triumph, apart from one young lady and this was my mother. She said she now felt sorry for him as he stood there alone and so plucking up courage she approached him. My father now realising that his days work was over bent down to pick up his jacket off the ground, only to find it being handed to him by a very beautiful girl. He was he recalls speechless for a moment as she congratulated him on his famous victory, but my father was never quiet for long and he was soon answering all my mothers' questions. By now they were both very tired and hungry and my father suggested that he would buy some food from one of the many stalls at the fair. Unknown to them my mother's parents and her sisters were combing the fair looking for her as they were now very anxious to start their long journey home. On finding his daughter chatting to a stranger her father was not very pleased and quickly ushered her away.

During the long walk home she wondered if she was ever to meet the wrestler again, but it was then she remembered that he had told her that after Puck Fair he was heading to the town of Kenmare. This town was over twenty five miles from her village but she at once made her mind up to go there as she knew she must see my father again. As they neared home, she suddenly realised

3

that because of everything that had happened she was still in the possession of her sixpence piece. The next day all the family were busy saving the hay and when they stopped to have the midday meal she told her father of her intention to meet the young stranger again. She was very surprised she said when he agreed to go with her to Kenmare. He wanted, he said, to buy some young pigs but she found out later that this was just an excuse as he knew he would never be able to stop her from meeting my father again.

The journey from her village to Kenmare was very hazardous at that time because it was across many miles of wild mountain paths and bogs and although they left at first light they did not get to their destination until well after dark. Once in town her father she remembers, found the house of a friend who thankfully gave them lodgings for the night. Although very tired from the long walk she still woke up very early the next morning as she was anxious to find out if my father was in town. After a hurried breakfast it was decided that she would make a search of the fair whilst her father made his purchases. Much to her annoyance after making many enquiries, she could not find any trace of her wrestler friend and was getting very despondent, but when she met up with her father he had good news. The wrestler John Casey, would, he had been told be wrestling Vincent Foley the pride of Castletownbeare that afternoon. On hearing this she made her way to the fairground and found my father who was constructing his makeshift ring. On seeing him she was filled with apprehension, worrying that he might have forgotten her. But all her fears quickly evaporated, as he was obviously very elated at seeing her once again. He immediately stopped what he was doing and lifted her high into the air. On seeing that her father was with her he became embarrassed and slowly lowered her to the ground. But on seeing his embarrassment my mother and her father started to laugh and assured him that they understood his actions.

As they stood chatting they were interrupted by the arrival of Vincent Foley and his supporters. My mother recalls that suddenly fathers whole demeanour changed, one second he was his happy smiling self, but now with the realisation that his fight was imminent he became the warrior that she had witnessed at Puck Fair. The brutal affair that followed in the next hour was talked about for years afterwards. Foley was well known for the dirty tactics he used and on that day he employed every trick he knew. My mother covered her face in horror for most of the fight fearing that her man would be beaten to pulp, but father, as always, waited for his opponent to tire and become reckless before he pounced with all the ferocity of a wild animal. On this occasion as he was so incensed at Foley's behaviour during the fight, he showed him no mercy and had to be dragged off his opponent. After they had carried his opponent away my father again issued his challenge to the vast throng that had gathered, but once again there were no takers. The crowds quickly realising that their sport was over for the day soon drifted away. My father was obviously very pleased with his performance and both my mother and her father showered him with praise.

By now the three of them were extremely hungry and so they decided to have a meal together. As they chatted that evening my father and mother both realised that they could not bare to part. This it seemed was very evident to mother's father, who sat in silence closely observing the pair of them. Before parting that night mother arranged a meeting with her hero before she returned home. The next morning the three of them had breakfast together but my mother said she was inconsolable at the thought of never seeing John Casey again. She need not have worried because as they ate their meal my father told her he had decided not to wrestle again that year but was going to help a friend who lived in the nearby village of Sneem bring in the harvest. Fortunately Sneem was he said, only about eight miles from their village and with her father's permission he could come and visit. This they all thought was the best solution to the problem. That morning the three of them set out for the mountains, but sadly they had to part again when they reached the crossroad for Sneem. Before leaving my father promised that he would visit my mother in Dreenagh the following weekend.

The next Sunday he left Sneem at daybreak for the long walk to see my mother and on his arrival was introduced to her mother and two sisters. They all welcomed him with open arms and as the weather was ideal for haymaking, he insisted on helping them in the fields. At the end of that first visit he felt like one of the family and when he left, my mother accompanied him on part of his return journey. He returned each Sunday for the rest of that year and it was no surprise when he made a proposal of marriage on Christmas Day. My mother's parents although worried about my father's occupation, realised that the two of them were now inseparable and consented to the wedding. Although my father had spent that autumn and winter farming, he had also kept his fitness by a stringent exercise regime. He was he told us, determined to return to wrestling as soon as possible with the intention of fighting for the All Irish Championship.

My mother and father were married at Shrovetide, in eighteen hundred and two and soon after the wedding they left my mothers village. Sadly she was never to return home again and I know that she never forgave herself for this. But our father had to make a living especially as he now had a wife to support. With the coming of spring they began their first tour together of the fairs of Southwest Ireland. Times were good for them that first year and by the time winter arrived they had managed to save a good portion of my father's winnings. At Christmas time they made their way to my father's hometown of Charleville. Although both of his parents had died, his brother Michael and many relatives still lived in the area and so that Christmas my mother was introduced to all of his family.

At Easter, when they left Charleville my father said he was ready for any challenge that he might face after three months of intensive training. That summer he decided to tour the fairs and race courses of the Irish Midlands as he had heard that they attracted vast crowds. During the first year together they had began to work as a team. On their arrival at a new venue, mother would spend the day handing out handbills that issued a challenge to anyone who thought they could beat her husband. In the mean time her husband was looking for a suitable sight on the fair ground to set up his makeshift ring. For the first couple of months it seemed that father's decision to seek new challenges in a different area of Ireland was paying off. They were both pleased with the amount of money they were making and there were rumours that the Midlands Champion had issued a challenge to fight my father. But tragically a disaster was about to occur that would ultimately finish his wrestling career.

On Whit Sunday, after attending Mass in the town of Ballingarry, mother toured the town giving out her handbills, while our father looked for a site for setting up his ring. They had heard that the Whit Monday Fair Day attracted hundreds of visitors but they were not aware of its terrible reputation. A traveller writing about the scenes he had witnessed years before wrote 'Whit Monday Ballingarry Fair Day, the most vicious fair in Munster or Leinster. For there is many a devilish blackguard with a stealthy stick, many a yeoman, tricky lout and a large- headed rogue with a white knobbed ash -plant cracking senseless skulls and brainless mindless mannerless heads.'

On the Monday morning they were both hoping for another successful day, and it seemed as if their prayers were answered because a large crowd soon gathered to watch my father wrestle. By mid afternoon he had fought and beaten five challengers and a queue of local men had formed all eager to take on the Champion of County Cork. Unfortunately without any warning faction fighting erupted between two rival gangs. My father said later, that he should have realised from the large military presence in the town that trouble was expected. The fighting began in town but gradually spread to the fairground, with more and more of the town's ruffians getting involved. As the fighting intensified the fairground soon resembled a large battlefield, with many of the stalls being wrecked in the melee.

My parents realising the danger began to gather their belongings together but in the confusion they somehow became separated. What happened next was to change their lives forever, my mother thinking that her husband was following her ran as fast as she could away from the fighting, but my father was not so lucky, because as he tried to follow his wife he tripped and fell. Suddenly he could hear the sound of the soldiers advancing on the rioters; he has never been able to say what happened next only that he heard the sound of rifle fire. As he tried to get up he felt a searing pain in his shoulder and then he passed out.

With the arrival of the militia the marauding gangs quickly dispersed, leaving many people injured and at least five men dead. Meanwhile my poor mother was becoming very anxious wondering what had happened to her husband. She now realised that she must return to the fairground to search for him. On reaching the spot where they had set up the ring she became frantic at the sight of a pool of blood nearby, somehow knowing that it was my fathers. By now she was frantic with worry so she ran back into the town fearing the worst. Once in Ballingary she stopped everyone she passed asking if they knew the whereabouts of the casualties from the riot. Eventually she was informed that the seriously injured were being treated in the church by local doctors. The lady who gave her this information, on seeing my mother's condition took her by the hand and led her to the church. She has never forgotten the scene that greeted her; she said the church was full of the dead and wounded. For a young person who had lived in a tiny remote community, the sight of the carnage and the plaintive cries of the dying were almost too much for her. Luckily her companion insisted that they look for her husband. By now father had regained consciousness and was being attended to by one of the doctors. The doctor informed him that although his shoulder was shattered and he was obviously very weak from the loss of so much blood his condition was not life threatening.

It was heartbreaking for my mother as she wandered in a daze looking for my father, but suddenly to her eternal joy she saw him, he was at this moment having his wound bandaged. With a cry she rushed to his side and cradled him in her arms, her companion on seeing the two of them reunited quietly slipped away and sadly they never saw her again. My mother nursed him in that church night and day until she was able to move him to lodgings nearby. It was fortunate that he was in the peak of condition when the tragedy occurred, because within weeks he had made a good recovery. As soon as he was able they made their way back to Charleville, where they spent the rest of the year living with my father's relations. During those long months he worked on farms in the surrounding area trying to regain his strength and fitness. He knew in his heart that his wrestling days were over but he was determined to have one last attempt at resurrecting his career.

In the spring of eighteen hundred and four, father once again began his usual training regime in readiness for the new wrestling season. Then in early April, as they prepared to leave Charleville my mother told him she was expecting her first child. When he heard the news he was overjoyed and wanted to postpone his wrestling activities, but mother would not hear of it, as she knew they were desperately short of money. This time they decided not to return to the Midlands, but to go back to the Fairs in the South West. But after a couple of successful bouts the pain from his injured shoulder became excruciating. My mother quickly realised that he would be seriously injured if he carried on and pleaded with him to stop at once. Sadly he did not listen and he was to have his last wrestling match in Killarney in June eighteen hundred and four. He had only received one challenger that day which he had easily beaten. But with no sign of any other challenges they decided to go for dinner. As they were taking down their makeshift ring my father was surprised to hear a voice saying, "I will wager two pounds that I can beat you". Turning round he saw the blacksmith from Killorglin who he had beaten two years before. The man was obviously looking for revenge and father said he could not refuse the challenge. News of the pending wrestling match quickly spread and soon a large crowd had gathered. My mother could not watch the fight as she knew how much pain her husband was suffering. Unlike the previous occasion, father realised his only chance was to quickly finish his opponent. Each time they grappled each other, my father said he kept goading the blacksmith hoping he would lose his temper. This strategy he recalls was sound, as spurred on by the crowd the man from Killorglin once again rushed in for the kill. My father was ready and sent his opponent crashing to the ground, but in doing so felt a searing sensation in his bad shoulder. On hearing the tremendous cheers coming from the vicinity of the wrestling match my mother rushed back fearing the worst. Obviously she was delighted that father had won, but when she saw how much pain he was in her delight soon turned to anguish.

That summer they slowly made their way back to Charleville, both worrying how they would survive now that my father would never fight again. Fortunately their friends and relations all helped them through that terrible time. In November a friend of my father told him that after the death of his mother her cabin was available. This was the best news they could possibly have, because with my mother expecting her first child at any time they obviously needed their own house. During the weeks leading up to Christmas they both worked hard cleaning and painting their first home. They spent Christmas Day on their own as mother was feeling very tired after all of her endeavours, but that night she woke my father as she was in a lot of pain. He immediately went to a neighbour's house who advised him to go for the midwife as they thought the birth was imminent. The neighbour stayed with my mother until my father returned with Mrs Finn the local midwife and I was born early that morning.

The earliest recollection I have is when my brother Owen was born. I think that I was only about three years old at this time. The two of us were always very close until his untimely death. He was the best friend and brother a man could ever have and although he died many years ago, I still pray for him. My mother, I now realise was determined that the two of us should be able to read and write as both of my parents were completely illiterate. But if you sent a child to school before the advent of the National Schools a fee was charged by the school master. As our fathers wages were always a pittance she had to work from dawn to dusk to pay for our schooling. I was six years old when I was sent to the local hedge school. These schools were normally very primitive and our one was no exception. The building was a small hut well off the beaten track, as in those far off times secrecy was essential because education for Catholic children was outlawed by the authorities. Any school master that was caught teaching at a hedge school was fined or in some cases sent to prison.

It is hard to believe now, but when I attended school every scholar took a turn each day on sentry duty. We were instructed to keep watch for strangers because they could be a danger to our school. On one occasion the authorities in our area became aware of our schools existence and sent a party of militia to destroy it. But the schoolmaster was warned in advance and luckily the school was empty when they arrived.

The news that the hedge school had been wantonly destroyed quickly spread around the parish and within days an alternative site had been found. My father, together with a group of helpers, assured the school master that he would soon have a new building. They were as good as their word, as it was built in three days. I can still remember its construction. On the first day the four walls were built, the next day the timbers for the roof were put in place and on the third day a thatch was put on. Our master was overjoyed and thanked all those that had helped. Strangely this building was never targeted by the authorities and was still being used until the National School was built over fifty years later.

When I attended school we were only taught the basic three R's, which were reading, writing and arithmetic. Fortunately in spite of a bad start I soon began to enjoy my lessons and eventually did well at school. This obviously pleased my mother because my brother Owen hated school as he was always in trouble with the master and struggled with his lessons. He was happiest when he was out in the countryside and he hated losing his freedom. For me having the ability to read had opened up a whole new world, reading books have always been my favourite pastime and I am eternally grateful to my mother for giving me an education.

As I have said Owen was the outdoor type and as soon as he was old enough acquired a dog. This dog was to be the first of many, because for the rest of his life he would always have at least one by his side In the summer holidays the pair of us together with Owens dog would roam the countryside trying to catch a rabbit or two. Our mother was always pleased if we brought something back from one of these trips. She was especially grateful if it was in the months of June and July when food was always scarce. When the harvesting season began our father would go off in search of work, this meant that our mother had to manage on her own. Obviously as we grew older we were expected to help her while he was away. As part of the tenancy agreement my parents were entitled to farm a couple of acres of poor land. But after years of hard work they transformed the soil and it generally produced enough potatoes to keep us fed during the year. Our work on the land started in the spring when the potatoes were sown; both Owen and I soon became expert at planting the seed. But my favourite job in those days was always hunting for chicken eggs. The chickens would normally lay their eggs in the thatch of the roof of our cabin; for me it was great fun to search in the thatch for the eggs, especially when mother boiled them for our breakfast.

Also I might tell you that in my childhood every family kept at least one pig, the pig had his own crib in the house and my mother always insured that its bed had fresh straw and was changed every day. Each year in February we would   all go to the annual pig market in Charleville. This was the only time my parents argued, as they could never agree about which pig they should buy. But once they had made their purchase, we would all proudly set off for home with our new addition to the fore.

As we walked home from the market each year we all sang at the tops of our voices the following song.

There are brown prolific pigs,
Black handsome pigs,
Spotted pigs that fill the sty,
Grey unwanted pigs,
And thin dun-coloured pigs like goats,
But a sturdy wide-backed light-headed pig,
Is the one for me?

Owen always became much attached to the pig that we bought and his first task when we reached home from market was to give it a name. My mother and father would pull his leg unmercifully for doing this but each year the pig received a name come what may. But sadly Owen was always missing on the day the poor pig was slaughtered, as he could not bare to hear its last terrible squeals. The pig you must understand was an important part of our lives in those days. My parents were very poor and like most of the peasants of Ireland meat was a luxury. Most families had their pig that they fattened up for the most important meal of the year, the feast at Christmas. After being killed, my mother would utilise every scrap of the animal, not a morsel was ever wasted. The week leading up to Christmas was always my mother's busiest time of the year our cabin was cleaned from top to bottom, ready for the many visitors that always came to visit us. Very occasionally an old friend or relative from mother's village in Kerry would arrive to have Christmas with us. These visits were the highlight of her year and she would talk about them for months after. But for me and my brother her visitors seemed strange, as they talked a language that we could never understand. What we also found difficult to comprehend was that our mother spoke exactly the same way when they came to see her.

Those wonderful years of my childhood, growing up in that very close knit community now seem like a distant dream. The young people of today often ask me what life was like in those days, before the famine and emigration carried thousand upon thousand of Irish people to far off shores. I try to explain that although we were extremely poor (new clothes and shoes were virtually unheard of) the generosity and the community spirit cannot now be imagined or understood. In the bad times the shopkeepers and moderately well-off farmers always gave food to the poor and hungry of the parish. Also it was normal when a penniless pauper died for a collection to be made for the funeral. Sadly many of the old traditions were lost at the time of famine as everybody's obvious priority was keeping alive.

Because of the popularity of my parents, our cabin was always the focal point of the local townland. It seemed that whenever my father was at home on a Saturday evening in the summer, musicians from far and wide, fiddlers, flutists and various other entertainers would appear. The dancing and singing would normally start in the late afternoon and usually carried on until dawn. As if by magic crowds would arrive, some of them walking miles to be there. On these occasions my father acted as the master of ceremonies introducing the musicians, being the caller for the jigs and reels and most important of all making sure everybody had plenty to drink. My mother being Kerry woman had been taught to dance from an early age by the best instructors in a County renowned for its dancers. I can still remember being spellbound watching her as she danced, as on many occasions the whole room would stop to watch and admire her. She was so amazingly light on her feet and I can honestly say I have never seen her equal. Both of us boys were lucky because from an early age we were taught all the various steps to the jigs and reels. Unfortunately she was wasting her time on me, but Owen was in later years well known for his dancing prowess.

As I sit here and reminisce, it seems that life then consisted of enjoyable days at school, followed by the long summer holidays, exploring the rivers and mountains with Owen and his dog. Then picking the potato crop when it was ready and as we grew older helping our mother when she worked in the fields gathering in the hay for the large farms in our parish. Another vital task we had was bringing home the turf that my father had cut in the spring.

The bog where the turf was cut was far off in the Mountains, this meant that we had to borrow a neighbour's stubborn old donkey. The donkey had a harness onto which two panniers were attached and these were filled with the turf. The work we did was hard but for me it was great fun and when our father arrived home after spending month's away working, he was always full of praise for the help we had given our mother. On many occasions he would bring us all a small present and normally mine was a book, one of which I still have. These happy times passed in a flash and at the age of fourteen I had to finish my education. On leaving school sadly it was also time to leave home and find work as my parents could not afford to keep me any longer.

As I have said my father had many friends all over County Cork, but his best friend had always been Brian Sullivan. Fortunately for me, Mr Sullivan was the farm manager for the local landowner Sir William Wrixon-Becher of Cecilstown which is a village not far from Charleville. On the first of March eighteen nineteen, I went with my father to meet Mr. Sullivan. Obviously the interview was only a formality, because after a brief discussion he agreed to employ me. I was to work initially as a farm labourer, but if I showed promise he told me there was always the prospect for advancement. I will never forget that my first wage was one shilling a week; this was given to my mother every Saturday evening. In later years she told me that as my father was finding it increasingly difficult to work; my wages were a godsend to them

At first I found the work very hard because the weather that spring was very cold and wet. But when the summer arrived the work became enjoyable and I was to learn a great deal about new methods of farming. This knowledge became very useful to me in later years. I realise now that Mr Sullivan must have found me very annoying because during this period I was always asking him questions. Luckily for me he eventually became like a second father to me and he would always have time to respond to my questions. At that time the farm was mainly tillage and I was put to work helping with the ploughing, sowing and reaping of the crops. Ever since my first year on the farm at Cecilstown, the saving of the hay strangely has always been the highlight of the farming year for me. The fun of working in the fields on hot August days with the sun on your back with the other young people from the farm is a memory I will never forget. Then when the hay was ready it was drawn into the yard where an enormous hayrick was built to feed the animals during the long winter months. This long tiring day was always followed by a huge meal for all those that had helped. On many occasions Sir William Wrixon Becher and his wife came to the dinner and personally thanked everyone for their efforts at harvest time.

After two years at Cecilstown, Mr Sullivan called me into his office to discuss my future. He told me that he had noticed that I was particularly good with the horses on the farm and he wanted me to work in the stables as a groom. Obviously I jumped at this opportunity especially when he said my wages would be doubled. After I finished work on the following Saturday afternoon I rushed home to tell my parents the good news. My mother was overjoyed at hearing about my new position and I knew the extra money I would now earn was always welcome to her. At that time the stables at Cecilstown were renowned in the South West of Ireland as they had some of the best hunters in the country. For me the next couple of years working in the stables were extremely interesting and rewarding. The Wrixon Becher family were all very good horsemen and took a great interest in their animal's welfare and so obviously our work was very important to them. During my employment as a groom they always respected my industry and hard work and in time I became quiet friendly with some of the younger members of the family.

One person stands out in my memory and this was Martin Becher who was a nephew of Sir William. Martin was attending school in England at the time, but he enjoyed spending his summer holidays on his uncle's farm. He would arrive each summer in early June and his first port of call was the stables where he would then question us about every horse in the yard. Martin and I being both of a similar age soon became firm friends during these holidays and in later years I was thrilled to hear of his horse jumping exploits. During those summer months he would participate at all of the local horse shows, winning many cups and prizes. Everyone at Cecilstown became very fond of Michael and we always looked forward to seeing him each summer. The feeling was mutual because he always became very remorseful when it was time for him to return to England.

As I previously stated, I always returned home after work on Saturday afternoon. Owen on leaving school had also been fortunate as he found a job working on a farm near Killmallock and so we usually had much to discuss each weekend. For Owen it was always the girls he had met or the girls he would like to meet. On one particular occasion he surprised me by saying that he had heard that a gang of men he had met that week had returned from a place called Newfoundland. They had told him that they had worked on the fishing grounds there. The work was hard but the wages were very good and they were going to return the following spring. Over the coming weeks he convinced me that we should both seek our fortune in that far off land. I gradually came to realise that if I was to achieve my ambition and become a tenant farmers sadly I would have to leave Ireland.

Once I had made my mind up there was no going back and in early March eighteen twenty-three, I informed Mr Sullivan of my intentions. He was obviously very sad that I was leaving but he understood the reasons and wished me luck. At the same time Owen also left his employment. Sadly our parents did not approve of our decision because many of the young of our parish had left never to return. But after promising that we would return home for Christmas with heavy hearts we set out on the long walk to Waterford. Once in the city we soon found out that no ships were sailing to Newfoundland due to the treacherous weather in the Atlantic We were advised to wait for a couple of days to see if the conditions improved, but in fact they worsened. By now our funds were running low, so when we were offered labouring work in England we both jumped at the opportunity.

On the twenty first of April, I left Ireland for the first time not for Newfoundland, as we had planned, but for the English city of Bristol. For both of us country boys everything we did that first year was an adventure. It all started with our first crossing of the Irish Sea, on that occasion I was terribly sea sick and I must confess that I have never enjoyed sea travel since that day, but Owen was a born sailor, a fortunate trait that was to stand him well in future years. The crossing seemed to take an age and at times I wished I had remained at Ceciltown, but we eventually landed at Bristol harbour. Once in the city we were amazed at the hustle and bustle of this enormous seaport. Everyone it seemed was in a hurry, in complete contrast to the leisurely pace of life in Ireland. Owen and I, along with about ten others boarded carts and were driven through the city into the English countryside. After a twenty mile journey we finally arrived at our destination. By now it was getting dark and we were all very hungry and thirsty after all the travelling. Luckily the owner of the farm had prepared a meal for us after which we were shown to our sleeping quarters.   Both of us enjoyed working in England that first summer, though the work was hard, the farmer treated us very well. He soon came to realise that I was more than a labourer and that I had a good working knowledge of horses. Unlike Ireland where most farm work was done manually, in England many of the tasks were now being carried out by horses pulling various machines. Obviously it was very important that they were well looked after, especially on the large farm where we were working that summer. As I have said, horses have always been a passion of mine so when I was offered the chance to work in the stables I jumped at it. There was also the added incentive that my pay would increase. After the harvest most of our colleagues left for home but Mr Edwards, our employer much to our satisfaction wanted both of us to stay on and help him until December. Obviously as we needed the money we readily agreed to his request. But by the middle of December we could not work any longer as the ground was saturated from the heavy rain and snow that kept falling. Also with Christmas approaching we were anxious to return home and so after collecting our pay, Mr Edwards kindly arranged for us to be driven back to Bristol.

Unfortunately it was a very stormy passage back to Ireland and I was again sick for the duration of the journey. While I was being sick and feeling sorry for myself, Owen had worked out how much money we had left after paying for the crossing. I can still remember how pleased we both were as we had managed to save most of our wages by being very frugal. On landing back in Waterford we hurried home to Charleville as it was now the week before Christmas and we were both looking forward to the festivities.

Our joy on arriving home was short lived; as we found that our father was very ill with pneumonia and fading fast and our mother poor soul, was in a terrible state as she had not slept for weeks worrying about his welfare. He had, she told us not worked for many months as he had been so weak. On hearing this I realised that they must be destitute without my father's wages. I found out later that they even sold their pig to purchase food and had been living on the goodwill of her friends and neighbours for the past months. My first action was to go into town for the doctor whilst Owen comforted our parents. The doctor was very busy but promised to come that evening after he had finished all his calls. Before returning home I made sure that I purchased plenty of groceries to fill my mother's larder. When I got back Owen had been very busy tidying up the cabin ready for the arrival of the doctor. He had also got a good blaze going and so we cooked some of the food I had bought. It was very late when the doctor finally arrived, but he still gave my father a very thorough examination. Before leaving he told me he wanted to speak to me alone. In this conversation he told me that my father was a very sick man who had only days to live. When I heard this terrible news, I asked if in the circumstances there was anything we could possibly do. He replied that we must at all costs keep him warm and comfortable and when possible feed him some hot soup.

Obviously our Christmas that year was a very solemn affair, but our timely return did help our mother because within a few days she was thankfully back to her old self. Sadly our father's condition worsened and on January the tenth eighteen twenty-four, we called for the priest who administered Extreme Unction. After the priest left, we all sat by his bedside and late that night he passed away by the will of God. At the end he was a shadow of his former self because he had tragically just wasted away. My mother was very distraught, so it was fortunate that we were there to comfort her.

As the eldest son it was now my duty to arrange the funeral. There was at this time still many ancient Celtic customs that had to be fulfilled, most of which have long since vanished. The first thing I had to organise was the wake, as I knew that everyone in the parish would come to pay their respects. The preparations for this I left to Owen, who went into town to purchase everything that was required. My second task might now seem strange, but when the mourners arrived the first question they always asked was what time did the deceased die? With this in mind, it was traditional to stop the clock at the time of death. Next with the help of my grieving mother we dressed my father in his best suit of clothes and laid his body out on the kitchen table. By this time Owen had returned with sufficient tobacco, snuff and whisky that had to be made available for the mourners. During the evening our relatives and close friends arrived and the women started singing the caonine (which is the haunting lament for the dead). The atmosphere was very sad, as each new arrival offered their condolences to our mother who was by now very distressed. Owen being her favourite was the only person who managed to comfort her that terrible night. The strange thing was that having to organise the wake and make the necessary preparations for the funeral, I did not have time to grieve for my father until weeks later.

The next morning I went with my father's best friend John Farrell and his son Michael to the cemetery at Dromina to dig my father's grave. There had been so much rain the ground was very wet and the three of us toiled for hours before we completed this task. The funeral took place on the following afternoon, when the coffin was carried on our shoulders from the house to its place of rest. To be asked by the deceased's family to be a carrier was always considered a great honour. With this in mind I had to be very careful in the choices I made as I did not wish to upset any of my fathers many friends.

Hundreds arrived that afternoon and it was only then that we realised how popular my father was. Owen, myself, John and Michael Farrell lifted the coffin and started out walking to the Dromina Cemetry, a distance of around four miles. As we tired relays of pallbearers took it in turns to carry the coffin; this was achieved with military type precision. The funeral procession also had a certain traditional order. The men followed the coffin many of whom were ready to relieve the carriers. Then came the women mostly dressed in black and taking up the rear was the priest riding slowly on his horse.

As we passed the houses and cabins along our route the curtains were drawn and their occupants joined the procession. By the time we finally reached the cemetry it was estimated that there were over a thousand mourners in attendance. At the graveside the parish priest gave the eulogy in which he spoke at length about the highs and lows of my father's life. It was a wonderful speech from a man that had obviously known my father well and most of the mourners were in tears by the time he had finished. Then came the moment I had been dreading, as four of my father's oldest friends lowered the coffin slowly into the grave. Then sods of grass were laid on the coffin to deaden the sound of the heavy earth that was now shovelled into the grave. Sadly we now all turned for home, with Owen trying to comfort our mother on the long walk. Fortunately on reaching our cabin we found that our neighbours had kindly replaced all the furniture and prepared a meal for all our close friends and family.

The weeks following the funeral were very difficult for the three of us, as we all knew that with our funds sadly depleted by the costs we had incurred we would again have to seek employment in England. How would our mother cope on her own this was the question I kept asking myself. Luckily my prayers were answered when she managed to find work at Fortlands a large estate near Charleville. In early April, we gave mother most of the money we had left and set out on our travels. Obviously she was very distressed to see us go but we knew that the local community would help her once more in our absence

This year our destination was the city of Liverpool, this was because Michael Walsh, Owens old school friend was now a contractor who lived in that City. On this occasion our plan was to walk to Queenstown Harbour as we had been told there were many sailings from there each day that went directly to Liverpool. For once the sea was calm, although the crossing seemed to take an age, but finally we sailed into Liverpool. At that time Liverpool was the busiest sea port in the world and both Owen and I were dumbstruck at seeing so many ships and people. On landing we found it very hard to find cheap lodgings, so in desperation we went to the home of Michael Walsh. Ever since that first meeting Michael and I have remained firm friends and even now we still keep in contact. That evening when we called he immediately invited us into his home and after dinner his wife insisted we stop for the night.

The next morning we were up very early because Michael wanted us to meet one of his associates who was hiring men. During the meeting we were warned that the work would be very hard and that only the toughest men survived this work, but we were told that they were paying very good wages and obviously when we heard this, we were desperate to get a start. At the end of the meeting we were told to wait outside and by this time crowds of men had also turned up all looking for work. Hour after hour we waited to see if we would get a job and by the evening we were both getting very despondent. Eventually the contractor came out of his office with a list of those he wanted and fortunately we were both accepted. That night we returned once more to Michael's house and during dinner he told us about the conditions we would have to endure. He also advised us to be on our guard at all times, because the contractors and workers were always out to fleece newcomers. The wages he again emphasised were very good but most of the men wasted it on drink and loose women. Both Owen and I on hearing this advice vowed to be vigilant and steer clear of all the temptations that were on offer. Early next morning we thanked Michael and his wife for their kindness and hospitality and promised to heed his words of warning.

On leaving our friend's house we returned to the contractor's office to await instruction. Eventually we were told to go to the company's depot. On arriving there we helped load supplies onto waiting wagons and then set off on the long journey to the construction site. This site was near the town of Ironbridge in the County of Shropshire where a new canal was under construction. On our arrival we were told we would be working for a ganger named Thomas Kelly. In the weeks that followed we found out that Kelly had a terrible temper especially when he was drunk. But on that morning he was very friendly and he quickly introduced us to the rest of his gang. These men, like every man working on the site were known to outsiders as navvies. Navvies were to become infamous in future years for their drinking and riotous behaviour, but they were also to become famous for their amazing strength and stamina.

The next day we were put to work with a team of horses, our task was to haul away all the soil and debris that had been dug to make the canal. The team of horses that we were given were the largest horses I had ever seen, big strong and willing and the locals told us the breed were called Shire Horses, and that they had been especially bred for heavy work in the fields of England. They were wonderful to work with and I have often wished I could have brought one back to Ireland. The project had been severely delayed by the bad winter weather so we were soon having to work seven days a week trying to make up for lost time This suited us because that year we were managing to save most of our wages, but the non stop work meant that many of the horses began to break down. Since my arrival I had kept quiet and did my job to the best of my ability. Unfortunately this situation could not last because the ganger Thomas Kelly started to become very aggressive towards my brother Owen.

The construction engineers and contractors always dreaded the end of the month as this was when the men were paid. Obviously with the majority of them working seven days a week they all had plenty of money to spend on paydays. At the end of our first month we witnessed at first hand the unbelievable behaviour of the men that our friend Michael Walsh had warned us about. With alcohol freely available in the shanty towns the men in our gang on receiving their pay immediately started drinking. Sadly within hours they became unrecognisable from the men we knew as all too soon the fighting began. That evening Owen and I were having a quiet drink with another native of Charleville, John Shea, when Kelly the ganger spotted us. Rushing over, he picked up Owen and threw him to the ground and then started to violently attack him. I have never been a fighting man and have always tried to keep away from trouble, but my father being a wrestler had taught me many tricks of his trade.

On seeing Owen lying defenceless on the floor my blood began to boil, but as I rose to confront his attacker my father's words came flooding back. "Do not under any circumstance ever lose your temper," he would say. "Keep calm and wait for your opponent to make a mistake and then make sure that you finish him." With these words ringing in my ears I confronted Thomas Kelly, who flushed by his easy success could not believe that I would stand up to him. Within seconds a large crowd had gathered to see me get a thrashing, because the ganger had a fearsome reputation amongst the men. At first we circled each other and then he caught me with a couple of heavy punches in the early exchanges, but egged on by his friends he became very careless and I managed to catch him with good solid punch to his ribs that sent him crashing to the floor. As he picked himself up I could see the look of amazement on his face, I found out later that this was the first time he had been knocked down. What followed I owe to my fathers hours of tuition in the finer points of the art of wrestling. Kelly was now in a terrible rage and with a tremendous roar he rushed at me throwing caution to the wind. Remembering what I had been taught I now seized my chance. As he charged at me I crouched very low and by using my fathers old trick I caught him by legs, his momentum did the rest. All I can remember is that everyone went quiet for a moment as my opponent flew across the room and hit the wall. Then the whole place erupted and I was lifted up onto men's shoulders and paraded around the site. Luckily Owen had only sustained a few cuts and bruises, but I never found out about Thomas Kelly's condition because he left the works that night and was never seen again.

Fortunately from that day on both Owen and I were left alone and it would appear that my reputation preceded me, because I was always treated with the utmost respect on all the construction sites I worked on in England. We had both learned a valuable lesson and we very rarely visited the alehouses on pay days again. In future we agreed we must keep ourselves to ourselves and try to save every penny for our aim was to rent a farm back home in Charleville.

The ganger that replaced Thomas Kelly was our friend John Shea, who quickly received the loyalty and respect from the navvies in our gang. John was a hard task master, but unlike his predecessor he listened to his men's grievances. My main worry during that long dry summer was the welfare of our horses. We were working the poor beast's non stop seven days a week with no respite. These Shire Horses were their own worst enemy because they would work until they dropped. Being fond of horses I could not stand idly by and watch them suffer. With my worries about their condition increasing I approached John Shea and informed him about my misgivings. At first he ignored my warnings but when the horses started to go lame he realised that I was right to be concerned. Work on the site was soon being affected and the bosses quickly became worried because of our lack of progress. The navvies now had to haul away the debris by hand, because of the shortage of horses. It was soon realised that this situation could not continue and strangely I was asked by the site engineer for my advice. I told him that in my opinion we were working the poor animals too hard especially during the hot weather that we were now experiencing. Extra water should always be available for them to drink and every horse should, I said, have a weeks rest every month.

On hearing what I had to say the engineer looked at me in amazement, but after much discussion my advice was finally heeded and gradually the horses recovered. As it had become very obvious to everyone how important the wellbeing of the horses were, both Owen and I were put in charge of the animal's welfare. For the rest of that long hot summer we both worked from dawn to dusk making sure that our animals were well watered and were turned out into the fields on a regular basis. Luckily because we were so heavily involved in our task, we had little or no time to spend our hard earned wages. This obviously meant that we had to take extra care with our savings, because most of the other men were continually broke and would steal anything to buy drink. We carried on working that year until bad weather caused the construction to shut down in early December. Personally I was sorry to leave those wonderful Shire Horses, but elated at how much money we had managed to save.

We had a very long journey home that year in appalling weather, Firstly we had to get back to Liverpool and then take passage back to Queenstown. Then it was the long hike back to Charleville to be with our dear mother for Christmas.

On our arrival in Charleville, everyone was so pleased to see us and our mother seemed very well under the circumstances. That year has a special memory for me as sadly it was to be my last ever Christmas with my dear mother. In those far off times Christmas was always a very special occasion when every family would where possible prepare and cook a pig for the Christmas feast. For most people this was the only meat that would be tasted in the year. On Christmas Eve all the houses in the village would have every candle possible shining from their windows. Neighbours would go from house to house wishing everyone the compliments of the season and on their arrival it was considered an insult if you did not offer them food and drink.

That Christmas morning we attended early morning mass and rushed home with our mother to prepare the feast. As normal we had invited some of our friends and neighbours who had helped mother while we were working in England. The harvest had been very poor because of the long dry summer, followed by a wet autumn. So it was fortunate that we had managed to come home with most of our wages. This had enabled us to purchase sufficient food to also invite some of the local families who had fallen on hard times. We were not alone in making sure that everyone in the parish enjoyed the Christmas feast, because the community spirit and generosity of the people, rich and poor cannot now be imagined. Not one poor soul in our parish ever went without food at Christmas. The meal my mother cooked that day was sadly the last Christmas meal we ever had with her, but obviously we were not to know that at the time. The dinner I remember was as good as she had ever cooked and both Owen and I after months of the terrible food we had endured in England really appreciated all her hard work. After the meal it was customary for every one of the guests to sing or play an instrument and very soon with the drink flowing the dancing started. Before long we were all begging our mother to dance a Kerry reel and to great cheers she reluctantly agreed. The house went silent for a moment as I led her out into the middle of the room. Then to thunderous applause she started to dance. Owen on hearing the music came in from the yard and instantly joined in. It was magical to see the two of them that Christmas night dancing together; it was an experience that all those present would never forget, for they were undoubtedly the best two dancers I have ever seen.

The next day St.Stephen's day as it was my birthday the three of us decided to go into town for the annual hurling match. On our arrival in Charleville that morning we found that many of the young men from our townland had gathered at a large field near the Parish church, all carrying their hurling sticks. It was then the tradition that a team from Kilmallock were invited each year. The rivalry in these matches was intense, as our rivals always had some of the best hurlers in the County. These contests were very violent with many a swollen ankle or broken bone being inflicted, to the obvious amusement of the many onlookers. Owen I must say was always a great hurler, but I was usually a spectator. This was because in a previous match my temper had got the better of me and I had done something stupid that I later regretted. That year if my memory serves me right Charleville gave Kilmallock a tremendous thrashing for a change. My brother was in fine form that day with all the players saying how much he had been missed in the previous months. After the game everyone wanted to celebrate the famous victory and obviously talk for hours about the match.

Sadly for all of us Christmas was soon over and we had to face the prospect of returning to England and finding work. Our first responsibility was to ensure mother had sufficient money for the coming year. Fortunately she was still employed at Fortlands and although the wages were a pittance, with our help she could afford to buy a pig that year. This purchase was made by Owen and as usual we had to give it a name which that year I recall was Grunter. Our mothers face lit up when we brought him home as she now had something to look after and rear in our absence. With mother provided for, both Owen and I went to The National Bank of Ireland in Charleville and made our first ever deposit with the remainder of our savings. That day was one of the highlights of my life, because at last we were a step nearer to the realisation of our ambitions.

With spring approaching and the weather improving, we again said our sad goodbyes to our mother and all our friends and neighbours and then set off on the long walk to Queenstown Little did we know that this would be the last time we would ever see our mother. The year of eighteen twenty-six, changed our lives for ever, because for Owen and me, tragically life would never be the same. As we turned our backs on the town of Charleville on that fateful morning and headed towards the coast, little did we know then that we were leaving behind the carefree days of our youth. We hiked and hitched lifts back to Cork City, and then on to Queenstown Harbour, where we quickly found a cheap passage back to Liverpool. Once back in Liverpool we went straight to the house of our old friend Michael Walsh. As usual Michael and his wife Bridget made us very welcome giving us dinner and putting us up for the night. After dinner we sat and talked, with both of them bombarding us with questions about affairs in Ireland. When later I broached the subject about our chances of finding work, Michael told us we had fortunately returned to Liverpool just at the right time. He said that contractors he knew were now hiring men for a new undertaking that was to be built between Liverpool and Manchester. This project he said was to be the first passenger and goods railroad to be constructed in the world. There was he informed us a great deal of local interest in building the railroad as it was envisaged that it would improve transportation between the two large cities. Travel then was very expensive with very few people being able to afford to travel on the stage coaches. Also roads in England and Ireland were appalling, virtually impassable in the winter and choking with dust in the summer months. The work, he knew was going to be extremely arduous, but with the experience we had gained when working on the canal the previous summer, it should not be a problem to us.

Within a week Michael had arranged for us to meet one of the Irish gangers who were hiring men for the construction. His name was Gerry Flynn, Gerry very sceptical about employing us, as he had heard about my altercation with Thomas Kelly and thought I was a troublemaker. It was only after our friend Michael Walsh, begged him to give us a start that he reluctantly agreed. Gerry

Flynn would in time prove to be a colleague who I am proud to call my friend. After he agreed to give us a chance he also stressed that the work would be extremely hard and very dangerous. But the wages the best workers could earn was the unheard sum of fifteen shillings a week. This was music to our ears and we could not wait to get started on the following Monday.

When we arrived on site on that Monday, we never dreamt that it would take four years to build the railway. During that time we would hardly ever have a week off; in fact on many occasions we worked none stop for months on end. On our arrival we were taken to the typical shanty town that immediately seemed to spring up wherever there were navvies. Gerry the ganger soon sorted out somewhere for us to sleep and then took us to meet the rest of his gang. We were soon to find out that every gang on this vast construction site were given names and we were called the Tipperary's, this was because Gerry Flynn and most of his men hailed from that County. We the Tipperary's, were to become notorious over the following years, firstly we quickly became renowned for our ability to tackle and complete the most dangerous of tasks. The second reason for Tipperary's notoriety was their amazing capacity for drink, which ultimately lead to fighting and causing mayhem every payday. Both Owen and I, on seeing the riotous behaviour of our colleagues on our first payday decided to build ourselves a small mud cabin. I knew that if we carried on living with the other men sooner or later one of them would want to fight me because of my reputation. Each evening in early summer we rushed back after work and by utilising discarded materials from the site we soon made our new home very comfortable.

Every navvy had a nickname, for many of the men this was essential because they were wanted by the law, or for other misdemeanours. Within days of the two of us joining the Tipperary gang, Owen was named "Blarney," as he was always telling the rest of the boys about all the lovely young girls he had left behind in Charleville. I quickly became known as the "Gent" because although I had gained a reputation amongst the navvies after my fight in Iron Bridge, it was soon realised that I always treated everyone with the utmost respect.

With the Tipperary's soon gaining a reputation for undertaking the most arduous tasks possible, we were ordered to report to the site engineers at a place called Chad Moss near the large city of Manchester. We had heard other gangs talking about the trouble they were having at Chad Moss and so we were eager to tackle this latest challenge. The problem the engineers faced at this location was that when they attempted to lay the track quicksand had swallowed up all of their efforts to build a solid base. At first we experienced the same problem as we built embankment after embankment, only to watch them all disappear silently into the boggy moss. In some of the areas we excavated the moss and quicksand incredibly went down to a depth of forty feet before it reached thick clay. At that time we had to use planks of wood strapped to our boots like skis, to sustain our weight by spreading the pressure.

Week after week we toiled, working twelve hours a day seven days a week but with nothing to show for our Herculean efforts. The problem seemed insurmountable with even Gerry Flynn our ganger at his wits end when he reported to the contractor that we had not achieved a thing after months of hard work. Fortunately for us the first sign of progress came when after four wasted months it was decided that we were to dig four parallel trenches each forty eight feet apart. These trenches were then drained and filled with dried moss that we had previously removed. Heathers and brushwood was then piled on top of this, followed by tons and tons of sand and cinders. This process finally solved the problem and at long last we had a firm but elastic base that would be able to carry the weight of the locomotives. As I have said that summer we had worked sometimes fourteen hours a day, but as the pay was good we were both happy as we were managing to save most of the money we earned.

After we had completed the nearly impossible task at Chad Moss the reputation of our gang was enhanced even further. In the preceding weeks we had heard that the most ambitious part of the project was the boring of a great tunnel under the city of Liverpool. The tunnel it was said would be over a mile and a quarter long and was thought to be the largest construction of its kind that the world had ever seen, but because of the many problems that were being encountered, the tunnel project was now months behind schedule.

The site engineers were obviously very worried by this lack of progress and so they sent for us and the other elite gangs. We were told that we must be prepared to work non-stop until the tunnel was completed and we were warned that anyone failing to report for work, especially after pay day would be dismissed. None of us were prepared for the tremendous noise and appalling conditions that we encountered on our arrival on site that first morning. Little did we realise that we were to spend months working in this living nightmare. It seemed that we spent our lives living ankle deep in water and soaked to the skin. Added to this there was very little light in the tunnel, as the darkness was only illuminated by a few candles that were constantly going out. The noise I have already said was virtually unbearable and together with the danger from the constant dynamiting of the rock face, it was a wonder any of us survived the ordeal.

As the construction site was in the city we decided that we should look for accommodation in the local vicinity. Fortunately once again our friends Michael and Bridget Walsh came to our rescue when they arranged for us to meet an acquaintance of theirs called Mrs Sharpe. On meeting this lady we discovered she had recently lost her husband and for financial reasons needed to take in lodgers. From the outset I realised that we had been lucky to have Mrs Sharpe as our landlady because she always treated us like her sons during the years of our stay in Liverpool. From time to time I had to tell Owen off for being so untidy, but he soon came to realise that we would never find anyone to match Mrs Sharpe's kindness and hospitality. Another reason for us to be thankful was that her house was only a mile from the construction site. Livings so near was obviously a godsend, especially when we were now working fourteen and fifteen hour days.

Each day we toiled hour after hour at the rock face gradually inching forward, with an army of carpenters on hand erecting props and stays to hold back the tremendous pressure from above. We all knew that one day our luck would eventually run out, our main fear being that the roof of the tunnel might collapse on us before the artisans could complete the arch work. Worryingly on the second of September eighteen twenty-seven, our fears were realised when the roof of the tunnel did collapse. As a result, it was estimated that thirty feet of earth and rock crashed down onto the area where we had been working a couple of minutes earlier. Fortunately we had all heard a terrific rumble and sensing the possible danger everyone ran for their lives. Later when a roll call of the navvies working in the tunnel was made, amazingly everyone was accounted for. This near disaster would eventually lead to a change in the way the tunnelling progressed. For safety reasons all dynamiting would in future be carried out at exactly the same time each morning. Before it commenced warning whistles were to be blown, to ensure that everyone in the tunnel was aware of what was about to happen. These measures restored the confidence of the men and happily we did not experience any other catastrophes.

Every evening after finishing our long shift at the rock face we could always be assured that Mrs Sharpe had a hot meal ready for us. We were also very fortunate as she washed and ironed all of our filthy clothes. The other reason I am eternally grateful to her was her insistence that we both had a hot bath at least once a week. At first we were both very much against her proposal, but we very quickly realised that it was a good idea after spending hours working in the dust and grime. I now realise that without her kindness I would not have survived those terrible months working in that tunnel. The only thing we ever looked forward to during this period was pay day. After receiving our wages Owen, always went straight to the Liverpool branch of The National Bank of Ireland and deposited our savings. As I have said, we usually worked seven days a week, but there were a few odd occasions when we were not required to work. On these very special days I left Owen to his own devices and spent the day exploring the city and its surrounding areas. I always marvelled at the hustle and bustle and the wide selection of goods that could be purchased in the shops of Liverpool. For a country boy like myself coming from a tiny rural town in Ireland, the cosmopolitan nature of the docks with shipping from every corner of the globe amazed me. It was said that the Liverpool docks were seven miles long and I can honestly say that I have explored every inch. In the docks there were hundreds of drinking establishments that served the sailors who thronged the quayside. These sailors came from every corner of the known world. Every colour and creed was represented and it fascinated me to hear the many languages that were spoken. Usually when I returned to Mrs Sharpe's after one of these tours, Owen would tell me in great detail about the latest beautiful girl he had met. Girls the world over were attracted to my brother because of his good looks and charming nature. I often thought that one day his philandering would get him in trouble, but fortunately it was never to happen. Those rest days away from noise and the dust of tunnelling were very brief interludes in our lives at this time.

Back at the rock face with the now frequent use of explosives we at last started to make steady progress. To plot the way forward the site engineers undertook frequent readings with a marine compass. These readings were then checked each day with the readings made by the engineers working on the tunnel that was going to link up with us. During the later stages of the tunnelling, I started to find myself getting more responsibility; this was to lead me eventually to become Gerry Flynn's deputy. I was always very ambitious and thrived on this extra responsibility that was now thrust upon me. Thankfully my promotion also meant an increase in wages, which obviously increased the amount we were saving each month. Little did I know then that the knowledge and experience I gained was to stand me in good stead during the worst period of my life.

Week after week we toiled on in that hell hole, wishing and praying that one day we would finally link up with the navvies tunnelling towards us. Each day we hoped to hear the sound of their approach and our patience was eventually rewarded when on the morning of the tenth of December we heard the rumble of explosions. This was obviously the engineers in the other tunnel blasting their way towards us. During the next couple of days we cautiously inched our way forward as we were worried that another cave-in might occur when the two tunnels met. But our worries were unfounded when the final boulders were removed and we gleefully shook hands with our colleagues who had tunnelled through from the other side. That afternoon as we cleared away the remaining debris, the bosses and senior site managers came to thank us for our endeavours. The measurements and calculations that linked the two tunnels so accurately, was a wonderful feat of engineering, which I have always been proud to have been part of.

Many of the local dignitaries and ordinary people of Liverpool came to see the finished tunnel and the local newspapers called the whole project a modern day Wonder of the World. The pay day that followed the completion of the tunnel will always live in my memory. Many of the navvies because of the dangerous conditions that had prevailed in the tunnel had been warned not to come on site if they were intoxicated. This had caused much resentment amongst the men, especially when some of them had been sacked for being drunk. But now with the tunnel finally finished and with plenty of money in their pockets, the navvies went on a huge randy (a randy was a tremendous drinking binge). This was what the bosses had been dreading, as the navvies were always notorious for their drinking and fighting. Once the randy started most of them would not return to the workings until they had spent all of their hard earned cash. But on this occasion after many months of forced abstention, and pockets bulging with money, the men were in no mood to end their drunken orgy. This time the randy was to last for three long weeks, with the police being summoned on numerous occasions. The situation ultimately deteriorated to such an extent that eventually the local militia were sent for and the magistrate read the Riot Act. As a result of this action many of the navvies were arrested and charged with various offences. Fortunately both Owen and I managed to keep clear of the trouble, I on one of my sightseeing tours, whilst my brother courted his latest young lady. But the most important thing of all was that on that pay day we again added a tidy sum to our growing bank balance.

Over the next few weeks it was hard to sympathise with our work colleagues as they gradually returned to work. But these fools had slaved for months in appalling conditions and had then wasted their hard earned cash on one mad drunken spree. Sadly most of them could never see the folly of their ways and they were to end up destitute when the railway project was finished. Fortunately no one from our gang had been arrested on this occasion and so with the tunnel now complete we were sent along the line that was now nearing the great city of Manchester. With the Tipperary's reputation further enhanced by our super human efforts at the rock face, we were called upon wherever tricky sections needed completion.

During our long stay in Liverpool, I had occasionally written home to my mother who as I have previously stated could not read or write. But I knew that on receiving my letters she would have asked my uncle Michael to read them out to her. I have always felt guilty that I did not return to Ireland during that four year period, sadly this guilt has remained with me. Let me explain. It was on a Saturday morning, in October eighteen twenty-eight, that we received a letter from home. Ominously before opening the envelope I knew that a tragedy had happened in our prolonged absence. Sadly my premonition was proved to be correct, for as I read the letter from my uncle Michael Casey my whole body started to shake uncontrollably. Owen quickly realised something was terribly wrong and made me sit down. He then snatched the letter from me and started to read it. At first he could not comprehend its contents, but he slowly came to realise its full implications. My uncles devastating letter told us that a cholera epidemic had swept across Ireland and our dear mother had unfortunately became one of its tragic victims. He told us that the epidemic had claimed many lives in the Charleville area, most of them we knew and loved. He went onto advise us not to return home at present, as the epidemic was still raging. When Mrs Sharpe our landlady arrived back from the shops that morning she was surprised that we were still at home. But from the tears running down our faces she quickly realised we had received bad news. That morning she was a great comfort to both of us and endorsed our uncle's advice not to return home. Later that day she helped me to compose a reply to my uncle. In my reply I thanked him for all that he had done to comfort my mother during her last days on this earth. Also I informed him that I would ask the National Bank of

Ireland, Liverpool branch to send written authority to its branch in Charleville, to release sufficient funds from our account to recompense him for the cost of the funeral.

The death of my mother devastated both of us, but during the rest of that year and all through the year of eighteen twenty-nine, with the ganger Gerry Flynn confined to his sick bed, I took on all his responsibilities. I cannot imagine how many hours I worked that year, as we were all under constant pressure from the bosses who urgently wanted the vast undertaking completed as fast as possible. By this period the Tipperary gang's reputation was so high that we were always summoned when problems arose. My elevation to acting ganger seems to have changed my character at this time and for a very brief period I stupidly fell out with my brother. Let me explain, when I became acting ganger, I began to lose sight of my ultimate ambition which was to have that small farm I had always dreamed off. The reason for me thinking seriously of staying in England and making my career in the construction industry was that the engineers were confident that there was a tremendous future for railway building in England. My arrogance and obnoxious behaviour, towards my brother became so bad that he finally packed his bags and threatened to return home to Ireland. His threats ultimately made me realise how stupid I had become and reminded me of why we had come to England in the first place. I knew deep down that he was right when he argued that I would always regret not fulfilling that promise I had made to our dear mother. She had always wanted us to be our own boss and not be at the beck and call of anyone unlike our poor father, who had spent his last years begging for work. As I lay in bed that night pondering my future, for the first time in three years I became home sick and longed to return home to the peace and tranquillity of the Irish countryside. The next morning I promised Owen that when the railway project was completed, I would definitely return home to our beloved town of Charleville.

Our gang of men had been very fortunate during the many months of dangerous work in the tunnel, but other gangs had not been as lucky as us. Serious injuries or even fatalities were common place as short cuts were taken in the rush to complete the construction. Unfortunately our luck finally ran out in November eighteen twenty-nine, when tragedy struck the most popular member of our gang. His name was Tommy Stack who was about to emigrate to America and was only waiting for the confirmation of his sailing date. On the fatal morning of twenty second November, I had given Tommy permission

31

to check if his sailing date had been finalised by the shipping company before coming to work. I in fact did not see what happened, but Owen told me later that when Tommy eventually arrived on the site he was very excited as his sailing date had been fixed for the first of December. On hearing his good news it appears some of the men began to give him some light hearted banter. Tommy always the joker obviously gave as good as he got, but then the accident occurred. The banter turned into a friendly wrestling match but as Tommy tried to get away from his assailants he tripped and fell under a passing wagon. The wagon driver tried to stop but to no avail and poor Tommy was instantly crushed to death. Obviously we were all inconsolable that our happy go lucky friend had died in such horrific circumstances. His unfailing good humour had helped Owen and myself through many a hard day and we knew he would be sorely missed by all those who knew him. Tragically his young wife who had been looking forward to starting a new life in America was now alone and far from her family and friends in Kilkenny

Every navvie on the site contributed generously towards the cost of the funeral, the amount that we collected was then boosted by a large donation from the site engineers. As Owen was the best friend of the deceased, it was his duty to make the arrangements for the funeral. Fortunately the local parish priest was very helpful in getting all the formalities sorted out. Tommy's funeral was a very sombre and moving occasion that took place on the following Saturday. As a mark of respect the construction site completely shut down for the day, thus enabling everyone to attend. Hundreds of navvies arrived at the church for the funeral service. Each man having a traditional white favour pinned to his coat lapel as a mark of respect for the deceased. On the previous day all the gangers had asked their men to behave in dignified way during the service and the internment. Surprisingly they all behaved impeccably and the priest in his eulogy praised them for their behaviour. The next day being Sunday we both went to mass and afterwards Owen asked to see the priest in order to pay him for conducting the funeral service. The priest told us that he could not possibly take any money from us as he was sure that poor Tommy's wife would now need every penny in order to return home. It was thanks to the priest's very fine gesture that Owen was able to give most of the money he had collected to Tommy's widow.

After the terrible events we had encountered at the end of eighteen twenty-nine, the following year passed rapidly with the finishing touches to the railroad gradually being completed. We were still under tremendous pressure from the bosses that summer, as the deadline for completion had been set for the middle of September.

When the great day finally arrived, we were as anxious as the owners and engineers that the Grand Inauguration Day would be a huge success. Looking back now in hindsight, no one at that time realised the full implications of what we had achieved. Before the coming of the railroads, travel was very expensive and out of reach for most of the population. The revolutionary Liverpool to Manchester railroad would eventually change people's lives forever. No one could ever have imagined that the passenger and goods railway we had built would be the forerunner of railroads that would eventually span the world… culminating in the huge task of linking both coasts of the United States together, an astonishing distance of over three thousand miles. It was and always will be a proud boast that I worked on the project that changed all our lives forever.

So let me tell you about the historic Inauguration Day, Wednesday the fifteenth of September eighteen thirty. In the preceding weeks we had seen the locomotives being tested on the now completed railroad. We felt that the eyes of the world were watching us all on that Wednesday. At dawn both my brother and I were working in strong winds and pouring rain. Our task that morning was to make certain that no stray chippings or lose clumps of earth had found their way onto the rail lines. Carefully we checked the links on the line making sure that there were no broken joints; our strict orders were that nothing should impede the smooth running of the locomotives. During the early morning the rain gradually ceased but worryingly the wind increased making our task virtually impossible. The management had also impressed upon all of us navvies that it was a great honour for us to be involved on this historic day. They also stressed that we were to keep clear of the locomotives because they would be travelling at unprecedented speeds, but what really interested us most was their promise of a large bonus if no problems arose and the trains ran smoothly.

Fortunately the skies soon cleared and the strong winds abated as we frantically tried to ensure that no debris had found its way onto the tracks. The final thing that the engineers stressed upon was that a total of eight locomotives would pass us that morning each pulling carriages packed with highly distinguished passengers. These included The Duke of Wellington who was Prime Minister at that time, also the Marquis and Marchioness of Salisbury and many other dignitaries. In total seven hundred people would travel on that inaugural rail journey. Also we were informed that trains would be travelling from Liverpool to Manchester on two separate tracks side by side, The Northumbrian Locomotive would pull the Duke of Wellington and his guests on one track, whilst on the other track the seven other locomotives, would transport the other dignitaries to Manchester.

At twenty minutes to eleven a large cannon was fired to mark the official start of proceedings. This was followed by the sound of cheering and shouting from the enormous crowds that had gathered to see this historic event. By now like everyone else that morning I found the tension overwhelming, as we were all fearful that an accident might happen on our section of the line. But fortunately our worries were unfounded... Owen and I, with the rest of our gang were stationed on the Hyton embankment about six miles from Liverpool, where by mid-morning we had been joined by hundreds of onlookers, many of whom, on finding that we had worked on the project shook our hand and asked us all sorts of questions about the construction work. By now, with the imminent sighting of trains expected at any minute the excitement became unbearable. Then we were thrilled to see the eight locomotives flash past at a tremendous rate, with everyone cheering and waving their hats at the various dignitaries. When they had passed we suddenly realised how hungry we were so we all went off in search of some much needed refreshment. Luckily we found that there were many small stalls selling food nearby.

After eating our well earned breakfast, we returned to our section of the line at Hyton and once again started searching the line for any obstructions. As we waited for the locomotives to return from Manchester rumours started to circulate that there had been a very bad accident involving William Huskisson. Mr Huskisson, it was said was the man whose foresight and drive had accomplished the wonder that we saw before us on this historic day, he was then the very popular Member of Parliament for Liverpool. Little did we know that afternoon that we would have to wait for hours, before one by one the locomotives returned? By the evening the weather had turned stormy and we became soaked from the heavy rain and hailstones, but obviously our day was not finished until the last train had passed. When the storm began most of the crowds quickly departed from the scene. After all the noise and hullabaloo when the first trains had passed by that morning, it was eerily quiet when the last locomotive returned that evening.

The following day we celebrated our success, firstly we met our gang in a local hostelry. It was wonderful to see Gerry Flynn, the ganger as he had finally recovered from his long illness and he seemed like his old self again. Obviously the only member of The Tipperary's that was missing was our sadly deceased friend Tommy Stack. Before we left the inn Gerry thanked us all for our support during his illness and said he hoped we all might work together again one day. At the time this was the last thing on my mind as I could not wait to return to Ireland. But years later I was to be eternally grateful to Gerry Flynn for his help when I needed it. After leaving the hostelry we went to Liverpool station, where the bosses had laid on a huge feast for everyone who had contributed to the success of the project. Sadly the death of William Huskisson overshadowed the proceedings on what should have been a joyous event. For both me and my brother that meal was a bitter sweet occasion, because when we said our last goodbyes to our friends and colleagues that evening, we knew that we would never see most of them again. For many of them the party was just getting started when we left, but as was usual both Owen and I resisted that great temptation to stay and enjoy ourselves. For us our priority was to return to Ireland as quickly as possible. But when I left the construction site that night for the last time it was with very mixed emotions as I wondered what the future would now hold me.

During the next couple of days while waiting in Liverpool for a passage to Queenstown, I read about the tragedy that had happened to William Huskisson. I have still retained the following cutting from a local newspaper written by Mr Thomas Creevy.

On the nineteenth of September I obtained the following eyewitness account concerning the tragic death of Mr William Huskisson given to me by Mr Jack Calcraft.

"About nine or ten passengers in the Duke of Wellington's car got out to look about them when the car stopped. Calcraft was one, Huskisson another, Esterhazy, Bill Holmes, Birch, amongst the others, then the other locomotive was seen coming up to pass them. There was a great shout to those without to get in. Both Holmes and Birch were unable to get up in time, but they stuck fast to its side, and the other engine did not touch them. Esterhazy being light was pulled in by force. Huskisson was feeble in his legs and appears to have to have lost his head, as he did his life. Calcraft tells me that Huskisson's long confinement in St George's Chapel, at King William's Hospital, brought on a complaint that Mr Taylor, his surgeon was very afraid of and had made a severe operation necessary. The effect of which has been, according to what he told Calcraft, to paralyse him in one leg and thigh. This no doubt must have increased, if it did not [cause him] to lose his life. He had written to say that his health would not let him come to the inauguration and his arrival was unexpected. Calcraft said he witnessed at first hand Huskisson's brief meeting with the Duke of Wellington and saw them shake hands shortly before Huskisson's death."

The subsequent funeral was attended by thousands of mourners and most of the shops and business's in Liverpool closed for the day as a mark of respect. We had other things on our mind at this time. The most urgent of which was the transferring of our savings to our account in Charleville. Sadly we were also leaving our landlady and great friend Mrs Sharpe, who had looked after us like a mother over the past few years. It was very upsetting for both of us to say goodbye and I feel she had shared the same emotions. On leaving I promised to keep in touch, and we were to regularly correspond until her untimely death in eighteen forty. With all our business now complete we took passage on route to Queenstown harbour. Strangely this was to be my last ever journey by sea as I was never to leave Ireland again.

CHAPTER TWO

On arriving back in our home town of Charleville in the winter of eighteen thirty, we went straight to our Uncle Michaels house to thank him for the kindness he had shown our sadly departed mother. It was a great surprise for him to see the both of us again; and he instantly invited us into the house and within a few minutes the table had been laid and our Auntie Hannah was busily preparing a meal for us. Later they told us about our poor mother's brief illness and also that that our bank had given him the funds we had arranged. He then went onto tell us that our parents cabin was now occupied by the O'Farrell family who I knew were distant relations of my father. We sat there chatting that night not realising how late it was, but fortunately both our Aunt and Uncle insisted we stayed with them until we found somewhere of our own to live. Before we went to sleep that night I thanked Owen for insisting we return home as I now understood his reasoning.

The next morning after a leisurely breakfast we went to visit our parent's grave with Michael and Hannah where we paid our belated respects to our dear mother. On seeing my mother's grave for the first time tears flooded from my eyes and I realised that I should have been there in her hour of need. All my life she was always the one I turned to when I needed help and advice and she had never let me down. As far as I can remember we had never had a cross word and she had always encouraged me to make something of myself. Both her and my father had struggled for years on a pittance and she had great hopes that Owen and I would better ourselves. When I finally stopped crying I asked my companions to leave me as I wanted to grieve alone, I must have stood there for hours thinking of all the wonderful times I had shared with my mother and before I left her graveside that day I made a solemn promise that come what may I would keep my promise and one day have my own farm.

In the weeks leading up to Christmas Owen and I began to look for a small farm to rent, but we were soon found that everywhere was now closed until the New Year. In the meantime we helped our Aunt and Uncle prepare for the Christmas celebrations. For them money was tight and so they were grateful for the financial help we were able to give them. Both Owen and I had not realised how tired we were after four years of very hard work and so this brief interlude was like a holiday for us. For me Christmas Day at my Uncle Michael's, reminded me of many previous Christmas's spent with my parents in the past, firstly we went to early mass, then home to help our Auntie prepare the feast as she had invited lots of our old friends for the traditional dinner. Later the music started with the party carrying on until the early hours of the morning. Next day St Stephens was my birthday and much to my surprise for the first time in many years Owen bought me a present. His gift was unusual as it was a spade, but for me his gift was symbolic, as it meant that I would succeed in the search for a farm. Later that day we all went to see the traditional hurling match and because as Owen was such a renowned hurler everyone wanted him to play but he reluctantly declined. He told me later that he wanted to play, but he could not take a chance and get injured as he hoped we would soon find a place to rent.

Early in the New Year we decided to pay a visit to my old friend Brian Sullivan at Ceciltown. It was an icy cold day and I knew from past experience that Brian would be at home in front of the fire. He was pleasantly surprised to see both of us and invited us to stop for dinner. Obviously as we had not met for a number of years we had lots of news to catch up with. As we chatted the conversation eventually turned to our reason for returning to Ireland. When he heard that we hoped to rent a small farm in the Charleville area his ears pricked up. Suddenly his whole manner changed and he became very business like and he asked us a series of searching questions, mainly about our financial situation. I explained that the two of us had worked virtually non stop for the past four years. Also I said that during our time in England we had earned very good wages, most of which we had saved. Now back in Ireland we were hoping to realise our dream which was to rent our own small farm. From his manner I could see that he was impressed by what we had said. On our departure that evening he kindly promised to obtain an interview for us with Mr William Grogan, the local land agent for Sir William Wrixon Beecham. Brian was as good as his word, because when we met him after mass on the following Sunday he told us to be at Mr Grogan's office at ten o'clock on the following morning.

The next morning we were both up at the crack of dawn, polishing our shoes and putting on the new suits we had purchased in Liverpool for special occasions. Before we left for town, Auntie Hannah insisted on inspecting both of us, as she knew that we needed to make a good impression at today's meeting. Fortunately we did not need to worry as our interview with Mr Grogan went very well. Brian Sullivan had he said, spoken in glowing terms about the two of us and his recommendation was good enough for him. He then mentioned how sad he was that our mother had died and how unfortunate it was that we had not heard the terrible news for many months. As we talked he asked Owen about our employment in England. Owen in reply, gave him a brief description of our work on the railroad in Liverpool. Mr Grogan on hearing this asked us many questions regarding the construction, as he said that even the newspapers in Ireland had hailed its completion as one of the Modern Wonders of the World. Our interview obviously went very well and he seemed to be impressed by both of us, because he now handed us for signing, the tenancy agreement for a small farm of ten acres. He said that it was now available at Springfort, near Charleville as the former tenant had recently died. The farm he said had been neglected but we could lease the land for twenty five years, which was the normal tenancy arrangement at the time. Owen and I were both elated at the news and thanked Mr Grogan for allowing us to have this wonderful opportunity. On leaving Mr Grogan's office we rushed back to tell our Uncle and Auntie the good news and by the end of that hectic week we had signed the tenancy agreement and made our first rental payment.

On Saturday morning the twentieth of January eighteen thirty-one, we went once again to Mr Grogan's office where we met William Grogan's son James. This was the first time I had met James Grogan and it was to be the start of a life long friendship that has endured until this day. James had been instructed by his father to take us to view the farm at Springfort. It is a three mile walk from Charleville but the three of us being young and fit and in high spirits, made quick work of the walk to what was about to be our new home. I shall never forget the first time we turned off the road and walked up the little lane to the farmhouse. This is what we had dreamed and strived for and now at last our dreams had been realised. After showing us round, James left but before leaving he handed us the keys to the farm and then he shook both our hands and wished us good luck for the future. Owen and I quickly realised that morning what a tremendous amount of work was required both on the house and also the land. After mass the next day, some old friends kindly offered to help us renovate the farmhouse, these offer's of help were very much appreciated. But before we could start work I had to go to town and purchase the building materials and also the provisions we needed. Whilst I was doing this Owen went back to Uncle Michaels for our belongings, as we had already decided to start living in our new home.

We then decided that I would concentrate on making the house habitable, while Owen worked on clearing and manuring the land preparing it for the coming spring. It was very fortunate for us that I made the farmhouse my first priority, because on the twenty ninth of January we had the coldest day in living memory. This was followed by gale force northerly winds and heavy snowfall that lasted for the next ten days. Fortunately the weather changed and by the middle of February we were both able to start work digging the land preparing it for planting our first potato seed

Easter was early that year as I remember, and we decided to invite the friends and family that had been helping us to dinner on Easter Day. With this in mind we both went to early mass and on returning home we started to prepare the feast helped by our Auntie Hannah. In the evening the music started and Springfort held the first of the many parties we were to enjoy over the years. I could not help noticing how many young girls that came, knowing that they all had their eyes on my brother Owen. But it was soon obvious that he was only interested in a local girl called Maureen Kelly.

On a bright sunny morning in the middle of April, Owen and I set off in high spirits for Buttevant Fair, as we had arranged to meet Brian Sullivan there. He had promised to help us purchase the livestock we needed and with his years of experience we gladly took up his offer. It was Market day and we followed Brian as he met and talked to his many old friends and acquaintances. At the time I thought he was just passing the time of day with them, but I found out later he was asking who was selling the best livestock. Once he had received the information he required, we went with him to make our purchases. I have witnessed in my time many farmers haggling, but none can compare with Brian. That day I received an education that I would never forget, it was a lesson from a master. As a result of his haggling we were soon the proud owners of a milking cow and five young pigs. With his work for us over Brian set off for home, as he was very busy on the farm at Churchtown. We both thanked him for taking the time to help us and promised to buy him a drink the next time we met.

I left Owen with our purchases and went in search of the various farm implements that I needed. One particular purchase I thought I would make was a scythe with a cradle attachment. A reaper using a cradle-scythe, can cut it is said, as much oats and barley as it would take four men with sickles. Luckily I managed to buy the last one in the store, together with a quantity of potato and grain seed. With this task completed, I found Owen and we somehow managed to struggle back to Springfort. That evening very tired but elated we sat by the fire and celebrated a very successful day.

During the next couple of months we worked from dawn to dusk planting potatoes and turnips, sewing oats and barley and also building outhouses for the cow, pigs and the chickens we now owned. It was at this time we started to put into practice the knowledge we had gained during our time in England, our main purpose was to improve the condition of the soil. Whilst in England we had seen that all the land was annually manured and dressed with lime, this they informed us was the most important task in their farm year. One of the English farmers advised me that you have got to put back into the soil what you take from it. Future years at Springfort were to prove the wisdom of his advice and when I saw the great improvement in our yields, it was only then that I realised the importance of this back breaking work. Although the work was very hard that first year we both appreciated the peace and tranquillity of the Irish countryside after the noise and bustle of the railway construction. In that first summer Owen worked harder than any man alive, in fact his ambition to succeed was even greater than my own.

That autumn our first harvest was not the success we had hoped for. Sadly we only managed to recoup some of the years' expenses when we sold our produce at Buttevant Fair in late September but fortunately the potato and turnips we had grown for our own consumption were more than sufficient. We now realised that we urgently needed to make improvements to our soil, so we immediately purchased as many barrels of lime as we could afford. All through November, we worked at turning over the soil in our fields and we then gave them a good dressing of manure and lime hoping that the winter rains would wash it in. I thought I had worked hard on the railway construction, but that was comparatively easy compared with trying to keep up with Owen that winter. Luckily for us the weather was reasonably good until the middle of December, but by then all our digging was finished and we could now relax and enjoy the Christmas celebrations. That year we were invited to spend Christmas with our Uncle Michael and Auntie Hannah and we both insisted on killing one of our pigs for them. It was at Christmas time that year, when Owen first started to visit the home of a neighbour John Kelly. As usual with Owen a young lady was the attraction and I soon found out that this time it was Mr Kelly's daughter Maureen.

During the winter months Owen seemed to spend more time at the Kelly's house in Doneraille, than he did at home with me. But as the weather improved and the ground began to dry out, our days were once again taken up with farm work. Also along with the tenancy of Springfort came a section of the local bog in the mountains. From the bog we dug enough turf to heat the house and cook our meals. We decided that I should cut the turf that spring whilst Owen concentrated all his efforts on the farm. Once again the pair of us worked long hours with very little rest, but we were very confident that we would have a much better harvest this year. Very occasionally Owen would go to meet Maureen and I somehow knew that his infatuation for this young lady was totally different to that of any of his previous girlfriends.

On a Sunday night in the middle of February, Owen had not arrived back from Doneraille so I went to bed only to be woken up by my very excited brother. I thought at first that he had been drinking, but I soon realised he was drunk with happiness. Dragging me out of bed he said he was going to make the most important announcement of his life and I was obviously the first to hear his good news. Owen went to the dresser and found two glasses into which he poured a large amount of whisky; he then said that he had asked Mr Kelly permission to marry Maureen. Mr and Mrs Kelly it seems were both very pleased to give their consent. As we sat there chatting Owen confessed to me that his only worry was how I would react when I heard the news. I have always been a man of few words, but that night sensing that my dear brother was in need of assurance I got up from the table and drank a toast to Owen, and his future wife Maureen. It was, I said wonderful news and shaking his hand I wished him and his young bride every success for the future. In those times the traditional date for announcing engagements was Shrove Tuesday which was on the sixth of March that year. I was greatly relieved that Owen was at last going to settle down. Also I knew that we needed someone to look after both of us as we sadly missed a woman about the house. Tragically this was not to happen and in the next few months our lives were thrown into turmoil. The following events were to totally alter my outlook on life leaving me with the feeling that social injustice will always be present in Ireland while we the Irish people are treated as an underclass in our own country.

Let me explain what the situation we encountered on our return to Ireland after spending four years working in England. Ireland and the Irish people were facing many problems at this period in time. Since the end of the Napoleonic Wars agricultural prices had fallen, obviously for a country like Ireland whose main industry was farming this was proving disastrous. As farm prices fell, more and more people began to rely on the potato as their only source of food. In the bad years when the potato crops failed many families were evicted when they failed to pay the rent. These evicted families were thrown out of their homes and were left to wander the roads begging for food. It was also during this period that large scale emigration started which was eventually to lead to millions of Irish people leaving Ireland with most of them never returning to their homeland. Another burden on the poor people of Ireland at this time was the universally hated Tithe that was levied on all households and paid to the Protestant Church of Ireland. Not only could we the people ill afford to pay it, our real objection was that the majority of us were Roman Catholics so we resented paying this alien tax.

Both Owen and I like our father before us had never become involved in any of the many secret societies that abounded all over Ireland. But when in the bad years evictions increased and families were being thrown out onto the road once again this agitation became rife throughout the country. Large groups of men calling themselves Whiteboys, or Ribbonmen, attacked wealthy landowners burning their crops or killing their livestock. It was also not uncommon for them to raid houses, or in some instances even attack the land owners or their agents in broad daylight. Mostly these acts were carried out against greedy land agents who had evicted their tenants, or greatly increased rents to the detriment of small local farmers. These Whiteboy gangs would meet at the dead of night all wearing a white shirt for identification purposes. The normal procedure they followed was the pinning of a notice threatening the landowner or his agent. This notice usually stated in no uncertain terms, that unless rents were reduced and evictions ceased certain repercussions would be forthcoming. If the warning went unheeded then retribution quickly followed.

The County of Cork was then at the centre of Whiteboy activities in Ireland and acts of terror went on daily. The authorities in Dublin sent various detachments of soldiers and militia to Charleville as the problem was getting out of control locally.

On the night of the twenty seventh of February eighteen thirty-one, the house of Samuel Hutchins at Fortlands near Charleville was attacked by an armed party. It was later reported that they then threatened Mr. Hutchins and fired shots at his house. Finally a notice was pinned to his front door that stated that this was the final warning. It went onto say that there were to be no more evictions, and no further rent increases. If this warning was ignored it warned terrible retributions would be forthcoming. Somehow one of the servants had managed to escape from Fortlands and rushed to the military barracks in Charleville to raise the alarm. A detachment of cavalry was at once sent to Fortlands House, but as they heard the soldiers approaching the Whiteboys scattered across the countryside fleeing for their lives. They all knew the dire consequences of capture; either hanging or transportation to the colonies was the harsh penalty at the time.

It has never been adequately explained to me how my brother Owen, who was coming home from visiting Maureen Kelly on that fateful night got caught up in the mellee that ensued. I have always maintained that the soldiers had orders to arrest anyone who they caught in the vicinity of the raid. Obviously he contested his innocence, but under the Martial law then in existence no one was prepared to listen to what he had to say. He later told me that he then went berserk when he realised what a terrible situation he now found himself in. I have on occasions witnessed Owen losing his temper so it was no surprise to me that it needed six solders to apprehend him. The military rounded up all those they thought were involved that night and they were then taken to the barracks in Charleville. Here they were put in chains and sent under heavy armed escort to Mallow County Jail. Owen still protesting his innocence was obviously taken with them.

When I woke up the next morning I was moaning to myself that Owen had not returned home again, thinking that he had spent the night at the Kelly's house. As the day wore on I began to worry because he was always home for breakfast. When it reached midday and there was still no sign of him I decided to go to Doneraille. By now I was certain that something terrible had happened to him and I had a sense of trepidation when I arrived at the Kelly's home. I was immediately welcomed by John Kelly and his family who insisted I sat and had a bite to eat with them. It was soon obvious to me that they thought I was paying them a social visit, but when I explained that Owen had not returned home the previous night Maureen said that he had left there at ten o'clock as usual. By now alarm bells were ringing and accompanied by John Kelly I headed for Charleville looking for my brother. On our arrival in the town everybody was talking about the sensational events of the previous night at Fortlands House. On making enquiries we soon found out that the military authorities had made numerous arrests and the arrested men, had already been sent under military escort to Mallow for trial. By now I was in a state of shock, because I realised why Owen had not returned home. But John tried to reassure me by saying he had probably met some friends after leaving Maureen and gone drinking with them and he was certain that Owen would be back home by now. Sadly somehow I knew that he was wrong and knowing that they would have a list of those arrested I headed straight to the barracks.

After many hours of waiting, my worst fears were realised when it was confirmed that Owen Casey, of Springfort, Charleville was one of the Whiteboy's that had been taken after the attack on the residence of Mr Samuel Hutchins. He was they confirmed one of the felons that had carried out this terrible deed against a gentleman and his innocent young family. On hearing that my worst fears were confirmed, I told John Kelly to hurry home and tell his daughter what had happened. Obviously I now had only one thought in my head; I knew I had to get to Mallow as soon as possible. Fortunately I managed to get a lift from a friendly carter who put me down in Mallow town square. By this time my shock had turned to a feeling of anger and frustration. But realising that it was imperative for Owens sake that I calmed down, I asked for directions and made my way to the jail.

At the jail I was again treated with total disdain by the prison guards who told me to wait and then ignored me for hour after hour. By ten o'clock that evening I realised that I must find a bed for the night and return to the jail the next morning. On the next day I again requested permission to speak to my brother and the only answer I received was to wait there and they would see what they could do. After a whole week of frustration and delays I was finally allowed to see Owen. My heart sank when I saw him because he was in a pitiful state, his face covered in congealed blood and he was unable to stand after the fearful beatings he had endured. Lying on a bed of filthy straw, with his wrists and ankles manacled it was truly heartbreaking for me to see him in such a terrible condition. But as always he still had that twinkle in his eyes and he vowed that whatever the future held for him no one would ever break his spirit. With our enduring bond of love and respect for each other I knew that he would somehow come through this terrible ordeal.

Summary justice was quickly dispensed in those troubled times; the fifteen men caught that night were tried and sentenced in one day. The trials were a complete farce as the only witness called, was the cavalry officer in charge on the night of the raid. In his brief account of the events at Fortlands House, he described how terrified the occupants were on his arrival. He then went onto explain how his men had rounded up the fleeing ruffians. When the Judge asked him were the men he had arrested those now in the dock, he replied undoubtedly they were. Finally he told the court that James Hussey and Patrick Griffin when arrested were found to be carrying firearms, but the evidence to collaborate this fact was never produced before the court. This lack of evidence did not appear to effect the trial, as both were sentenced to hang. To my eternal horror theses two unfortunate young men met their maker the very next morning, although they were without doubt totally innocent. The rest of the accused were sentenced to transportation to the colonies, which meant they would be sent to Australia. When Owen Casey's name was read out in court, I let out a howl of anguish as the judge pronounced his sentence as transportation. For this indiscretion I was seized upon by the militia and thrown out into the street. To this day I cannot believe that someone who was completely innocent like my brother could receive such a savage sentence. This harsh treatment of my brother would haunt me for the rest of my life, and I have never lost the feeling of injustice and anger that I felt at that time. This feeling of hatred against the authorities that governed Ireland would fester within me and was eventually the reason I became a member of the Fenian Party.

After being thrown out of court, I decided my only course of action was to return home, as I was getting very worried about the farm. Fortunately both my Uncle Michael and John Kelly had been to Springfort in my absence and had kindly kept things under control. Sadly when I arrived home Maureen Kelly was also there with her father. They could instantly see from my face that the news was bad. Poor Maureen was shaking with emotion as I described what had happened in the courtroom that morning. At first she could not comprehend what I was saying when I told her that Owen had been sentenced to transportation, because she was such a state of shock. But when she finally realised what I had said, the poor girl fainted and collapsed to the floor. Both John and I rushed to pick her up and gently laid her down on the bed. We then decided that I would sit with her, whilst John hurried home to fetch Mrs Kelly as we were both very worried about her condition. As I sat there by the bedside looking at this young girl, who now had her life completely shattered it occurred to me that it was all a nightmare and when I woke up everything would be as normal, but obviously this was wishful thinking.

As I sat there I realised that before Mr and Mrs Kelly returned I must plan ahead. My main priority was the welfare of my brother, but there was also the farm to consider. Fortunately it was not long before Maureen's parents returned and they sat by her bedside until she revived. Over the next few days her condition rapidly improved and she was soon able to return home.

The news of Owens plight spread rapidly and over the coming days I was overwhelmed with offers of help from his many friends. This help was to prove invaluable over the coming weeks and I doubt that I could have survived on the farm without it. Each Saturday morning I left Springfort at the crack of dawn for my weekly visit to Mallow Jail and luckily on many occasions I managed to hitch a ride. Over the coming weeks the wagon- masters and carters on hearing the reason for my visits to Mallow were all very sympathetic. This sympathy eventually led to me being given regular rides to and from the jail; this was especially helpful when Maureen Kelly came with me. Prison for Owen was a living Hell; he was just   like a wounded animal as he could never bear to be incarcerated. For a man like him, losing his freedom was bad enough, but knowing that you were the victim of a terrible miscarriage of justice was heart breaking.

On my last visit to the jail we talked about the farm and he was pleased when I asked him for his advice on the many problems I was encountering. As usual he was very interested in the running of Springfort and the work that I needed to do, obviously wishing that he could be there to help me. The strange thing was that in talking to him on that final visit before he was transported, instead of being totally dispirited; he was gradually coming to terms with his predicament. To my eternal shame it was me that broke down as we hugged each other for what I thought was the last time. On parting he vowed that someday he would return to Ireland and I was to make sure not to lose Springfort. I knew in my heart of hearts that this was just a dream, because to my knowledge no one transported had ever returned from Australia.

I was never to visit him in jail again because on Tuesday the sixth of April, my brother and fifteen other prisoners were taken from their cells still dressed in the stinking and flea ridden clothes that they had on when they were arrested. Then they were chained at the wrists and ankles and placed in three carts with a military escort for the long journey to Queenstown. The next morning one of the wagon masters I had befriended came to tell me that he had seen a convoy on the road that was carrying the prisoners from Mallow Jail to Queenstown Harbour. He was certain that Owen was one or the convicts in the party and he thought that I should be informed. Thanking him for his kindness, I set out at once for the Kelly's home in Doneraille to tell them the news. When I told John Kelly that I was going to follow the military convoy to its final destination and hoped to speak to Owen for one last time he promised to look after the farm in my absence. When Maureen heard what I was proposing to do, she immediately asked if she could accompany me.

Under the circumstances I obviously could not refuse and so after having dinner with her parents we set out at once on the long road to Queenstown. We reached Mallow that evening where we found comfortable lodgings for the night. The next morning we were up and out at the crack of dawn, as we hoped to catch up with the convoy that day. Once again I was fortunate as we were offered a lift by one of the many carriers that were heading in our direction.

The carrier who gave us a lift that morning had made all his deliveries and was returning to Cork with an empty wagon. So when we told him the reason for our journey, he immediately shook up the reins and we were soon rattling along the road. The convoy in contrast had made very slow progress as it was being hampered by the weeping wives, and children of the prisoners. By noon the convoy came in sight, and so after thanking the carrier we jumped down from his wagon and started to follow the procession of carts. Thankfully Maureen Kelly was an optimist like my brother and her optimism helped keep my spirits up in the following days. The forty-mile journey to Queenstown was to take five long weary days with every step filling my heart with a feeling of dread and foreboding for my brother's future. Each evening when the convoy stopped for the night, Maureen somehow managed to speak a few words to Owen. In these brief conversations they talked about their future together and Owen made Maureen promise that she would someday join him in Australia. Although I knew that this would never happen I kept these thoughts to myself. Sadly we reached our journey's end when we finally arrived at Queenstown Harbour.

Once there the authorities wasted very little time in readying the prisoners for their transportation. From the quayside we could see the prisoners being issued with the clothes of a transportee. Each man being issued with three shirts, two pairs of trousers, and a pair of shoes, they were also given a Guernsey smock, a woollen cap and handkerchiefs. All of their own clothing was discarded and burnt. Once they had been kitted out for their long voyage, they were immediately ferried out to the waiting ship. This was all carried out as though they were cattle being sent to market all their dignity had been stripped from them and from now on they would be branded as convicts.

On speaking to a sailor on the quay I found out that their ship was named "The George" and he had heard that it already had on board one hundred and twenty convicts from other parts of Ireland. He went onto tell me that he had heard that another two convoys were expected from Galway and "The George" would not leave until they arrived, In the intervening days before the ship departed, Maureen and I managed to pay a local boatman to row us out to see Owen exercising on deck. From our small boat we managed to attract his attention and Maureen called out her last ever words to her loved one. This brief interlude was soon over because the very next day the ship departed for Australia. That last sighting of Owens mass of black curly hair and smiling face has haunted me to this day.

And so "The George" set out on its five-month voyage to the other side of the world, with both of us waving frantically until it was a tiny dot in the distance. Slowly Maureen and I turned our back on the sea and began our slow journey back to Charleville. For the next two days we hardly spoke a word as we were both deep in thought, I was trying to understand how such a tragedy had occurred. While poor Maureen was now too distraught to speak. As we neared her house in Doneraille she at last unburdened herself to me. For the remainder of our journey together we both confided in each other because we now realised how much we had become to rely on Owen. Sadly we had both lost the one person in the world that we loved. The future for both us we knew was bleak in those troubled times, but before leaving I made Maureen promise to come to me for help if ever she felt the need. Many years later when both her parents had perished in the Famine I was in fact able to help her.

It was strange to see Maureen all those years later and at first I did not recognise her. When last we had met she was a very attractive young girl, but now she was a haggard women who had lost her will to live. My wife Catherine brought her into the house and gave her the first good meal she had eaten in weeks. Maureen stayed with us for a few weeks while she regained her strength. At the end of her stay with us she finally plucked up the courage to ask me for financial help, as she was trying to raise the fare to emmigrate to America. Her only brother was now living in Boston and she hoped to join him there. Obviously I gave her what I could afford, but this sadly was the last I ever saw of that unfortunate girl, who through no fault of her own had lost everything.

As I sit here reminiscing about that tragic period in my life, it is a wonder how I survived the following twelve months. On arriving back at Springfort my thoughts and feelings were in turmoil. Deep depression, anger and despair gripped me for months on end. Also for the first time in my life I realised that we as a nation should not continue to be ruled by a tyrannical government that was only interested in the Ascendancy Class. I vowed to myself that one day in the future I would somehow fight back against the establishment that had taken my brother away from me. During that time I channelled all of my fury and anger into the improvements that Owen had said we had to do if we were to make our farm profitable.

Working from dawn to dusk for months on end, the only rest I had was when I made my occasional visits to the Charleville reading room to peruse the newspapers. My main reason for doing this was to check on the shipping movements of vessels arriving at Queenstown. This information was generally in the local Cork papers. On each visit I hoped to read that "The George" had returned from its long journey to Australia. The months slowly passed with my hopes gradually receding that I would ever read of the return of "The George." Then suddenly over a year later I read that "The George" had arrived back in Queenstown.

It was reported that there had been many arrests after the recent wave of unrest in Ireland, with most of those arrested being sentenced to transportation. Obviously that was why "The George" had returned to Ireland for another batch of transportees. In the report I read it stated that these convicts were bound for the notorious settlement called Tasmania. Over the last months there had been numerous reports of unrest in the colony of Australia. This had lead to a new penal settlement being built in the island of Tasmania, This settlement was eventually to house the most dangerous prisoners and employ the most sadistic guards. The knowledge that "The George" had returned, after hopefully taking Owen safely to Australia, allowed me to concentrate fully on my task of making the necessary improvements to the farm.

Apart from my visits to town for supplies, Sunday mass was my only other relaxation of the week and during this period the underlying tension of the people of our town land could be plainly felt. The Emancipation Law for Catholics in Ireland had been passed, this was to give us Catholics some limited freedom but in April eighteen thirty-one, Martial law was brought into force once more. The long felt grievance of the giving of tithes to the Ascendancy,

Church of Ireland was still with us. Intimidation and agragarian violence was again part of life in Ireland and the town of Charleville soon began to resemble a military camp. It was usually after Sunday mass that I caught up with all the local news, as all I did during the rest of the week was work and sleep. Fortunately my hard work and efforts at improving the soil gradually increased my yields. Also I have always been an avid reader and it was at this time that I joined the circulation library that had been started in town. This allowed me to read periodicals at my leisure instead of going to the Charlevile reading rooms.

The big event of my farming year was always in October, when I went to the market at Buttevant. At that time and for many years after it was the largest and best market in North Cork. Buyers came to Buttevant from all over the West of Ireland, as the animals sold there were always in very good condition.

That lovely autumn morning, I set off very early with the intention of buying a cow and a couple of young pigs. My harvest had been very good that year and for the first time in months I found some of my old optimism returning. As I neared the town the roads were teeming with people, livestock and carts full of local produce. As I picked my way through the crowds that morning I met and greeted many old friends and acquaintances, who were as always hoping that prices would be good. On reaching the town the sights and sounds of the market were amazing. Dealers, huxters, tinkers, musicians and singers, all trying to be heard above the noise of the crowd.

When I reached the area set aside for the cattle sale, I immediately started to question an old friend of mine John Sugrue, who I knew had a good eye for buying cattle. When I told him that I wanted to purchase a milking cow he led me straight to a farmer he knew and pointed out the one I should buy. After being introduced by John, I began at once to haggle with the farmer as I realised that all the best animals would soon be sold. The process of haggling over the price of an animal is still the custom in some parts of rural Ireland. It could on some occasions be a long drawn out affair with bids and counter bids and also much banter between buyer and seller. But as I recall, my cow was soon purchased that day and John Sugrue's advice as usual was very good.

After having a quick bite to eat, I met some of my relatives who fortunately did not mention my brother, but discussed instead the high prices that the cattle were fetching that year. In the early afternoon with all my money spent, I set off at once to return to Springfort with my new cow and young pigs. By walking as fast as possible I quickly left the fairground with all its bustle and noise. My intention was to get as far away as possible from Buttevant before the crowd decided to leave. That evening as I neared my farm, I wondered if Owen would have been as pleased with the livestock I had bought that day. All our hard work was now starting to reap dividend's, but sadly he was not there to share with me my success. But deep down I did feel a little bit of pride in what I had achieved that year.

Soon the Christmas of eighteen thirty-one, was upon me and my intentions that year was to ignore the celebrations, as I still could not get over the deep depression that still hung over me. But my family and friends had other ideas and I was invited to come and enjoy the festivities with them. Surprisingly we had a wonderful time and as the harvest had been good everyone had plenty to eat On Christmas Day, as I was staying with relatives who lived near the village of Dromina we attended the local chapel for mass. After the service like Irishmen the world over we stood around chatting about the latest news. Little did I realise that this would be the day that change my life. As I have previously said Owen was always the one for the girls, but on that occasion by some strange chance the McGrath family came up to speak to us and my cousin John Keane introduced me to them and we all shook hands wishing each other good luck for the coming year.

As we stood there chatting I noticed their daughter Catherine. She had left the chapel late and had then hurried over to be with her family. After being introduced it was for me love at first sight. As I was a confirmed bachelor, this chance introduction was to give me a reason for living again after the trauma of losing my brother. I have often said over the years since that chance meeting that I could not recollect ever meeting such an attractive girl as Catherine. That morning I tried to make some small talk, but unfortunately this is something I have never been very good at. It seemed the harder I tried to say something worthwhile, the more tongue tied I became. Luckily Catherine seemed to understand my predicament, because she brought up the subject of my brother's transportation and asked if I had received any communication from him. I explained that all I knew was that the ship that had taken him to Australia had reportedly returned to Ireland. This fact I thought was a good sign, as I had read many accounts of ships floundering in the stormy seas on the long voyage.

During the coming weeks I could not get Catherine out of my mind and so I started to regularly attend mass at Dromina, hoping against hope to speak to her again, but every Sunday she was usually surrounded by many of the local young men of the parish and completely ignored me. My cousins quickly realised my reason for going to their chapel each Sunday and ribbed me unmercifully. This was to go on for many months, but I was determined that somehow I would speak to her again. Finally just before Easter, I managed to at last speak to her alone. This was the chance I had waited so long for and so plucking up courage I asked her if she would accompany me to a dance in Charleville on the coming Saturday and to my great surprise she readily agreed.

During the following week I spent a great deal of time practising the steps my mother had taught me as a child, luckily I could still remember most of them. On the Saturday afternoon, for the first time since my interview with the Land Agent, I put on the suit I had purchased in Liverpool. Then with butterflies in my stomach, I set off for Dromina, but how I now wished that Owen was at home on that day, for he would surely have given me some good advice on what to say and do on this occasion. But I need not have worried because as soon I arrived at the McGrath's house, they immediately invited me to sit and have dinner with them. Mrs McGrath fussed over me as though I was one of her sons; I found out later that both of her boys had emigrated to America. When we sat down to eat Catherine insisted on sitting next to me and from that moment on I began to relax.

It was so good to sit and eat a meal with a family again after months of eating alone. There was obviously the added attraction that at last I was in the company of Catherine the girl that I was smitten with. After the most enjoyable meal I had eaten in years, we set off for the dance with other couples joining us on the way. By the time we got to the dance there was a big happy crowd of us, all in high spirits. Catherine looked wonderful that night and I could see everyone admiring her. When the music started we danced the jigs and reels, not missing one dance all evening. All my inhibitions left me and at the end of the evening I told Catherine that I had not felt this happy in years. Before I left her at Dromina that night, I plucked up courage and asked take her out again. At first she pretended to say no, but then burst out laughing and said of course I could.

After I left Catherine I had even forgot about Owen for a few brief hours because I was so happy. I strolled home without a care in the world feeling really pleased that the evening had gone so well. For the next couple of months I met her after Sunday mass to discuss which dance we would go to that week Then the days would drag by until we met again. Soon we were inseparable, and luckily both of her parents were very kind to me. But with no one to advise me what course of action I should now take, I decided to pay a visit to my Uncle Michael and Auntie Hannah. Obviously they had heard that I was seeing Catherine, as by now it was common knowledge. When I asked them how I should now proceed, they said if I was sure of my choice I should arrange an interview with Mr. McGrath. At this interview I was to ask Catherine's father if we could announce our engagement as was the custom at that time. Armed with this advice I could not wait for my next meeting with Catherine. Unfortunately we were not seeing each other until the following Sunday as I was busy on the farm.

That week passed by very slowly, but as I worked I tried to think of what I was going to say to both Catherine and her father. On that Sunday I awoke early and spent hours trying to make myself look presentable as I was obviously hoping to impress. After mass that morning I seemed to wait an age before Catherine appeared. Her first comment was that I looked as though I was dressed to go to a wedding. There was now nothing more I could say but to blurt out what I proposed to do. On hearing of my intentions her face lit up and she said she had been wondering how long it would be before I plucked up enough courage to ask her father, this was music to my ears and we decided to go straight back to Catherine's home. As we neared the house I walked slower and slower wondering what kind of reception my proposal would receive.

On our arrival Catherine quickly disappeared saying she was going to help her mother prepare dinner. Mr McGrath then came out and asked me to stay for dinner, I must say he was a wonderful man and in the coming years we became firm friends. On this occasion I felt very nervous and as we sat there chatting about the weather and other farming topics I realised that Catherine and her mother were keeping well out of our way. Finally I stood up from the table and told Mr McGrath what I had in mind. He greeted my proposal with a stony silence and as I waited for his reply, the room was so quiet I could hear the clock ticking. Then much to my great pleasure, John McGrath, who I found out later was always a joker, winked at me and then started to laugh saying, Patrick nothing would please me more than to have you as my son-in -law. On hearing her father laughing, Catherine and her mother came running into the room. Soon a bottle of whisky was produced and we all drank a toast to the future. Then we had dinner and Mrs McGrath certainly excelled herself that day later it was a very drunk but happy man that made his way slowly back home to Springfort that night.

During the next few months I went to Dromina on every possible occasion to see Catherine and looking back, I realise what wonderful days they were for both of us. At harvest time John McGrath and I agreed that with both his sons now in America and with Owen in Australia, it would be sensible to pool our resources and work together during the busy times. This idea worked so well that John and I co-operated every year up until his sad death in eighteen forty-five. With all the harvesting finished, we began to make preparations for the forthcoming wedding. After nearly two years of living alone in Springfort the house had become sadly neglected and I was ashamed of it when Catherine and her family came to visit for the first time. On this visit it was traditional for the father of the bride to be shown around the farm where his daughter was going to live. I could tell that John McGrath was impressed by the improvements I had made and with the ideas for the future. Sadly both Catherine and her mother were not so complimentary about the house which they said was in a sorry state.

Before they left that day the only problem we had to resolve was the amount of dowry that I should receive. This was the conversation I had been dreading as I knew that the McGrath's would insist on paying me a sum they could ill afford. Many families then and up to this day have had to borrow money for their daughter's dowry at exorbitant rates which have left them in debt for years. Money lenders, or as we called them Gobbeen Men, are notorious for their greed and I did not want John McGrath to get in debt on my behalf. We eventually came to a compromise; I was to receive a total of fifteen pounds. Five pounds was to be paid on the Wedding Day and the rest when he could afford to pay me. He was as good as his word, because over the following years I received every penny that was owed. With this very embarrassing matter resolved, I could now look forward to spending Christmas at Dromina with my future wife.

During the next few months Catherine and her mother made many much needed improvements to my house. When the work was completed it was unrecognisable from the shambles I had lived in. They had me painting from dawn to dusk, the outside walls were scrubbed and then white washed. When the outside of the house was finished they then purchased paint for the inside, by the time the painting was completed my arms were sore and my neck was aching. The next step was to buy some much needed additional furniture. When the house was eventually ready for Catherine's arrival, I was given strict orders by Mrs McGrath to keep it tidy.

Christmas that year was a very special time, because when I went to visit friends and family, Catherine came with me for the first time. During the holiday festivities we obviously also had to visit all of the McGrath's friends and so that Christmas was a very memorable occasion.

In the first weeks of the New Year we made arrangements for the wedding to take place at Shrove Tide, which that year was on the sixth of March. It was up until recent times traditional to marry at Shrove Tide. I can remember before the terrible famine years that on some occasions there would be ten or more weddings in our Parish on the same day. Fortunately for us, ours was the only wedding in Dromina that year; this meant that the Parish Priest was able to stay for the whole day which was a real honour.

Finally after all the preparations the wedding day arrived. I made my way to the McGrath's very early that morning, accompanied by my Uncle Michael, who because Owen was obviously not available had agreed to act as my best man. The house was a hive of industry when we arrived and we were soon put to work helping to finish the last remaining tasks. During the morning I was introduced to Daniel McGrath, who on hearing that his sister was to be married had made the long journey home from Boston in America especially for the wedding. Neighbours and friends brought presents of fowl, bacon, bread, cakes and beverages of all kinds. On speaking to my uncle he suggested that as Catherine's brother had made the long and hazardous voyage to be at his sister's side on her wedding day, it would be the prudent to ask him to act as a master of ceremonies. When I mentioned my Uncles proposal to Daniel, he readily agreed. The master of ceremonies duties were vital to the success of any wedding as they included making sure the musicians were well lubricated. They were expected to call for the next song or dance, in fact it was an onerous task, but it was also regarded as a great honour to be asked.

Fortunately it was a lovely bright spring day and by eleven o'clock we had finished all the arrangements. By now I was getting very agitated, worrying that something would go wrong, then suddenly we heard shouting and laughing and then much to my great delight I could see a number of riders on horseback approaching down the lane led by John McGrath with Catherine riding pillion,. The arriving of the bride and her father signalled the beginning of the festivities. Then just before noon the priest arrived, with his arrival the music and feasting stopped and all the guests crowded into the house to see the wedding ceremony.

Obviously I was very nervous and apprehensive because throughout my life I have never liked being the centre of attention and I knew that the occasion was about to overwhelm me and I would be overcome with emotion. My body was shaking when the priest instructed me to say my vows, but when I tried to speak my voice was so feeble he had to keep urging me to speak louder. The more I tried the harder it became, but also it seemed as though I was having a wonderful dream. There beside me was this beautiful young girl of eighteen and I was at last getting married. After the terrible things that had happened in the last few years, I thought this moment would never happen, then while still in a daze I heard the priest pronounce us man and wife. Only at that moment I realised that at last all of my dreams had come true.

After the ceremony the priest called for witnesses, many of our guests pressed forward as it was considered an honour .to have your name recorded on the wedding register. Then the party really got under way and this was the moment I had been waiting for, to have the first dance with my beautiful young bride. I can still picture her now, with her long flowing black hair and that irresistible twinkle in her eyes. My only regret was that Owen was sadly absent. His presence on this the best day of my life would have been the answer to all of my prayers. But I realised that for once I must forget about my beloved brother, as I knew he would want me to be happy and enjoy my wedding day. With this thought in my mind I threw myself into the merry-making. Even Catherine complimented me on the way I danced that day. But when she danced the reel with Daniel her brother, she put everyone to shame as she was a truly wonderful dancer.

During the evening as was tradition a group of Soupers, sometimes called straw boys arrived. There were in all seven of them, all had straw cloaks and wore masks with one of them being a fiddle player. Before coming into the house they had to ask my permission to enter. On entering, their leader approached Catherine and asked her to dance. Three of his companions then asked three other girls to step onto the floor and then they all danced an eight handed reel to the music of their own fiddle player. Thunderous applause greeted the end of the dance and then Daniel as master of ceremonies called for a round of drinks. Fergal Dermott one of the Soupers was renowned all over County Cork as a talented singer and he was then asked to entertain us. After much persuasion and another couple of drinks he called for quiet and began to sing in Gaelic. The songs he sang for us were haunting ballads that had many of the ladies present reaching for their handkerchiefs, but his final song was a rousing rebel tune that lifted all our hearts. Then raising a cheer for Catherine and me they left the party to tremendous cheers.

On their departure my wife and I boarded a hired trap and left to begin our new life together at Springfort. As we headed towards home Catherine started to sob, the excitement of the day and the realisation that she was leaving her home and family for the first time in her life now overwhelmed her. But I tried my hardest to reassure her that she had made the right decision and by the time we reached our farm the tears had been replaced by smiles. Before entering the house I picked Catherine up and carried her over the threshold welcoming her to her new home. Once inside the house we were greatly surprised to find that our neighbours had come to the house and left a meal and placed bowls of fresh flowers in every room. But by now we were both extremely tired after our long and hectic day, so ignoring the food we went straight to bed.

In the next few wonderful months I soon realised how lucky I was, Catherine although only a young girl was both practical and hard working, she was also was very good at managing our finances. Life for me soon changed dramatically, the house was now always spotless and I had to reluctantly mend my ways. She would not tolerate my untidiness in any shape or form and every farm implement had to be cleaned and stored after use. The changes that she instigated were in the long run to be very beneficial, although at the time I was very sceptical. My marriage was the turning point in my life, because from the age of fourteen when I left home to work at Ceciltown until our wedding; I had only myself to care for but obviously everything was now so very different and fortunately I quickly adapted to my new circumstances. We were both fortunate to have a long happy marriage together and I know that without Catherine by my side I would not have survived the catastrophic events of the coming years.

During the summer we started to make plans for the farm. A kitchen garden was started near the house and various vegetables and fruit were grown to supplement our diet. My investment in liming and manuring the soil now started to pay off with improved yields and that year the harvest was excellent and gave us sufficient funds to increase our livestock. Another cow and some pigs were purchased and we also decided to build a shed to keep our chickens. These purchases were made as usual at Buttevant Fair in October, but this year was different as I now had Catherine with me. For her market day was always a big event and she insisted that we dressed up for the occasion. On reaching Buttevant, she always went off to meet many of her old friends. Fair

Day in Buttevant was always the highlight of Catherine's year; it was the day she purchased the materials for the clothes she made during the long winter nights. But most importantly it was also her chance to hear all the latest local gossip. That year and every subsequent year, we returned home very late laden down with the materials for Catherine's dress making and the livestock that I had purchased.

We both enjoyed those wonderful early years of married life attending all kinds of social occasions. It seemed not a week went by without us being invited to some sort of merriment or other, culminating during the Christmas period when it seemed that everyone made an extra effort to enjoy the festive season.

Unfortunately the underlying tensions of agrigarian violence still existed. I purposely did not involve myself, but my sympathies were for the poor people who were being evicted by the greedy land agents. Another grievance at this time, as I have previously stated which caused great anger, was the tithe system. This was a tax on all farms. This tax was used for the upkeep and stipends of the Church of Ireland the Protestant ascendancy. As most of the population were Catholics this obviously caused widespread resentment, especially when the harvest was bad, because it was only in the good times that small farms broke even. The poverty and misery of evicted families led to an increased Whiteboy agitation. This led in turn to the authorities reintroducing another Coercion Bill in the English Parliament which was immediately followed by Martial Law. The current situation in Ireland I knew could not continue.

Apart from the literature I received from the circulating library, it was still my practice to go on a weekly visit to Charleville reading rooms. I was always on the lookout for news from Australia, trying to ascertain if any of the convicted men ever returned to Ireland. Although now very happily married, my brother Owen was never far from my thoughts and I always lived in hope that someday he would return. With this thought in mind, I scoured the newspapers for any reports of prisoners coming back home. Very occasionally there was mention of one or two men returning, but worryingly it was the harrowing accounts of the terrible treatment they were suffering that caught my imagination. Newspaper articles carried stories of prisoners who had received fifty lashes for very minor offences, with many men dying as a consequence of the severe lashings they received. Every night before we went to sleep Catherine and I would say a prayer for my brother's safe return, it was always my wife's wish that someday she would meet the brother that she had heard so much about.

For me the newspapers and periodicals have always been my main source of information about new farming methods and the latest livestock prices. Strangely my young wife also became very interested in these articles and some of the new ideas that we tried were to prove highly successful in the future.

In eighteen thirty-five, the headlines in all the local newspapers were dominated by the exploits of an old acquaintance of mine Martin Beecher. As you may recall we had become acquainted when I was a young lad, working on a farm owned by one of his relations. This relation was Sir William Wixom-Beecher the largest land owner in our part of County Cork. Martin Beecher had subsequently become one of the most famous horsemen in England. He was, it was reported, to be seen riding at all the major racecourses. His achievements in the saddle had it seems brought him much success over the past years. But his name will always be remembered for his exploits at the Aintree racecourse near Liverpool, which was the venue for The Grand National of eighteen thirty five. From my knowledge of horse racing I knew The Grand National had the toughest obstacles of any racecourse in the world and each year very few horses completed the course. In the reports of the race that year the newspapers wrote that Martin Beecher had been unseated by his horse at the largest obstacle in the race. He was we are told leading the race at this time; but he quickly realised his situation and formed up cavalry style just under the bank of the jump. This prompt action enabled the rest of the field to clear him and his horse in safety. When the race officials heard of his chivalrous act they decided to rename the offending obstacle Beechers Brook in his honour. This story was the talk of Ireland for many months and as far as I know the name of the obstacle still remains the same until this day.

When I returned that week from my usual trip to the reading room in Charleville, I told Catherine about Martin Beecher, but she was more interested in the local gossip. Unusually on this occasion I did not have any news for her, apart from hearing of a dance in town on the following Saturday. Dancing was always Catherine's passion; she would have gone to a dance every night if it had been possible. But our hectic social life came to an abrupt end in eighteen thirty five, when to our great joy she found that she was pregnant. I had great difficulty trying to stop her helping at harvest time that year; I had to eventually persuade her to return home to her mothers to rest. Obviously all our family and friends celebrated our good news, especially at Christmas festivities. Our first child, a baby boy was born on the seventh of March eighteen thirty-six. We called our son John as a mark of respect for Catherine's father.

We were both obviously very happy and overjoyed with his birth, as Catherine had always said she wanted to fill Springfort with our children. But our joy soon turned to sadness as poor John only lived for five months. Our lovely bouncing boy unfortunately caught pneumonia and tragically died after a short illness.

Catherine was obviously broken hearted and it was many months before she got over our terrible sadness. Gradually we managed to overcome our grief and in January eighteen thirty eight, Catherine thankfully announced she was pregnant again. This time unlike her previous pregnancy her confinement went exceedingly well and on the twelfth of October eighteen thirty- eight, she gave birth to another boy. This son we named Michael, in honour of my uncle who had been a great comfort to me when Owen was transported. Michael was a bonny baby and we were both delighted with him. After his birth Catherine quickly regained the strength and vitality that she had before the tragedy of losing John.

Our lives now settled down to the slow pace of country life, much enhanced now that we had a child around the house. Deep down I still harboured a terrible hatred against the authorities, who had ruined the life of my brother Owen and I still after all these years, can never forgive those who sent an innocent man to a far distant land without a fair trial. But although my heart was filled with this injustice, I had never become involved in politics. This all changed in the summer of eighteen forty- two, when after coming out of mass in Charleville on a Sunday morning with Catherine and my son Michael, I noticed a group calling itself the Loyal National Repeal Association collecting funds.

My curiosity was aroused because during the previous twenty years, I had heard and read in great detail about Daniel O'Connell and his fight for Catholic rights, culminating with his victory in the winning of Emancipation for the Catholic Church in Ireland. After this success he had turned his attention to the Repeal of the Union between England and Ireland. The ultimate aim of his new campaign was to be the return of Irish Members of Parliament from London. This was to be followed by the reinstatement of our own Parliament in Dublin. His valid argument was that the Union was a total disaster for the people of Ireland and Repeal and self government free from outside influences would improve the lives of millions of Irishmen. I could after living in England for a number of years understand the opinions he expressed. We were a small very poor country with our economy totally dependent on agriculture. But most of the land was owned by rich English landowners who mainly lived in England. This meant that the high rents they received from us tenant farmers did not benefit the economy of Ireland in any way, but was spent in England. Ultimately he argued that this situation would eventually lead to disaster, unfortunately this prophecy would come true, but even he did not realise the scale of the catastrophe that eventually overwhelmed us.

That year Daniel O'Connell addressed meetings all over Ireland, with ever increasing attendances. Very soon the newspapers were calling them Monster Meetings and it was reported that the authorities in Dublin Castle became alarmed at the enormous popularity that O'Connell now enjoyed. At each of his meetings he pressed home his basic argument; this was that only a native Irish Parliament could bring about the over-riding need for change in Ireland. This simple message struck a chord with everyone that heard it at the time and if only it had been heeded by the Members of Parliament, in London what was to follow might have been partially eliminated.

Over the next few weeks I discussed the aims of the Repeal Association with my wife before I decided to join the organisation. Once I had committed myself it was not long before I became a prominent member of the local Charleville branch. So when Daniel O'Connell, came to our town on May the eightieth, eighteen forty-three, I was in the leading contingent headed by the Very Reverend Doctor Croke that marched into Main Street behind our local band. Next in order were units from Kilbolane, Freemount and Kanturk, led by Mr Robert MacCarthy with his band, Rockhill, Colmanswel and Bruree, then followed contingents from Ceciltown, Ballyclough, Kilfinane, Ballyhea, Ballingarry, Dromina and Drewscourt. Bringing up the rear was the Pastor of Mallow the Very Reverend Doctor Collins, with their band playing the rousing marching tune The Rake of Mallow.

At this moment the enormous crowd that had gathered caught its first sight of Daniel O'Connell, or as he was now known The Liberator. As he stepped down from his carriage the crowd erupted into a frenzy of cheering and clapping. But as at all such meetings that had taken place all over Ireland, the stewards kept the throng in good order and no trouble was allowed to take place. As usual the Government had an aversion to such gatherings and our meeting at Charleville was no exception. The presence of a large police force, together with a company of the 45th Infantry Brigade only added to the tremendous tension of that day. When the meeting started the military took up their position outside the Market House and they were obviously looking for any excuse to break it up.

Mr O'Connell addressed the meeting from the home of Michael Spillane in Main Street. Fortunately I was in a good position to hear his speech that called on our support for his endeavours in obtaining Repeal. The first words he quoted were "That every man who is a Repealer put up his hand" a forest of waving hands went up over the head of the assembled thousands, whilst the cheering became deafening and went on for some ten minutes. When the cheering eventually subsided Mr O'Connell recounted to the meeting the momentous events that had occurred during his forty years in public life "I have been at the helm and no mischief has ever occurred," he said. "I have steered the ship through the shoals that beset emancipation. I have pulled down the flag of Protestant ascendancy that so long waged in insolent triumph over the heads of my fellow countrymen and I will steer the vessel of Irelands hope into the secure haven of Repeal." After this final sentence the crowd again cheered and clapped and each man bared his head and waved his hat in the air as O'Connell withdrew from the window.

That evening a Repeal dinner was held at the Old Mill, as no suitable accommodation could be found elsewhere in the town to seat the four hundred people who were to attend. Luckily I managed to get a seat and again was moved by Daniel O'Connell's address to the gathering on the purpose of Repeal, these were the restoration of Ireland's rights, protection of her trade and commerce and the giving of her manufacturers an impetus such had not been received since the year of seventeen eighty two. "I throw out these thoughts and cast my bread upon the waters, which it will be for you to receive with the sentiments with which they are given. I hope my faculties shall not fail me or, my judgement deceives me in moving to the next step, which will be to College Green, the site of the old Parliament of Ireland." With these words he sat down amid thunderous applause and so ended the most momentous day in the history of Charleville, never was there to be another event like it in my lifetime. That evening I could not wait to get home to Springfort to tell Catherine about the events of the day and the charm and charisma that had emanated from Daniel O'Connell the Liberator. We both sat down and discussed at length all that I had seen and heard and that night we were convinced that, Mr O'Connell would in time obtain Repeal. But with hindsight I now know this was all wishful thinking.

By this time our family had grown, we now had three lovely boys, Michael who was now nearly five, James who was born on the eighth of June eighteen -forty and William our last child was born on the sixth of April eighteen forty-two. Catherine was obviously kept very busy caring for our growing family and we also continued to increase our livestock and the land we cultivated with the funds Owen and myself had saved while working in England on the railway. Our first ten years of marriage were the best days of my life. I know that it is wrong to look back at the past and be nostalgic, but those years were golden for myself and Catherine. Although we now had a growing family which restricted us from going to dances and other social events, on most weekends the house was usually full with friends and neighbours. At that time before the terrible famine decimated the rural population of Ireland our year was dominated by the ancient Saints Days, many of which had also become holidays.

Our year started on January the first, or as we knew it then Little Christmas Day. The next Feast Day was January the sixth, the Twelfth Day of Christmas.

This was followed by St.Brigids Day Eve. The ancient custom that occurred on this day, was that the little girls of the parish would go from door to door with Bridgeogs,

[Images of St Brigid dressed up in lovely clothes] asking for halfpennies.

February the first, St. Bridgids Day, we celebrated as the first day of spring.

Shrove Tuesday was one of the main Feast Days of the year for the poor it was one of the few days in the year that they tasted meat. It is also the traditional day for weddings to take place.

Ash Wednesday, A fast day with milk or any food containing milk was forbidden.

First Sunday of Lent, the Sunday of Tears- the tears of the young girls who were not married this Shrovetide.

St. Patrick's Day, Seventeenth of March, when shamrock was worn by everyone.

Good Friday the day of the black fast, it was also known as Friday of Torture, so called because of the torturing of Christ on the Cross.

Easter Sunday, traditionally the day when the poor of the parish were fed by the farmers and shopkeepers.

Easter Monday or Easter-Egg Day the children's favourite day of the year.

May Day, the young boys and girls favourite day.

Whit Monday, large fairs in many towns in Ireland, usually followed by faction fighting between rival mobs.

Ascension Thursday. A holiday.

June the second. Corpus Christi. In times gone by it was the custom to spread fresh rushes and irises on benches, near the doors of houses in the country on which the old people used to sit telling Fenian tales.

June twenty ninth. Feast of St. Peter and Paul. A Holiday.

October eleventh. St Stefan's Day. Large Fair Days in most of Ireland.

November the tenth. It was customary on this day for the well of farmers to kill a sheep, cow, or pig, and divide it amongst the poor of the parish.

November the twenty fifth. St. Catherine's Day.

Obviously my wife and I always celebrated her patron saints day.

Christmas Day. Always my favourite day of the year, especially when I became a father and was able to celebrate the festivities with my young sons.

December the twenty sixth. St. Stephens Day. My birthday we always celebrated my special day.

We did not know in those happy years before the Terrible Famine that this traditional ritual that was part of all our lives would be swept away in the following years, as the Irish people struggled to stay alive.

Meanwhile Daniel O'Connell had continued to hold his meetings demanding Repeal and by now his message was now being heard all over Ireland. The numbers that were now coming to listen to his message dramatically increased and it was reported that at the historic Hill of Tara, in County Meath, there was a quarter of a million gathered to hear him speak. The Government now felt the Repeal movement was a menace and the Lord Chancellor was reported as saying that the peaceful demeanour of the assembled multitude is one of the most alarming symptoms. At forty meetings that year the only disturbance that the Government could discover was the accidental overturning of a gingerbread stall. During this period I myself went to see the Liberator speak again at a meeting in the town of Mallow and this time I was shocked at the large military presence. From the newspapers reports I read at the time it would seem that the Government was certain a civil war was imminent. But for me returning to the town where my brother was so badly treated, I felt that O'Connell's words caught the mood of the Irish people. We wanted a change and his message gave us all hope that change would eventually come.

In the autumn of eighteen forty-three, Mr. O'Connell announced that a monster meeting, the biggest of its kind would be held on Sunday eighth of October at Clontarth near Dublin. This historic sight was symbolic as eight hundred years before, The High King of the Celts, Brian Bora, had defeated the Norsemen, and driven them into the sea. On Saturday October seventh, the Government, convinced there would be a rising panicked and proclaimed the meeting. This outrageous act was compounded when a week later the authorities arrested Mr. O'Connell. Such was the discipline of his supporters at Clontarth that on being ordered to return home and directed by his Lieutenants, the vast crowd quietly dispersed. Sadly for Ireland after his arrest, trial, and imprisonment and subsequent release in September of eighteen forty four, O'Connell was a changed man. While in prison he seemed to have lost his nerve. By this time he was nearing seventy years old and the immense strain of his single handed fight for the well being of the Irish nation, had obviously taken its toll. The arrest of the Liberator was on everyone's lips and I quickly came to realise that we would never obtain our freedom by peaceful means. Daniel O'Connell's trial turned out to be a farce and he was given a hero's welcome when the jury found him not guilty. Tragically all his endeavours on our behalf were soon forgotten as the terrible events of the subsequent years unfolded.

CHAPTER THREE

In looking back at catastrophic events of eighteen forty five, I must explain that as a subsistence farmer in order to be able to pay our rent, we had each autumn to sell most of our harvest. This normally included any surplus livestock that had been reared and fattened for the October Fair. Most of these proceeds were then spent on rent and the ubiquitous land tithes. At that time our main food was of course the potato, to which we added if, available a drink of buttermilk. On special occasions normally at Christmas and Easter, we could in good years kill a pig to supplement our diet. But in the bad times we even had to sell most of the chicken eggs thus depriving our hungry children of their breakfast. But although by today's standards our diet of potatoes supplemented with a little buttermilk sounds very poor, unfortunately for most of the peasant population of rural Ireland as a result of the potato famine that was about to engulf us, even this meagre diet was to become a luxury that few could afford.

With hindsight it now seems a very strange coincidence that in January eighteen forty-five, at the suggestion of my wife Catherine, I began to keep a weekly journal. This journal has enabled me to recount the tragic events that I observed on my travels and also how we as a family managed to survive the most horrendous period in Ireland's history.

Every Sunday afternoon I religiously sat and wrote about the happenings of the preceding week. Sadly the exception to this routine were the weeks and months that I was obliged to spend working away from home. But when the worst of the famine was over and we could once again survive on the income from the farm, I again returned to writing my journal. Unfortunately most of these journals have now been destroyed or have been mislaid. But fortunately the most important volumes relating to the famine years have remained intact.

First of all I must explain to you the reason for keeping my journal. The initial reason was to check if we were making any progress in improving the condition of the land. In the preceding years, I had experimented by growing different crops, in the hope of improving the income from our harvests. Up to this juncture I had failed to keep a record of our successes, or failures. But now I hoped that my journal would eventually rectify this problem.

As I have previously mentioned our main crop was obviously the potato. Each year we tried to keep back sufficient potato seed for replanting. This seed was normally supplemented by the purchase of other varieties which were bought in March. Also just as important for us was the growing of the large Lumpur potato, this variety was normally given to the livestock, but in bad years we would eat them as a last resort. Preparations for the growing of the potato would start in November. The plot was dug over and then layers of manure and lime were left on the surface to be washed into the soil by the winter rains. Then in the spring, we drilled holes about a foot apart, into which the seed was planted. These plots were called lazy beds and in normal times this method of growing was very productive and usually gave us enough potatoes to feed us for the whole year.

From time to time I had known the potato crop to partially fail causing great hardship to the many thousands of Irish families who were totally reliant on it. Only the year before in eighteen forty four, the early crop was lost due to bad weather, but the main crop that followed was excellent and was sufficient to see us through to the following summer. On reading the entries in my first journal, I find that up to the beginning of July eighteen forty-five, the weather had been dry and warm. I also wrote that there was no sign of the problems that had affected the early crop of the previous year. But ominously, I had then recorded that we then had three weeks of totally inclement weather. During this period we had low temperature and continuous rain followed by a damp fog, all in all very depressing, but the signs were still good for the coming harvest.

One morning in early August, on one of my weekly visits to the Charleville Reading Rooms, I read a report in The Cork Gazette that I shall never forget. This report stated that a potato blight was affecting the crop in Belgium and had now worryingly spread into England. A Dr. John Linley, Professor of Botany at Kew Gardens in London, was quoted as saying "A fearful malady has broken out among the potato crop, on all sides we hear of the destruction. In Belgium the fields are said to be completely desolate, and there is now hardly a sound sample in Covent Garden Market, London. As for a cure for this distemper there is none, we are visited by a great calamity which we must bear."

I rushed home from Charleville as fast as my legs could carry me to tell Catherine, about this worrying news. Fortunately after closely examining our potato crop we found abundant growth with no sign of any problem. Obviously we were both very relieved and now had great expectations for the coming harvest. Unfortunately this would be the last occasion for many years that we had any reason to be optimistic. As tragically the potato blight was to return year after year, leaving terrible death and destruction in its wake.

In September I read with fearful trepidation that the blight had started to affect some farms close to Dublin. The first week of October, when we usually harvested our potato crop, my journal informs me that very heavy rain fell continuously for six days. Then on the seventh of October we were woken by a tremendous thunderstorm. But during the morning the skies cleared and we were able to finish the task of threshing the remainder of the oats we had harvested, 'The yield I noted was excellent that year.' We felt very pleased with ourselves when the last sack of oats had been filled and stored that afternoon. This feeling of euphoria soon turned to despair when Catherine suddenly sniffed the air and said, "That's strange," "What is," I replied, "That terrible smell, can't you smell something unusual?" In a blind panic we both started to run towards our potato field, praying that the terrible stench was not the dreaded blight that we had heard so much about. But to our horror the potato plants that only that morning had been full of luxurious growth, were now rotting before our eyes. Without hesitating I turned and rushed back to the house for my tools, knowing that every second counted if we were going to manage to save some of our crop. Once back at the house I grabbed my spade and immediately started to run to the potato field.

Within minutes I had started digging and Catherine and my sons soon joined me. As my wife and I dug, our sons with Michael the eldest leading the way began to pick the potatoes and stack them in piles. Fortunately for us, after working till after dusk that evening and then most of the next day, we managed to save all but four bushels of our crop. Although we were more fortunate than most we still had lost about a tenth of our usual harvest. With the potatoes lifted and sorted, we then had to immediately start on the next crucial process, which was the storing of our crop. Firstly I dug a long shallow pit, lining the bottom with dry ferns, on which we laid the potatoes in a tapering heap. The pit was then thatched with more ferns and withered stalks, then earth was piled on top of the mound, this was then battened down with spades until airtight. It was obviously extremely important that no diseased potatoes went into any of our pits, so Catherine, carefully picked out every potato that showed any sign of being diseased. After four days of frenzied work we were all exhausted, but elated that we had managed to save most of our potatoes. I was particularly pleased with the way our boys had helped us in our hour of need, so the very next morning I walked into town and bought them all a large bag of sweets.

During the next few days when our neighbours and friends came to visit, we soon realised how crucial our prompt action had been. This sadly was because

69

most of the other small tenant farmers in our town land had lost more than half of their crop. This tragically meant that they would probably have to sell most of their livestock in order to survive the approaching winter. Unfortunately false rumours soon began to circulate, claiming that the authorities were to give help to all those affected by the blight. But all that happened was that the local constabulary called at each farm, carrying notebooks and carbines and made an inventory of what potatoes had been lost. It was soon evident that the government had no intention of helping us and that we were to be left to our own devices to survive the coming winter. Traditionally, we now started to prepare for the local Fair, which was held at the end of October, when our harvest and livestock were sold and the rent paid. That year with the partial failure of our potatoes, we were obviously hoping that the prices we received on our sales would be high. As was usual on Fair days, I was up well before dawn; my first task was to scrub the pigs we were selling with soap and warm water. While I was scrubbing the pigs, Catherine fetched our old mare from the field and hitched it up to the cart. I then loaded our sacks of oats onto the wagon before having my breakfast. Catherine then dressed the boys in their Sunday best and then she put on her new dress that she had recently finished. Then before we left she fussed over me making sure that I too looked smart for the occasion. By now the three boys were all very excited as we set off for the Fair. The lanes and byways were thronged as usual with everyone making their way into town. As we neared our destination we met numerous acquaintances, whose sole topic of conversation was the blight and how it had affected them.

At this time more and more local tenant farmers, especially the prosperous ones were now talking seriously of emigration to America. This partial emigration had been taking place for several years, but not on the same scale as we now know happened in the following years. When we finally arrived at the fair ground, Catherine warned the boys not to wander off, as she was very worried that she might lose them in the vast crowds. That year there seemed to be hundreds more people there than normal and we found it was very hard to keep together. For this reason we decided to split up, for it was imperative that I had sold our livestock and produce as soon as possible.

The authorities must have expected trouble, because there was an unusually large police presence in town that day. But we farmers were only interested in going about our business at that time. After leaving my family I pushed my way through the crowds to where the stock jobbers were in attendance, praying that

I would obtain good price for my livestock. But although I desperately needed to make enough to cover the rent and buy supplies for the winter, I was still very determined to drive a hard bargain. With this in mind I spent the next two hours haggling with a local dealer before I finally sold my livestock at the price I wanted. Next stop was the corn chandler where I sold my crop and I was once again pleased with the price I received. I then went to meet Catherine and my sons with the good news that we had sufficient funds to keep the roof over our head for another year. My wife always enjoyed the days at the Fair, as it gave her a chance to catch up with all the local gossip. That day was no exception and she regaled me with all the news as we made our way back to Charleville that afternoon.

On our arrival in Charleville, Catherine managed to purchase the remaining items on her shopping list, while I headed straight to the land agents office. As I waited to pay my six-monthly rent I could hear many of the desperate small local farmers asking the agent to defer some, or part, of their rent because of the failure of their potato crop. Fortunately for his tenants Mr. Grogan, the agent for Sir William Wrixon-Beecher, was a very compassionate man, who because of kindness at that time and during the horrific years that followed, is still talked about with affection. Sadly for the people of Ireland his thoughtfulness and understanding of the perils we faced in those times was unique. This quickly became evident as many of the land owners and their agents were soon threatening their tenants with eviction orders.

When I left the agents office I met a fellow member of the Repeal Association who informed me that Mr. Tom Steele, one of Daniel O'Connell's associates was about to address a public meeting. On hearing this I rushed to find Catherine and our sons and persuaded them to make their own way back to Springfort. I then pushed my way through to the front of the crowd and heard Mr. Steele say the following "I have been sent by the Liberator in pursuit of a campaign to rouse the country from end to end in order that the government is forced to arrest the progress of a calamity which is threatening our national extinction. I refer to the blight that has fallen on the potato crop and the famine that will follow unless drastic measures are taken to prevent it. We the people's representatives realise that by a merciful providence there is more than sufficient food in this country as a result of a plentiful harvest to feed double the population. We want the government to immediately prohibit the export of this food and to throw open the ports to foreign foods and to stop distilling. By the application of our own money of which we are being robbed of year by year in excessive taxation the government must buy provisions for relief. The railways must be built and the labourers paid in food, we want absentee landlords taxed fifty per cent and residents ten per cent to provide the capital for railway building, which in England has reversed the condition of eighteen -forty when one and a half million were on the rates to the present one of comparative prosperity. As a representative of an ancient and glorious nation we are demanding justice not charity."

The cheering and clapping erupted and it was some time before he could proceed. "The corporation of the city of Dublin" continued Mr. Steele "under the presidency of the Lord Mayor John Arabin has appointed a committee and at a meeting on the twenty eighth of this month the Right Honourable Daniel O'Connell is going to put forward the plan of the people's representatives for dealing with this catastrophe." The remainder of his speech was drowned in wild cheering and the crowd surged forward and carried Mr. Steele on their shoulders to his jaunting car and then followed the car on the road to Limerick, cheering and clapping him on his way. On my journey home that evening I had a strange sense of foreboding and for the first time in my life I began to worry about my young family's future.

It was around this time when visiting the reading rooms, that I discovered a new publication that was to entirely change my political thinking. This newspaper was called "The Nation" and it was written by the younger more militant members of the Repeal Association. This journal gradually became more radical as the famine crisis deepened and its contributors or "Young Irelanders" as they were known soon distanced themselves from Daniel O'Connell's ideals of non-violent agitation. But all the political infighting between the various factions of Irish politicians soon came completely irrelevant to the average Irishman, as I will now try to explain.

The last weeks of October were usually the time for opening the potato pits and carrying the crop inside for the winter. In my journal I noted that at the end of October it rained non-stop for a total of seven days. On All Saints Day the first of November, the rain did eventually stop and after returning from early morning mass I hitched up our horse and made my way to the potato field. By now it was a glorious sunny autumn morning and I was feeling in a very good mood. My good humour soon turned to a feeling of utter despair. On reaching the nearest pit I started to carefully remove the covering of earth making sure that I did not damage any of my valuable crops. As I removed the first protective layer, an all prevailing stench of rot filled my nostrils. In panic I removed the final covering of ferns only to reveal the mass of corruption that my potato crop had become. With great trepidation I slowly returned to the house, where with tears in my eyes, I explained to Catherine what had happened.

My wife "God rest her soul" was always an optimist and without hesitation suggested we now open the other pits to see if we could salvage any of our crop. With heavy hearts we both returned to the potato fields taking our three young sons with us. With extreme caution I removed the coverings from the rest of the pits. Thankfully the potatoes in some of the pits had not been contaminated. Once again Catherine and my three young sons were a great help to me. Our eldest son Michael, who was now aged eight, was even then a great worker and on this occasion again showed a maturity well in advance of his age. We all worked like demons for the next few days, making sure that the potatoes we saved were disease free before we hauled them back to the house for the winter, luckily for us we had somehow managed to save about thirty bushels of our crop, but in total we had lost nearly half of our annual harvest. The position we found ourselves in although very precarious, could have been worse. Luckily for us the kitchen garden that Catherine had so carefully cultivated over the years had produced enough other vegetables that year to hopefully keep us fed over the coming winter.

Once again it would appear that we were more fortunate than most of the Irish population, because the terrible spectre of famine and starvation was about to sweep across Ireland, leaving a trail of death and destruction in its wake. Sadly many of our neighbours and friends had lost most of their crop and were soon depending on the charity of others to feed them. But unlike previous occasions when the potato failed, this time the blight would return for the next five years. This was to eventually culminate in many poor souls taking the dreaded journey to the workhouse, or emigration for the fortunate, as ultimately there was to be no large scale help from the authorities for the majority of the starving population.

On my next visit to Charleville I was shocked to find the town full of groups of people who had came in from the countryside in search of food for their families. Unfortunately this scenario was to become all to commonplace in Ireland, during the following years. In every town and village hungry, and desperate mobs would gather in search of any morsel of food or help they could find. Tragically in response the government increased its military presence and declared Martial Law in many areas.

That winter we helped as many of our relatives and friends as we could, but Christmas that year was vastly different to those of years gone by with despair and desperation everywhere. My wife Catherine to my knowledge never turned anyone away from the house during those times, even if it meant that she herself went without. During that long very cold winter we both agreed that we would plant alternative crops in the spring to supplement our potato crop, so when we had the occasional fine day we started to expand our kitchen garden in readiness for the better weather.

On reading my journal for April eighteen forty-six, I find that we had managed to obtain sufficient seed potatoes for planting and were hoping against hope that the blight would not reappear. Also there was a general feeling of optimism in the country, for the government we were informed had established a relief commission. Sufficient food had been purchased abroad and this would soon be distributed throughout the country. But the daily reports in every newspaper and journal in the land wrote eyewitness accounts of labourers and their families starving to death by the roadside, we somehow struggled through that summer as luckily I still had some of my savings so that we could purchase enough food to survive. During this period the government finally opened food depots, which sold Indian corn imported from America. At first we like may other families were very reluctant to try it, but Catherine, as resourceful as ever obtained a recipe and the resulting stir abouts and cakes she made with this corn were excellent.

The cold winter was eventually followed by heavy rain that spring, but fortunately we had warm and sunny weather in June. The potato plants showed every appearance of an abundant harvest and so we prayed to God that our problems were over. But ominously in late July, after more stormy weather we again smelt the terrible stench of the blight. Running to the potato fields we could see the spores virtually going from plant to plant. Appallingly what an hour before had been a field of luxuriant potato plants was now rotting before our eyes. Frantically we started to dig up what was left of our crop, the results were catastrophic less than eight bushels of potatoes were edible. Even with the harvest from our kitchen garden, we knew that we would never be able to feed ourselves until the following summer. Words cannot express my feelings as I knew that we faced total ruin, with the certain knowledge that we would eventually be evicted if the rent was not paid. That evening we talked long into the night both realising that we had to act quickly to try to stop the disaster that was about to engulf us. So after a long discussion it was decided that I must try to obtain employment as soon as possible. But the thought of leaving Catherine alone with my three sons horrified me, but fortunately Michael our eldest as I have previously said was always a great help to his mother and she was confident that they would be able cope in my absence.

On my next visit to the reading rooms in Charleville, I was interested to read about the proposed expansion of the railroad system in Ireland. The report stated that work was about to start on building an extension to the railroad, which would eventually run from Waterford across the middle of the country to the town of Limerick. As I read this article my thoughts returned to the railroad I had worked on in Liverpool, perhaps I thought one of my old colleagues might be involved in this new construction and there could be an opening for me. What happened next was a once in a lifetime coincidence. By the time I left the reading rooms that evening it was pouring with rain and with the evening approaching darkness was closing in. Knowing that I had a long unpleasant walk in front of me, I bowed my head and started on my journey. As I rushed passed the Hotel on Main Street, I collided with a gentleman who was endeavouring to get in out of the rain. To his immense annoyance the force of our collision had sent him sprawling into the road where he lay cursing me to the devil. Obviously I rushed to pick up the poor fellow, only to realise that it was my cousin from Clonmel, Jonathan Casey.

His cursing quickly turned to laughter, when he recognised his assailant. "You have always been a clumsy oaf," were his first words as we headed for the Hotel. Later after he had dried himself off in front of the fire he explained the reason for his visit to Charleville, "he was" he said "purchasing leather from one of the many Tanneries that were then in the town." Luckily he insisted on buying my dinner that night and although I knew Catherine would be worried that I had not returned my conversation with Jonathan that evening was to have a profound effect on our lives. All through the evening I sat and listened as he spoke about the terrible scenes he had witnessed on his travels throughout the West of Ireland that autumn. I sat there in silence until he asked about my family's wellbeing. I told him that our situation was perilous and I must find work. It was when I mentioned the newspaper article about the railway construction that his face lit up. Thumping on the table with excitement he exclaimed in a loud voice, "It was only last week that I was talking to our cousin James Stephens in Clonmel about his new employment, he is now working as an engineer on the railroad between Waterford and Limerick, surely with your previous experience and his patronage, an opening must be found for you. We must he said get you to Clonmel as quickly as possible."

With these words ringing in my ears, I left Jonathan and made my way back to Springfort hoping that this chance encounter would change our fortunes. It was very late when I finally arrived home and Catherine was now frantic with worry. But when I explained   the reason for my late return, she immediately understood the implications for us. That night before retiring to bed we both agreed in view of our present circumstances I must take the opportunity that had presented itself. The next morning after breakfast I explained to our three sons that I was leaving home for a little while and they were to promise to help their mother at all times. The two youngest obviously did not understand, but Michael I knew could be relied upon. Catherine tried not to make a fuss but we were both in tears before I left.

When I arrived in town I helped Jonathan load his wagon with the leather goods he had purchased and by noon we were on the road bound for Clonmel. Although I had witnessed some suffering due to the famine in Charleville, nothing could have prepared me for the scenes that I was about to encounter during the next couple of days.

The first town we passed through was Kilmallock, which in normal times was a busy thriving market town. But on this occasion wild eyed starving families were everywhere beseeching shopkeepers and merchants for any morsel of food they could spare. This was to become a familiar scene in every town and village we passed through on our journey. In some places these poor creatures, in desperation had surrounded and raided wagons carrying food that was destined for export. In other town's food riots had taken place, consequently the whole countryside was now full of soldiers and militia. Our progress was very slow on that first day because of all these problems so on the following day Jonathan decided that where possible we should avoid the main roads. This was to prove a wise decision because the rest of our journey passed without incident.

That night when we eventually reached Clonmel my cousin's wife made me very welcome and after a good night's sleep, Jonathan and I went to the construction site, hoping to meet James Stevens. Unfortunately we were told; he had been sent forward to reconnoitre the future passage of the railroad and was not expected back for a couple of days. There was nothing I could do but wait for his return as I was desperate for employment. Worryingly there were hundreds of men besieging the construction site all desperately wanting a chance to work. For the first and only time in my life I had to sit patiently waiting for Mr Stephens return, all the time praying that my patience would be rewarded.

Luckily my meeting with James Stephens when it finally took place was very fruitful. He began the interview by informing me that because the men that the company had taken on when the project started did not have any previous knowledge of railroad construction, they were way behind schedule. But he went onto say that in recent week's ex- navvies like me had been hired because of their previous experience. During the interview he questioned me closely about my working knowledge of tunnelling and other aspects of railroad construction that I had gained in England. Although we were distantly related, he conducted this first meeting in a very business like manner. But he must have been impressed by the answers I gave to the many questions he asked because he asked me to return the next day to meet Mr Brophy the site foreman.

John Brophy on hearing that I had been a member of the famous Tipperary gang during the construction of the Liverpool to Manchester railroad was obviously very impressed. We then talked about my extensive knowledge of tunnelling and dynamiting which he said would prove invaluable to him in the future. Thankfully John took a liking to me and the very next day I was put to work with the gang of newcomers who had also gained their experience working on railroad sites in England. Incidentally John Brophy was to remain a close friend of mine until his untimely death in eighteen eighty-nine.

During the first few weeks I found it very difficult to get used to taking orders again after working for myself for the last ten years, but I also realised how fortunate I had been to find work. The gang of men that I had joined because of our past experience soon began to prove its worth. The engineers and bosses were delighted because the construction work began to move rapidly forward in spite of the terrible weather that winter. The stormy weather went on week after week and during that period I greatly missed Catherine and my young sons. The food and accommodation on site was appalling as usual, which made the thought of returning to the comfort of my home even more appealing. Fortunately the site closed for the Christmas festivities and so I was able to return to Springfort taking with me the wages I had saved

On my long walk back home I tried to avoid the towns and villages where possible because the effects of the terrible famine intensified diseases such as cholera and famine fever. Sadly on this journey, I unfortunately had to pass through the town of Dundrum. It was here that I saw for the first time the full horror of the tragedy that was unfolding across the length and breadth of our small island. Hundreds of people were in the town and they were all desperately trying to get a docket that would enable them to get into the local workhouse. Tragically because it was full, the poor souls were being turned away. I stood watching near the gates of the workhouse the constabulary showed no mercy as they beat back the starving crowd with rifle butts.

The whole town was a dreadful sight, with scores of half dead and dying families shuffling through the streets begging. Some of the old people had given up and they were sitting down on the frozen ground waiting for their inevitable death. The worst thing of all I witnessed that day is something I will never forget to my dying day; it was the suffering of the tiny children. I can still hear their plaintive cries of hunger ringing in my ears; the memory of that day still brings tears to my eyes. Unfortunately apart from giving a couple of families a few coppers there was nothing I could do to help them.

As I hurried on through Dundrum that afternoon, in the Main Street I was shocked and appalled to see that all the shops had Christmas fare in abundance. The butchers shops were filled to capacity with geese, fowl and other meats, but the greedy shop owners had greatly multiplied the prices. Shaking my head in disbelief at the callousness of these people that would see their own country dying in their thousands, I quickly left that sorry town and was glad to regain the solitude of the countryside.

Thankfully I managed to avoid visiting another town that day, but it was very late by the time I reached Springfort. My homecoming was greeted with a mixture of happiness and sorrow. Obviously Catherine was delighted to see me and so were my young sons, but her pleasure was tinged with great sadness, because John McGrath her father and a true friend of mine had passed away in my absence. The shock of hearing this sad news cast a shadow over Christmas that year, but fortunately we were able to invite all our relatives and friends to our traditional Christmas Day dinner.

My short holiday was soon over and it was with great reluctance that I returned to the railroad construction site. On leaving Springfort, I gave my wife the remainder of the money I had saved hoping that it would provide for her and my family until I could return. On the return journey the weather began to turn very cold and strangely I was relieved when I reached Clonmel. Although as I have said the accommodation was appalling, the navvies working on the site at this time were hard working and mainly sober. It was very rare if anyone returned to the workings drunk after a payday, as we all realised how fortunate we were to have found regular employment in those troubled times.

During my first few months of work, I had rarely caught a glimpse of James my cousin and benefactor and had only managed to speak to him on one occasion. All this was to change in the New Year, as we were to converse regularly during the long dark evenings that terrible winter. From our conversations, I quickly came to realise how deeply concerned he was by the appalling suffering that our fellow countrymen were now having to endure. He was also angry and totally disillusioned at the complete inability of Daniel O'Connell and the Repeal Association to come to their assistance. In our many discussions he implied that the Young Irelanders, should if no help was forthcoming from the Government start an armed insurrection. All that heard him speak thought his words were the idle boasting of a brash young man, not thinking that in the near future he would be at the forefront of an armed rebellion.

Now on reading my journal it confirms that the winter that year was one of the worst in living memory. We have never been used to snow and ice in Ireland but together with the other calamities we faced it now seemed that country's misery would never end. I obviously was very worried about my family but luckily early in February Jonathan Casey came to visit me on the site. He was, he said, returning to Charleville on business and would call and see Catherine, at Springfort. Obviously I could not miss this opportunity to send my savings back to my wife, because I realised that she must now be running short of money to buy food and turf for the fire. Jonathan's kindness towards us at that terrible time was never forgotten and he has always been very welcome whenever he has visited us.

As every navvy working on the railroad was as desperate as me for money to feed their families during that terrible winter, we struggled on normally working seven days a week. Fortunately with my extensive knowledge of tunnelling and use of dynamite I soon found myself in great demand and as usual seized the opportunity. Thankfully my wages increased with this extra responsibility and I also began to have a closer relationship with the engineers. This afforded me more time to get to know James Stephens and during this period we became very close friends and that friendship has remained a strong bond between the two of us ever since.

During that terrible winter of eighteen forty six- forty seven, the government belatedly realising the catastrophe that had engulfed Ireland introduced soup kitchens. Every day we would see the starving and disease ridden people carrying their bowl or pot to the nearest town in the hope of being fed. On reaching the soup kitchen they were made to stand in line for hours and then they would eventually receive either one-pound of biscuit meal bread or one quarter soup thickened with meal and four ounces of either bread or biscuit. This was their ration for the day but if supplies ran out, the poor souls still waiting were turned away. Prior to the opening of the soup kitchens the government had introduced a scheme, which had given work on various projects around the country. But this system could not cope with the tremendous demand of the thousands who turned up hoping for work. The projects being inadequately funded soon ran out of money and so the outdoor relief project as it was called quickly closed down and the cheaper solution of soup kitchens was introduced.

Although we were the lucky ones with regular work and pay, the human suffering of the majority of the population confronted us from all sides. Obviously my thoughts were always with my family in Springfort, because apart from my Cousin Jonathan's visit to see them, I had not been able to get home in weeks. But at the beginning of March after two months of non stop work, I decided I must at all costs make the long journey home with the money I had saved. It was a very tiring journey that weekend with the mud knee deep in places from the persistent rains, but the joy on Catherine and my three sons faces made it all worth while. That night as we sat by the fireside I realised how much I missed being at home with my family. But by midday on the Sunday sadly I was on the road again, but not before promising Catherine that I would be home for Easter.

Back at the construction site it was agreed by the whole workforce, that a monthly collection for the relief of the famine victims should be taken up. James Stephens agreed to organise and to distribute these funds to the starving families in the local area. Although our charity was a drop in the ocean, we all felt that we should be helping in some way to relieve their suffering. James after distributing our funds would return shaking with emotion at the terrible scenes he had witnessed and I am sure that it was the complete lack of compassion and understanding for the Irish Nation by the authorities that convinced him that Ireland must have its freedom. For me, the more I saw of the way our people were treated the more I realised that my cousin's ideas although fraught with danger, could be the long term solution to Ireland's problems.

That long terrible winter continued throughout March and during that miserable month we had icy winds, sleet and snow showers, followed by days of torrential rain. This awful weather continued on into April and I note in my journal that on the twenty six of April, we had hurricane force winds and a storm of frozen hail. The weather was so bad during late April, that even the railroad construction was suspended for a couple of days. As promised, I did manage to get back to Springfort for Easter. But when I attended mass on the Sunday, I was shocked at the condition of many of my friends and neighbours; obviously the effect of the long cold winter and lack of any decent food was now taking its toll. Sadly many of the young parishioners had emigrated and the church was now only half full.

Fortunately the weather that weekend had improved and so after mass I managed to purchase potato seed in town. During the remainder of my stay at home that Easter, the five of us worked until it was dark planting our potato seed hoping against hope that the blight would not return that summer.

During May the weather continued to improve and thankfully I was able to get home most weekends. As the railroad steadily progressed towards Tipperary, my journey home became easier as I could now walk along the main Dublin Cork highway. Usually I could manage to leave the site at midday on Saturday and walk or hopefully hitch a ride to Charleville. It would normally take around five hours to get back to Springfort and then after a quick bite to eat it was time to start work on the farm. Catherine and I usually never finished until after sunset, as we realised my time at home was precious. Then on Sunday morning we all attended early mass and on our return we would endeavour to finish any of the farm work that was urgent. In my absence Catherine had taught our oldest son Michael how to prepare some basic meals. This certainly was a good idea because it enabled her to spend more time in the fields helping me.

On looking back now on those weekends although very strenuous they were most enjoyable. On many occasions one of our friends would arrive to give us a hand and I would hear all the local news. But all too soon the weekend was over and after saying our sad goodbyes I was again taking that long walk back to the construction site. On these return journeys I often wondered if my life would ever again return to normal, or was I to end up like my poor father who had always had to go in search of work.

It was about this time when we thought things could not get any worse for our tragic country that we heard the calamitous news that on the fifteenth of May, eighteen forty seven, Daniel O'Connell had died. The whole country was deeply shocked and saddened at the death of this great man who had worked tirelessly for the good of all the people of Ireland. "The Liberator" it was said had died of a broken heart fretting at the distressed state and suffering of his people. Just before his death, the Young Irelander's under the leadership of William Smith O'Brien, had split from O'Connell's Repeal party and founded a new organisation known as the Irish Confederation. This organisations ambition was to set up a confederate club in every town and district in the country. The ultimate aim of the Irish Confederation was an Irish Parliament in Dublin to be achieved by every means possible, this included armed insurrection. The purpose of the clubs was they envisaged, to educate and instruct its members to understand the principles of repeal and the self-reliance of the Irish Nation. Although only twenty persons were required to form the nucleus of a confederate club, only twenty such clubs had been formed by November eighteen forty seven. One of the prime members of the Confederation at this time was my cousin James Stephens. He was now very active starting the new clubs and trying to recruit members for clubs in the areas along the route of the railroad. The problem he faced was the total apathy of the people, whose only thought at that time, was obviously how they could find sufficient food to survive. On odd occasions I assisted him with his efforts at recruiting, but although he was always very optimistic that his message appealed to the population, at the meetings I attended, it was obvious to me that his words were falling on deaf ears.

On my weekend journeys to and from Springfort I could see the situation worsening week by week during eighteen forty-seven. During that summer even the small wealthy farmers were leaving their farms and heading in their hundreds to ports all over Ireland with only one intention to emigrate. The newspapers were full of stories about the people of Ireland leaving its shores in their thousands. Some landowners seizing their chance were clearing their estates of the peasantry by eviction, or in some instances giving them money to emigrate. How many of these poor innocents ever made it to America or Canada will never been known. The emigration ships were very old and un-seaworthy and the food that the passengers were given was generally inedible. This together with typhoid fever led to terrible mortality rates on these vessels with sometimes only seventy five per cent of the passengers surviving the crossing.

Unfortunately it has become in my lifetime an all too familiar happening the young leaving Ireland to better themselves in some far off country promising to return but in most cases leaving their grieving family and friends forever. Those countries that received our youth were always better governed than Ireland and there were usually prospects for advancement. We the Catholic majority in Ireland, had for years been treated as second class citizens by the authorities and sadly this was the case during most of my lifetime. This was most evident during the calamitous famine years when the government hardly lifted a finger to help our beleaguered Nation.

Just when I thought that our nightmare could not get any worse, another terrible disease spread rapidly through the country. This was called famine fever and it quickly became an epidemic with thousands dying, mainly in the workhouses which were by now were packed to capacity. It was during this period that I heard the following story, which fully illustrates the terrible times that we were then experiencing. A friend of mine was attending a court in Bantry Bay when he heard the following testimony.

A man had died from hunger and his widow had gone into the ploughed field of her landlord to try to find a few potatoes. She hoped she could find a few that might have been missed during the harvest. Fortunately she had found a couple of very small ones when the landlord saw what she was doing and sent the Magistrate to her cabin. To the Magistrates horror he found three children there in a state of starvation with nothing in the cabin but the pot which was over the fire. The Magistrate demanded that she showed him where the potatoes were, his question was met with silence He hesitated but then enquired what had she cooking in the pot, she was still silent. So he picked up the pot and looked to see what the contents were. He was shocked to find it contained the family's dog together with the handful of potatoes she had gathered from the field. The sight of the wretched cabin and the despairing looks of the poor silent mother and the famished children crouched in fear in the corner, so touched the heart of the magistrate that he took the pot from the fire, he then instructed the woman to follow him and they went to the courtroom in Bantry Bay together. He presented the pot and the handful of potatoes to the astonished Judge. The Judge called the woman and interrogated her kindly. She told him they had sat in their desolate cabin two whole days without eating before she killed the half famished dog; also she did not think it was stealing to glean potatoes after the harvest was gathered. The Judge gave her three pound from his own purse and told her when she had used that to come and see him again.

This story and countless others were told in these most troubled times. The tragedy was that some individual government officers did all that was in their power to help, but the government in London and the authorities in Dublin were totally indifferent to the continuing famine conditions that raged on throughout the terrible winter of eighteen forty seven- forty eight.

The irony of the situation was that due to the shortage of potato seed that spring very few potatoes were sown. Obviously this meant that although the blight did not occur that year the crop that was harvested was again insufficient to feed the starving people. Luckily with my wages we managed to struggle on through another year and were able to pay our rent on Gale Day that October.

As I have previously said, on the weekends that I journeyed home I always tried to avoid the towns and villages where possible. But in late November I once again observed the full horror of the famine. On reaching the outskirts of a small village called Kilteely, I saw men digging large trenches for the many poor souls from the village that had perished from starvation or the fever. Then I watched as three women fought over the remains of a small dog. All around this god forsaken place I could smell the stench of death and destruction with hardly a living soul to be seen. Also along the road that day were unspeakable sights, cabins and small farmhouses had been pulled down and burnt and their inhabitants evicted by the heartless agents and landowners. In one house at Glantane, tragically an entire family had perished the parents, four of their children and four old people. Two neighbours told me the last to die a boy of six had locked the front door and hid under the bed feeling too ashamed for his family to be found in this way.

With dreadful sense of foreboding I pressed on walking as fast as I could fearing that something dreadful had happened at Springfort in my absence. Fortunately my fears were groundless as Catherine and my young sons, although running short of food were well and very excited to see me home. That night after the children had gone to bed I told my wife about the dreadful things I had seen that day. That weekend we must have been at our lowest ebb, as for the first and only occasion we discussed leaving Ireland. All around us it seemed was death and destruction, we even heard at Mass that Sunday that our curate the saintly Father Croke had died from famine fever. The poor young man had contracted the disease because of his devotion to the welfare of the starving people of the parish.

That winter our work on the railroad progressed steadily towards Limerick and fortunately for me the construction was again stopped for the Christmas Holiday. Before leaving the site to return home for the holiday I had a long discussion with James Stephens. Although I did not know it at that time, my cousin had now risen high in the councils of "The Young Irelanders" and many of his radical ideas had been adopted by the organisation. His life, he told me in the strictest confidence was about to change entirely, as he and the rest of the firebrands in the "Young Irelanders" organization were determined to lead an armed insurrection and rid Ireland of English rule forever. This statement sent a shudder of apprehension down my spine as I feared the worst for my cousin and his friends. The people of Ireland I told him had other priorities at this time and were only interested in staying alive. I urged him to wait until the current crisis had passed, but he replied that their minds were made up and nothing would now stop them. That Christmas I gave a lot of thought to what James had said, but I did not mention it to anyone; I even kept it from my wife, fearing the consequences if the authorities ever heard of what the "Young Irelanders" were planning.

Once again Catherine tried to feed many of our friends on Christmas Day, as we were more fortunate than most at this time. Sadly many of our friends and neighbours had emigrated that year and so Christmas was a very sombre affair. Soon after New Year I returned to the railroad little knowing that eighteen forty-eight, was about to be one of the most mementos years of my life. During the first two months I was very busy on the site and worryingly could not return home but as the weather improved and we neared Limerick Junction on the final section of the railroad, I was at last allowed a weekend off. Having worked almost everyday for two months and being frugal as usual I had managed to save a fair amount of money, this was fortunate because by the time I returned most of our potato crop had been eaten and Catherine and my sons had barely a mouthful left to eat. Obviously on reaching home I was greeted with open arms and on this occasion I did not even stop for a drink, but rushed straight into town to buy all the supplies that we needed including three large bags of sweets for my young sons.

CHAPTER FOUR

Unfortunately because I was working seven days a week at that time, I could not return home again until Eastertide and when I finally did get back to Springfort it was late on the Saturday evening, but strangely no one came to greet me. In the current climate this was obviously very worrying and as I walked up the lane towards the farm my sense of foreboding increased with every step. My worries were to prove completely unfounded, because from the house I could hear cheering, and laughter and a great amount of hilarity. I shall never forget the scene that greeted me when Catherine saw me at the door that night. She came running towards me with tears streaming from her eyes. "Owen is home," she shouted hysterically, for a moment I could not comprehend what she was saying, but then I saw him sitting in his old familiar position by the fire. I stood in the doorway in a trance, thinking that I was having a wonderful dream, but when he got up from his seat and embraced me I knew that all my prayers had been answered. The day had come that I never thought would occur. By some miracle my only brother, my one true friend and the person with whom I had shared so many experiences with in the past had kept his promise and returned home.

That night we talked and talked and dawn was breaking when we finally got to bed. In our conversation I had told Owen about all those who had emigrated and also the many poor souls that had died in the parish. Strangely both of us managed to avoid talking about Maureen Kelly, the beautiful young girl that Owen had been betrothed to before his transportation. Finally I plucked up courage and told him about Maureen's fate, this news obviously devastated him for although he tried not to show it I knew that she was the principle reasons why he had returned.

The next day being Easter Sunday, we all attended morning mass. During the service Father Quinn the Parish Priest led the congregation in a prayer of thanks to celebrate Owens return from the penal colony. It was he said the one piece of good news in a time of great hardship and suffering for everyone in the Parish. The scene after mass that morning was unforgettable with family, friends and neighbours all saying my brother's return was a miracle.

Briefly before I returned to the railroad site, we talked about our future plans. Fortunately for us Owen had accumulated quite a sum of money and with this we could eventually achieve our ambition of restocking the farm with livestock. That Sunday evening I left the farm with great reluctance, but I was also glad that Catherine and my sons now had Owen to look after them.

On the subsequent weekends when I made it home Owen told us all about his journeys and experiences and the following narrative is his own account of the terrible hardships that were inflicted on him and his fellow convicts many of whom had been transported for very minor offences.

This is Owens own detailed account, of those years as told to me on his return to us in eighteen forty eight.

I will never forget the feeling of apprehension and dread on that fateful day, the fourth of August eighteen thirty-one when I left Queenstown Harbour on "The George" for the long voyage to the penal colony of Australia. As the sight of land receded, I was left wondering if I would ever see my brother Patrick again. It soon became obvious that my best hope of survival was to hold my own council, and keep a low profile. This I had learned from past experience in England, where I had been totally focused and had never become involved with the other navvies.

For the first couple of days of the voyage us prisoners were battened down and had ankle chains on to restrain us. I like most of the others was violently sick as we sailed into the Celtic sea and then out into the Atlantic Ocean. After we had sailed for a few days in the Atlantic and were clear of the Ireland much to our relief the ankle chains were permanently removed. Life on the ship then settled into a regular routine. Convict cooks were allowed on deck about five am each morning and they began working up a fire in the galley to cook our breakfast. If the weather was suitable the prison doors were thrown open and we were then allowed on deck. Seeing the vast ocean for the first time with its changing colours and dramatic skylines held a certain fascination for me and on the long voyage to the other side of the world it somehow made my miserable life more bearable.

Every morning as I had been given the job of what was called a "Mess Man" my first task was to go to the storeroom and draw rations for the six convicts that I represented. Breakfast was by then cooked and at eight all the convicts went below decks. Here they were served their meal from a central table running the length of the deck. After breakfast teams of prisoners cleaned and scrubbed the deck thoroughly using pumice stone and seawater. When this task was completed the Captain, made his daily inspection of every area of his ship making sure that it was spotless from top to bottom. This daily ritual I found out later was although seemingly tedious was of the utmost importance. The reason for this was that with so many men living in such close proximity the danger of disease breaking out was always possibility. After breakfast, weather permitting various classes was offered to the convicts. I joined such a class studying geography; because at that time I had little knowledge of the subject and hopefully would find out more about our voyage and the route we were taking to Australia.

Instructing us in this class was an Irish seaman named John Page. John informed us that he was a veteran seaman who had served in the Royal Navy during the Napoleonic Wars and he had actually fought at the Battle of Trafalgar. During the long voyage to Australia he loved to reminisce and regale us with stories of those times, always finishing by proudly flourishing the medals he had won. But it was his lessons that I always found fascinating and a great distraction from the monotonous daily routine. His detailed knowledge of geography and the route we were now navigating completely baffled me at first but with John's patient tuition during that long voyage I eventually came to understand the meaning of latitude and longitude.

During the first lesson our group had with John Page, he started by telling us that when the ship had left Queenstown Harbour, it had then sailed passed the Old Kinsale Head, this was our last sighting of Ireland. John then produced a large board and proceeded to draw a rough map of the world, and each day he traced our route towards our final destination Australia. When we passed Old Kinsale Head we had sailed out into the Celtic Sea. Very soon we left the Celtic Sea and were then sailing in the mighty Atlantic Ocean. The route, he told us, was in those early days predominantly south. John now explained that we were at present sailing across the Bay of Biscay where the weather could be at times treacherous, but fortunately it was very kind on this voyage. He then told us that during the Napoleonic War he had spent many years on ships blockading the ports of France and its allies along this very coast. Ultimately he told us, that this was to lead to the annihilation of the French and Spanish fleets at the Battle of Trafalgar. He explained that by keeping the French and Spanish navy's pent up in their ports for years had eventually caused their commanders to panic and leave port. The English fleet under the command of the legendary Admiral Nelson, were waiting, and although Nelson, himself was fatally wounded the English fleet won an overwhelming victory. In the years after Trafalgar, until

Napoleon's final defeat at Waterloo, the British navy had he said patrolled these waters but the enemy never ventured out of their ports again.

From the Bay of Biscay, we had sailed passed the northern tip of Spain, at a point called Cape Finisterre. "The George" then headed out into the South Atlantic, in this area the weather gradually improved and became much warmer. As we sailed south the next sighting of land was we were told the island of Madeira. By this time the temperature had started to climb and the weather became hotter than most of us had ever known. Unfortunately, as I was to soon find out, the hot weather effects some people in a strange way causing them to loose their heads. This phenomenon I unfortunately saw at first hand, when a Galway lad called Tom Griffin, attacked the boson of "The George," for no apparent reason. Sadly as a result of Griffins actions he was sentenced to forty lashes as a lesson to all of us. We were all marched on deck and made to watch the poor mans back being ripped to pieces by the lash; Tom Griffin never recovered from his ordeal and died in great agony three days later.

Unfortunately this was to be the first of many occasions that I was made to watch this barbaric practise being meted out during my years in Australia.

John Page now told us that the route our voyage now followed was parallel to the coast of Africa, the Dark Continent. Africa, he explained was a land, where very few white men had ever ventured into its interior, most of those who that had never been seen again. During the following days the wind dropped and "The George," became becalmed in what the crew called the "Doldrums." This meant that the crew had time on their hands and John, our tutor was able to scare the lives out of us with his gruesome stories about the savage tribes that inhabited Africa. Many of my fellow prisoners had lived all their lives in rural Ireland and so John's yarns about giant black men that were cannibals and enjoyed eating human flesh scared the life out of them.

The wind gradually picked up and we got under sail again continuing our southerly course along the coast of Africa. Unlike most of my fellow convicts I was fascinated by the wonderful wildlife and beautiful clear skies and the fantastic sights we were now regularly encountering. Under different circumstances I felt that this voyage into the unknown would have been an experience of a lifetime but like all the other prisoners I worried about how I would be able to cope with life in the dreaded penal colony of Australia.

During this tranquil period I tried to ensure that I was a model prisoner and endeavoured to keep on the right side of our guards. My brother's advice was always at the forefront of my thoughts and actions; "Keep your own counsel and keep yourself to yourself" and this was the best piece advice I have ever had. Time and again, during my long incarceration I kept myself out of trouble by heeding these words. As the ship sailed further and further south I continued with my geography lessons under John Page's tuition and with the help of his map of the world he explained we had now crossed the Equator. Once over the Equator he said, we were now sailing in the southern hemisphere. At this time he also showed us how the Captain plotted the course towards our final destination. Three times a day measurements were taken he explained, using a sextant and at the same time readings were obtained from the chronometer and the ships compass. These three measurements were then collated by the Captain and transcribed onto a chart or map to ascertain the ships current position.

Once passed the Equator the heat became even more unbearable, but fortunately as we had had been no further trouble from us convicts, we were all allowed to sleep on deck. This was a blessed relief to all of us because below deck it had now become impossible to sleep. About this time the food and water started to become rancid and virtually inedible. But as we were all continually both hungry and thirsty we were glad to eat and drink whatever we were given. As we carried on sailing south the temperature began to drop and John informed us we would soon be leaving the Atlantic and sailing out into the Southern Ocean, where with strong prevailing winds we should make very fast progress to our destination. As usual he was proved correct, but with the sudden tremendous drop in temperature many of the convicts became ill with bronchitis and many other ailments. The clothing we had been given proved to be completely unsuitable for the icy cold conditions we now encountered. Tragically two of our fellow prisoners succumbed to the appalling weather, Michael O'Reilly a small farmer from County Meath and the other poor soul was James Shea from Kenmare, County Kerry. After a brief ceremony both bodies were committed to the deep. Fortunately these were the only prisoners to die from sickness on this voyage.

After ten days fast sailing in the Southern Ocean, the Captain called his crew together and we heard him promise that the first sailor to sight land would get double rations of rum. This was obviously a great incentive to his men because they now scoured the horizon from dawn to dusk. By now after being at sea nearly five months even we convicts were praying for the end to our long voyage, and most of the convicts also spent every available minute looking for the elusive first sighting of Australia. It was not for another two days that we heard a great cry of land ahoy and there in the mist coming out of the sea was our first view of the colony of Australia.

My first sighting of Sydney our final destination was on the fifth of December, eighteen thirty-one. As we sailed into the harbour we craned our necks for a view of our new home. Having been to both Bristol and Liverpool docks, I was no stranger to the sight that greeted us. But most of my fellow prisoners were amazed by the enormous crowds and the hundreds of ships that were tied up in the docks. What astounded me most was that we had arrived in Australia, in the month of December and the weather was extremely hot, On speaking to John Page, about this he explained that in the Southern hemisphere the seasons were the opposite to ours in Ireland and we had actually arrived in the middle of the Australian summer.

On our arrival although we knew what was in store for us, both convicts and sailors were anxious to get ashore. The sailors were the lucky ones as they were soon given permission to go ashore. But we prisoners had a very long and frustrating wait onboard the ship and it was not until the twentieth of December after being inspected by the colonial surgeon and other officials that we were finally allowed to disembark at Sydney Cove. Once ashore we were again thoroughly inspected by various officials, and then ironically they asked all of us if we had any complaints. Obviously nobody stepped forward, because by this time even the most hardened criminals amongst us had realised that their best chance of survival was to keep their mouths shut and to see what developed in this totally alien environment where we had now found ourselves. Also the whipping that had killed Tom Griffin on board ship was still fresh in every ones minds and its ferocity had shocked us all. As I have previously stated the savage sentence had achieved its aim and life on board ship for the rest of the voyage had been trouble free. Consequently the Captain and his fellow officers had realised this and had then acted quiet leniently towards us. Once ashore this attitude quickly changed, because before moving off we were again chained together for the long march through the town to our new accommodation in a building called Hyde Park Barracks.

So it was that after five long months at sea, we all found it very strange walking on land again, and being chained together we needed to concentrate to stop us from falling over. Apparently we had unconsciously become used to the constant roll of the ship, and now our legs had to readjust to being on land. As you know I have travelled a great deal but, nothing could have prepared me for my first experience of the colony of Australia as everything I saw that day was amazing. The town of Sydney seemed to consist of hundreds and hundreds of what we became to know as Canaries. They were in fact convicts working for the government, who got their nickname from the brightly coloured jackets and trousers they wore. As we passed them by, they jeered and swore at us somehow knowing we were all Irishmen and as we were soon to find out, we Irish were looked upon as the lowest of the low all over the colony.

After enduring a long walk in the extreme heat of the day we eventually got to the barracks. Luckily my stay at Hyde Park Barracks was to be very brief because it would appear that a profile of every convict transported on "The George", had been advertised in the local papers. The reason for this was to inform prospective employers of the skills that some of us transportee's had. Fortunately for me my previous tunnelling and railway experience in England had attracted the attention of a mining entrepreneur named James Scully. As was the practise, he had immediately approached the local authorities for permission to employ me. Permission was soon forthcoming and all formalities were quickly completed, as it was quiet apparent that the government's intentions were always to keep the numbers of convicts the fed and clothed to a minimum. The first I knew about what had been decided for me was when I was introduced to a man called Thomas Edwards. My orders were to accompany Mr Edwards, who I found out later was an employee of a certain Mr Scully.

I was told that our destination was a town called Newcastle, which was about a hundred miles north of Sydney. So on the fourth or January eighteen thirty two, I left that hell hole called Hyde Park Barracks, accompanied by Thomas Evans. I was still dressed in my shipboard clothes but I carried with me a private employment ticket, which I had been informed I must produce on demand to any soldier or police constable who requested it. No transport was provided for us, so we set out together on the long dusty road to Newcastle. I found that first day extremely tough, due to the intense heat and my lack of exercise while on board the ship. After we left Sydney that morning we soon reached the countryside, or the bush as it is known to the Australian's, our walk then became very enjoyable as the wild flowers, unusual trees and fascinating birds were a joy to behold. During the next few days journey I saw for the first time, koala bears, platypus, kangaroos and wallabies all living in the wild. It is hard for me to describe to you these creatures as they are all so different to the animals we have in Ireland, but they are a wondrous sight to behold. But even more magnificent was the fantastic variety of birds that I saw, they seemed to be every colour of the rainbow, yellow, bright blue, and all different shades of red.

So although that first day's walk was very arduous, the experience was unforgettable and I was also very fortunate in that my companion. Tom Evans, a former coal miner from Wales, had spent many years in Australia and had acquired a vast knowledge of its wild life, and seemed to be able to answer my every question.

That first evening we were both very tired and hungry, when we stopped at a tiny village called Hornsby. Tom told me that he hoped to meet his old friend Robert Hughes there, as he would definitely find us both a bed and a meal. Hughes he told me later had come from the same town in Wales and they had both been transported for poaching salmon many years before. After serving their long sentences both men were now free and Hughes he said was now working on a local homestead for a settler raising cattle. As Tom, had predicted Robert was very pleased to see us and greeted the two of us like long lost brothers. He soon had a good fire going and a pot of tea was quickly brewed. After the long days trek the tea tasted wonderful and the food that followed has never tasted as delicious as by now both Tom and I were starving. Robert set before us some fine corned beef and a wheaten cake baked on the hearth, which is locally called damper. I recall that this my first meal in what was called by the Australians "The Outback" and it tasted particularly appetizing to me after the months of rations on board ship and the terrible food we were given at the Hyde Park Barracks. After the meal it is customary in Australia for pipes to be lit and the conversations to commence. That night I was so tired after the meal I informed our host I would retire to bed, but I must now tell you that the mysteries of Australian bed making, demand some explanation.

The following description of our accommodation is not a generalisation, but is purely my observation as a newcomer to the colony. The huts that the locals lived in I must explain are merely a few sheets of bark stripped from local trees, not brick built, or made of dried mud like our dwellings. The living space was only a single area of about nine feet long, by six feet wide, the roof too is made from bark but of the usual shape. The total length of one of the six feet ends was the fire place of the hut, where a log fire was constantly burning on the earthen hearth. At the other six feet end was a sort of berth also of bark, not unlike the bunks on board a ship, they were fixed about three feet from the ground, whilst at the nine foot side next to the road, was a door, which likewise was of bark and at the opposite parallel side was a little table and that too was of bark. The original architect of the building had used all manner of materials whilst they were green wood and so that on seasoning everything twisted to all different shapes, and as is usually the case, the worst example came from the most important item that being the table, which was the most crooked thing in the whole hut.

I made quickly my bed from all the old clothes that I could find, and then I pulled over myself half dozen good-sized sheepskins for blankets. As I have said, that night I was so tired after my exertions I thought I could have slept anywhere, but in fact I lay awake for an age listening to the strange animal noises that were emanating from the countryside that surrounded us.

The next morning I was very surprised to find that our host was already up and about. He had lit the fire and was boiling a piece of salted beef, and baking a fresh cake. The aroma from his cooking reminded me of the good times back in Ireland and for a brief moment my heart longed to see you again. But I quickly suppressed this romantic notion and helped Richard brew the tea. Our breakfast that morning and the wonderful hospitality of Robert Hughes I will never to forget and somehow in that brief meeting we struck up a friendship. This friendship would blossom in later years and apart from you Patrick, I have never known a truer companion. This was all in the future, as Tom and I reluctantly bid our kind host goodbye that morning and carried on with our journey, this time heading towards the township of Gosforth.

That day the heat quickly became unbearable and we decided that at midday we would stop at the township called Bourora and have bite to eat. Tom said we would then wait there for a couple of hours and continue our journey in the cool of the evening. Bourora was a small township in those days; and when we arrived there, Tom who I was about to find out had a fondness for strong liquor, straightaway headed for the local public house. After a couple of drinks Tom soon got into conversation with a party of farmers who had attended the Sydney market on the previous day. These farmers were mainly settlers from the Hawksby area and at this time all the talk was about the severe drought which had affected them for many months. Coming from Ireland, drought was a word I had never really heard used, but it would appear their cattle were tragically dying in their hundreds for want of food and water. From the conversation that we had with them, it seemed there was no sign of any imminent end to the drought. Consequently the price of cattle had fallen to ridiculous levels and many settlers were facing bankruptcy and ruin.

We sat chatting to these travellers until the early evening by which time Tom could hardly walk as he was so drunk. I fortunately had kept sober as I had no intention of giving anyone in authority any excuse for returning me to Hyde Park Barracks. Eventually my companion started to sober up and we regained the road that headed north. By now the temperature had thankfully dropped and so it was a pleasant walk that evening and we eventually reached our resting place just before midnight.

Our accommodation that night was a settlers hut run by an Irishman from County Clare, called Jimmy Roche and as usual the host was very welcoming. What was so surprising to me a newcomer to the colony was the realisation that the whole of the Australian population seemed to be constantly on the move. This night was no exception; every makeshift hut in the vicinity was full of wayfarers and travellers. It is always the custom wherever you went in the colony, that as soon as you arrived the kettle or a similar utensil for tea making was on the boil. While we were drinking our tea Mrs Roche's wife prepared an excellent supper for the two of us. After the meal pipes were again produced and as always, many a ballad was sung and in many instances these were old Irish familiar songs that brought tears to everyone's eyes. Luckily there was no liquor available for Tom to drink that night and so wearily we found a spot to put our blanket down and soon the whole hut fell silent.

The next morning after a quick breakfast we were soon on the road again journeying northwards we crossed the Hawksby River and by noon we had reached a small township called Wyong. Here sadly all my early illusions about life in this strange and wonderful country were shattered. On our arrival in Wyong we happened by chance to walk past the local courthouse. In the street in front of the courthouse I trembled to see a punishment triangle set up. On closer examination of this terrible instrument of torture I knew at once that it had been recently used. On enquiring we were told that convicts had been flogged for minor offences that very morning. The blood and gore were so fresh that the local dogs were still licking it off the triangles. Even more appalling was the fact that we saw where the punishment inflictor's foot had worn a deep hole in the ground from the force he had used as he whirled himself round to strike the victims back. One poor soul's punishment had only recently finished because I could see the trail of blood that had squelched from his shoes as he had walked back to the barracks. An observer told us that the prisoners back was a mass of swollen ragged sinews and his punishment had been so severe he must surely die.

Tom my companion counselled me saying any slight show of insolence or rebellion was just the excuse the authorities needed to inflict this terrible punishment on the convicts. His warnings were prophetic, because during the next ten years I was to see at first hand many terrible punishments handed out in Australia. Subsequently in recent years, after details of these brutal and inhumane practises were published in various English newspapers, the indiscriminate flogging of convicts for trivial offences is hopefully a thing of the past. But from my first hand experience I know that the Irish convicts were always singled out for the worse punishments, and there was definitely a bias against the Catholic religion and those that chose to practise it throughout the colony.

Passing quickly through Wyong, we continued on the road north to Newcastle, luckily for us later that afternoon we fortunately hitched a ride on a dray that was going in our direction I was very relieved as once again the heat was unbearable that day and by now my feet were in a terrible state. As I have previously said those months of inactivity on board ship had not prepared me for walking in the searing heat.

The owner of the dray told us he was originally from the County of Essex, in England, and he had originally been transported for stealing a chicken. His name we soon found out was George Thomas, George was a wonderful story teller and he regaled us with all the local history of the area we were passing through. His stories about his past life in England were hilarious and that afternoon both Tom and I laughed until our sides were aching.

Fortunately for us George, was travelling in our direction for the next two days and was delighted to have us for company. On the third day we reluctantly said our farewells to our new found friend who had lightened up our long journey. After leaving our new companion we still had two days of hard walking before we finally reached our destination. During those two days I pestered Tom with questions about my future employee Mr Scully and his mining activities. Tom assured me that as long as I was willing to work hard and kept out of trouble I would be well looked after by my new boss. Strangely on the last night of our trek we found lodgings in a small township called Swansea. This was ironic for my companion, as his hometown in Wales was also called Swansea. Never one to miss an excuse to get drunk I spent my last night with him listening to him reminiscing about his early life in Wales. Then like all his compatriots the world over he began to sing. Singing is something the Welsh are very good at and Tom, was no exception but once started he carried on singing until the early hours of the morning.

When he sobered up the next the day he told to me about the recent history of the town of Newcastle. It had, he said, been for many years a penal settlement where the most notorious convicts in the colony had been incarcerated. The first penal settlement was originally at a place called Lime Burners Bay; this prison was under the control of the military. Treatment of these prisoners was always very harsh and often barbaric. The lime that was produced by the convicts at Lime Burners Bay was much prized in the colony and was transported by sea to the various new towns then expanding all along the coast of Australia. In Sydney it was famously used on the construction of the Supreme Court, St James's Church and many other buildings. Sadly the convicts working at producing the lime had terrible health problems. The effects of the work on the prisoners were immense, as they were obviously continuously exposed to the lime. This exposure affected their eyes and over parts of their bodies that were not covered mainly the hands and arms. Without any eye protection the lime blinded hundreds of convicts, whilst others saw their hands and arms wither away from being in constant contact with that deadly substance. Tom said that many of the other poor souls became wearied and enfeebled by hunger and the endless whippings and collapsed and died. Fortunately in recent years the harsh military rule had ceased and the number of convicts in the penal settlement had drastically been reduced.

Freed for the first time from martial law Newcastle and the surrounding townships including Lime Burners Bay, had began to acquire the aspect of a typical Australian pioneer colony. A number of shopkeepers and tradesmen had arrived from England in the intervening years and during my stay I saw at first hand how the town expanded and prospered mainly due to the coal industry.

With much trepidation I finally arrived in Newcastle, where my companion Tom, seemed to be known by everyone we met and he introduced me to many of his acquaintances. Knowing that I was very apprehensive about meeting my future employer, Tom took me at once to the offices of Mr Scully's company. After a long delay I was shown into the office James Scully for my interview. My new employer seemed to take an instant liking to me and he was very interested to hear about my past experiences working on the Liverpool to Manchester railroad. [From this conversation it would appear that there was now a greater interest in building railways in England and this interest was spreading to other countries around the world]. Eventually he said we will soon have them here in Australia, as the transportation system in the colony was at that time very antiquated. Also from our conversation I gathered that the coal was in great abundance in the Newcastle area and with my previous experience in tunnelling and the use of explosives, he thought I could be a great asset to his business.

After the interview I went with Tom to find accommodation, he directed me to a local boarding house where he and a number of my future colleagues lived. That evening after they had finished their shift, I met some of them and we talked about their experiences at the coal face. Most of them were fellow convicts serving their sentences and hoping to eventually become free men.

On my first morning as a miner, I was kitted out with overalls and a pick and shovel and then put to work. We worked a ten hour shift with only thirty minutes break for a bite to eat at noon, but although the work was extremely hard and the hours were long, I was told by my new colleagues that compared to other mining companies in the Newcastle coal fields, we were very fortunate. James Scully, they informed me, was a former miner, with many years experience and knew that the welfare of his workforce was of prime importance in ensuring that his mines achieved their production targets. With this in mind he had been the first mine owner in the area to install baths for his men to use when they had finished their shift each day. Also he decreed that all work must cease at three o'clock on Saturday afternoon, to enable his workforce time to rest. As I was to find out later these concessions were revolutionary at the time and very reluctantly the other mine owners realised that Scully's ideas did increase output and soon followed his example.

Fortunately for the coal industry of Newcastle, demand for coal was booming in the colony and it was also now exported to many other parts of the British Empire. For the first few months I personally found it very hard to get used to working underground because of the heat of the Australian summer. Also I quickly realised how unfit I had become after nearly a year of incarceration in jail and aboard the transportation ship. It was to be many months before I started to regain my old strength and acclimatise to the heat down the mine. Luckily, my knowledge and expertise gained on the construction of the railroad in England soon became apparent. With this recognition came an added responsibility and I soon became responsible for most of the blasting work at the coalface Although this work was extremely dangerous, it was obviously better than slaving away with a pick and shovel for ten hours a day.

Gradually as the years passed, Mr. Scully began to seek my advice on a regular basis usually regarding the purchase of new machinery to improve production. Being a very shrewd business man, he was always looking for new ideas and so he always consulted the men he could trust and in time I had become one of this select band. Over the years that I was in his employment I saw his mining empire grow until he became one of the largest owners in Newcastle.

I quickly realised the reasons for his success was looking after his workforce and listening and taking advice from the men he trusted. So I was very fortunate in that by the time my sentence was finished I had become an integral part of his mining company. My sentence ended in December eighteen thirty-nine; this meant I could now apply for what was called in the colony, a ticket of leave. The granting of my ticket of leave was only a formality as my boss fully endorsed my application. Ironically once I obtained my new status I was entitled to seek employment wherever I wished in the Australia.

I had no intention of leaving James Scully's employment as by this time I was quite settled in Australia. But in my heart I still hankered for a return to Ireland. Every day since leaving Ireland I had prayed that one day I would be able to afford to return home and marry my beloved fiancée Maureen and to have you standing at my side in church as my best man. Obviously I had met many girls in those years in Australia, but I could never get the thought of my fiancée out of my mind. At first I thought that the idea of returning to Ireland was impossibility, but gradually over the years my circumstances changed. After I received my ticket of leave, my employer realised he would have to increase my wages as skilled miners were now in great demand. Fortunately I still remembered your advice and drank very occasionally and this enabled me to save much of my wages. As my savings increased, I started to hope that I could one day afford to pay for a passage home, but until that day I decided to close my mind to any thoughts of seeing Ireland again.

Although I now only met Tom Edwards on the odd occasion we had remained good friends since our walk from Sydney. On one of our infrequent meetings he brought along his old friend from Wales, Robert Hughes who was now also working as a miner in Newcastle. Subsequently after this meeting, Robert and I found we had much in common and we struck up an enduring friendship. In the years following the end of my sentence we decided that when it was possible we would go out into the bush and explore the region around Newcastle. So in late September, eighteen forty, after consulting the locals we purchased our equipment and supplies for the first of our many adventures together. You must realise that at this time the area we were exploring was very sparsely populated and there was always a danger we might get lost in this unexplored wilderness. With this in mind our list of equipment consisted of the following, four blankets and a tent, saddle bags filled with tea, sugar, flour, tobacco, dried meat, quarter pots for tea making, tinder box for getting the fire going an axe and various other sundry items. Eventually on the twenty fifth of September, having both received permission to have two weeks holiday, we were all packed and ready to go. We had we had also hired three good horses from the local stables as we required one to carry our equipment.

It was a wonderful spring morning we when set out along the Hunter River, towards a small settlement called Maitland. All along the beautiful river valley we saw signs of the extensive felling of the wonderful cedar trees that grew in abundance in that area. On being felled these giant logs were being manhandled into the river and lashed together from where they floated down river to the wood yards of Newcastle. Like the coal that we dug, much of this timber was destined for shipment around the world.

That first evening as we were both unused to horse riding, we ached from our long ride so we were glad to reach Maitland. As it was a Saturday there was a large gathering of thirsty bush men already starting on their usual weekend revelry. Our first priority was to find a bed for the night and luckily there was room at the local public house. Our second priority was stabling and feeding our tired horses and this was a task that Robert always insisted on doing as he always had a close affinity with horses. After a traditionally hearty dinner we joined the noisy drinkers to swap stories and hear the local gossip. Both Robert and I enjoyed a couple of glasses of ale after our dinner, but these Bushmen's usual drink was rum and their hard drinking reminded me of the navvies in England on pay day. The common saying amongst the Bushmen was that they earned their money like horses and spent it like asses; and during my stay in Australia I found that this was definitely true. Once they had relaxed with a glass of strong rum, most Bushmen, just like the navvies in England would not finish drinking until all their hard earned cash was spent.

Day two found us heading towards the township of Singleton, after the usual breakfast of steak, damper and plenty of tea to wash it down. Then we rode on through the bush aiming for a homestead near Singleton, which had been recommended to us. At noon we had a stop to have a light meal and gave the horses a drink at a nearby stream. As we were about to restart our journey a tribe of native aborigines suddenly appeared. Their appearance startled both of us, but as we were to find out later, most aborigines were friendly and this tribe were no exception. I had occasionally seen aborigines in Newcastle, but this group obviously still lived tribally in the bush. Robert explained that aborigines were migrants and that they had their traditional hunting grounds. They never stayed in the same location very long but spent their whole lives on the move, carrying their kangaroo rugs and cloaks, their weapons and their gourds, calabashes and bark dishes wherever they went. The local aborigines I had seen in Newcastle were mainly used as trackers by the authorities and sadly had a strong addiction for alcohol. But these natives seemed very proud and fortunately very helpful, giving us advice in their Pidgin English as to the best route for us to take.

That evening being Sunday, we once again encountered a large crowd of Bushmen at our destination. Sundays in the bush is always treated as a holiday and the men usually take the opportunity to do their washing, mend clothes and grind the wheat for the following week's damper. Many of them had already finished their weekend chores and the drinking spree was once again in full swing. As usual the owner of the homestead made us very welcome and begged us to stay for a few days but we declined as we wanted to head further into the bush. It was a hard decision to make, as his homestead was very comfortable and the food they served was excellent.

During my stay in the colony I found the average Australian is always very friendly especially those who live outside of the towns. Kindness to strangers seems to be an unwritten law, I think this is because many of them lead a very solitary life in the vast wilderness they call "The Outback" and they are glad of the company. Day three saw us heading towards Durami Creek, and that night we had hoped to be in Singleton. But the terrain suddenly became tougher as we headed towards the town along a track that quickly became mountainous. Once we rode out of the mountains we quickly descended onto a fertile plain. Here there was an abundance of Australian wild animals, kangaroos, wombats, possum and the occasional koala bear. These animals are totally different from any seen in Ireland and to see them in their natural habitat is a wonderful sight. As we rode along that afternoon I was thinking about how much I was enjoying the peace and tranquillity of this area after years of incessant noise down the mines. Strangely, it was as if Robert, had read my mind because at that precise moment he said how wonderful it was to be away from mining and mines, for a few days.

That evening it was getting dark when we finally arrived in the township of Singleton after a very long hard ride. What you have to realise is that summer evenings in Australia, are totally different to what we are used to in Ireland, because by eight o'clock it is pitch dark. This was always a worry to us when we were travelling as we did not want to lose our bearings and get lost Luckily for us we found a public house with a bed for the night before it started to rain and before long there was a terrible storm that continued all night and most of the next day. In the morning the rain was so bad we decided to stay at the public house for another night. So together with the locals we sat and traded stories and rested up for the day. It also afforded us time to look after and feed the horses as the poor beasts were very tired after the previous day's journey.

On day five we realised that because we had lost a day, any hope we had of reaching our target of Bathurst on this trip had disappeared as from the outset we only had fourteen days available to us. At each nightly stop Robert always closely questioned the Bushmen and settlers we met in the hope of hearing about a suitable spread he could purchase. During breakfast the locals advised us to head towards a township called Mudgee, as they said the land around that township was well known for cattle rearing. Taking their advice we turned our horses and headed towards our new destination. That night was to be the first of many nights over the following years that we slept under the stars. The reason for this was unlike in Ireland, in "The Outback" townships and homesteads became fewer and fewer and so we were obliged to bed down for the night wherever we could.

Day six found us waking up stiff and aching as we were not used to sleeping on the ground, but after a quick brew of tea and a bite to eat we were soon on our way again. That morning we had hoped to reach the small township named Buranii Creek by noon and purchase supplies and rest the horses. But the ride that day was longer than we anticipated and it was late afternoon when we at last arrived tired and hungry in the township. As we sat and ate our dinner at the local ale house a party of freemen had arrived from up-country. These men had earned huge wages sheep shearing and their primary intention was they said to have a half pint of rum and move on, but as was usual in the colony the first drink led to a second and then a third until typically all their wages were spent. Sensing that these men were dangerous, we quickly left their company and found a bed for the night. Fortunately our intuition proved correct, because their drunken spree ended in a violent affray, with many serious injuries. Of all the wild men in the colony of Australia at that time, the ones with the worst reputation of all were the shearers. These men were indispensable to the large landowners because of the vast sheep herds that they owned and for this reason they seemed to be beyond the law.

The next morning day seven, we quickly left Buranni Creek heading towards a homestead near the town of Kandas which had also been recommended. Today's ride was a distance of thirty miles, but it was easy riding for a change. Our route followed a lovely winding river and as the weather had become exceptionally hot we stopped at regular intervals to rest our perspiring horses. Although we did not hurry because of the heat we still managed to arrive at our destination by late afternoon. On our arrival we quickly realised why this homestead had a good reputation. As soon as we dismounted from our weary horses, the owner's son appeared and stabled them for the night. The owner, Jim Nolan showed us into his house and soon had the kettle boiling and the tea made. Then to our surprise he introduced us to his wife Anna, we were surprised, because at the time there were very few women living outside of towns in Australia. She was she told us originally from the town of Galway, but had come to the colony looking for work and had met and married her husband in Sydney. That night I ate the best meal since arriving in Australia, Anna was a wonderful cook and Jim Nolan being a singer and fiddle player of repute entertained us until the early hours.

The next morning we had a long conversation with our host Jim and he advised Robert to think carefully before making any decision about purchasing a cattle station. His reasoning we both agreed was sound. The prolonged drought had he said bankrupted many of the small homesteads and the rest were struggling to survive. Have patience he cautioned and in a couple of years hopefully the drought will break and things will return to normal.

Before leaving the kind hospitality of the Nolan family, we decided that going on to Mudgee would not be practical this trip as we had to report for work in Newcastle on the following Monday. So very reluctantly we retraced our steps and headed back in the direction we had come. On looking through my diary entries for the return journey that year I read that nothing untoward happened.

Arriving back in Newcastle, late on the Sunday afternoon we were both very tired but elated after our adventure. Although Robert had had his hopes of buying his own place dashed that year he was as always optimistic for the future. His optimism would always seem to rub off on me and combined with his infectious humour he was the ideal travelling companion. That evening as we sat having our dinner we both promised ourselves that we would make these trips of discovery an annual event. Unfortunately, because of the exceptional busy workload we both experienced the following year our next trip into the outback was not until the spring of eighteen forty-two.

In the preceding years as I was now a free man, James Scully, usually gave me a generous annual wage increase. Also much to his credit he realised that most of his miners usually spent all of their hard earned wages on payday, so with our agreement he withheld part of our pay and he opened an account for each of us at the local bank. Although I was not in the habit of wasting my pay on drink, this method of saving appealed to me and Mr Scully being a shrewd businessman managed to obtain a fair rate of interest on our savings.

Those following two years were extremely arduous but financially rewarding for both Robert and me. Each Sunday I met him after mass and we would talk for hours about our next trip. But frustratingly we had to wait until early October, eighteen forty-two, for this finally to occur. This time with the lessons we had learned from our previous adventure, we plotted a more direct route as we were determined to get to Mudgee. Luckily this year we both arranged with our companies to have three weeks off and so on Monday, the second of October, we thankfully left the noise and bustle of Newcastle.

Here I must explain why we had decided on Mudgee as our final destination; Robert, prior to this journey had met an old friend from his native country of Wales. His friend a former miner in Newcastle, had after a heavy drinking session one evening let slip that he had recently been panning for gold in the Cudgegong River. This river Robert knew was between the townships called Gulagong and Mudgee. The former miner had not it seems been very successful in his quest but had heard rumours that others had. Obviously we had kept this secret to ourselves and decided to tell anyone who was interested the purpose of our journey was to purchase a suitable station to run cattle.

On leaving the dirt and grime of Newcastle, we once again marvelled at the peace and tranquillity of the Australian outback. Spring is the ideal time for riding along the Hunter River, as I once again saw wonderful flocks of birds with magical colours, budgerigars, black cockatoos and the breathtaking king parrots. But on this trip we were obviously in a hurry, so every morning we were up early and on our way by sunrise and this year we made camp wherever possible so as to avoid questions from inquisitive Bushmen. Pushing on up country I didn't have time to write my diary, but I recall that after obtaining fresh supplies in Maitland, we bypassed the town of Singleton. Then striking across country and pushing our horses to the limit we finally arrived at our destination Mudgee. After five days of solid riding the horses were now obviously in need of a rest and luckily in the small township of Mudgee we found a very welcoming public house with good stabling. Here we both agreed that having made good time we should rest the next day and then continue our journey. This was to prove a wise decision as it gave the horses the rest they required.

On day seven we decided to head straight to Gulagong and so we got up very early and after a wonderful breakfast of steak, eggs and damper, we saddled our horses and rode out of Mudgee. We were both getting very excited as we neared the river Cudgegong and discussed the chances of finding our fortune in gold. Robert who had years of mining experience and also some geology knowledge, both in his native Wales and here in Australia informed me of his plan. We would he said ride along the river bank for a day or two and then if the river bed looked promising, we would stop and pan for the gold. This year we had allowed ourselves ten days for our search and had come prepared with plenty of supplies to keep us going.

That morning we had a pleasant ride along the river and in the afternoon we found a favourable camping site. Both of us then decided that I would prepare the food and pitch the tent whilst Robert made his way back to the river to start panning for gold. That evening Robert returned just after dusk quite disheartened because he thought that the early indications were not at all promising.

On the eighth day of our trip we again rode along the Cudgegon River on another wonderful spring day, although there was a serious side to our endeavour, I could not help but enjoy the wonderful countryside. But every now and again, we stopped to let Robert investigate the riverbed; fortunately we did not meet anyone again that day so there were no explanations to be made. Bushmen are notorious gossips and we knew that if they had any idea of what our motives were the news would travel like wildfire around the colony.

On days nine and ten we carried on our long ride, still in glorious sunshine keeping to the same routine. Although it now seemed the chances of meeting anyone was pretty remote, we had both agreed that if we had a chance encounter, we would still keep to our original story about looking for a suitable cattle station to buy. Our story was that we had heard that there was a decent spread on the market just past the townships of Gulagong in the direction of Dubbo, but during these two days we again only had ourselves for company. Unfortunately there were no sign of the elusive gold in the river and all of Roberts's hard work had been in vane. But after his earlier disenchantment, luckily he once again became his old positive self.

On day eleven we woke to the sound of thunder, lightening and torrential rain and as we had pitched our tent very near the river bank, we quickly decided to move to higher ground. In the past we had both heard stories of Australian rivers that would often rise ten, twenty and on occasions thirty feet in a few hours. So we deemed it prudent to move our camp site a good mile away from the raging river. The storm that day became more and more violent as the lightening lit up the grey sky. Then large hailstones started to fall, driven by strong winds. The hailstorm made both of us very worried, as at one stage we thought it might puncture our tent. In less than ten minutes when the violent squall had passed the ground was covered with hailstones to the depth of eight inches. After the storm passed, the heat of the midday sun quickly melted them and they mingled with the vast torrents of storm water which we could see sweeping down from the hills. Fortunately our campsite was not in the path of this torrent of water, but the only sound we could hear was the roar of the water flooding into the river. Thanking God that we had moved to higher ground we both agreed that our only course of action was to sit and wait until the water levels receded. But after a brief lull it started to rain again and although it was not very heavy it was to continue non stop for the next twelve hours. That night we both had to endure another wretched time cold, wet and hungry and we were also very worried about the whereabouts of our horses.

It was still raining on the morning of day twelve, but by midday it had eased and we now both decided to abandon our search for the elusive gold. Because we both realised that due to the storm it would be at least a week before the river was back to normal. Most of that day was spent searching for the horses, who when we found them the poor beasts were very frightened and obviously very hungry. While Robert tended to them I managed to pack up our very wet equipment. Unfortunately we still had a long ride that evening before we reached the welcoming public house in Mudgee. Although by the time we arrived there it was nearly midnight, thankfully the publican was once again pleased to see us and cooked us a hot meal before us two tired and weary travellers turned in for the night.

The next day was spent in Mudgee, resting up before our long ride back to Newcastle. After the terrible weather of the past two days it was really good to see the sun out again. As it was by now the end of spring, by midday the temperature had started to soar. Although I did not like travelling in the heat I thought at least the sun would quickly dry the trail. But while I spent my day resting, Robert was out and about around the town hoping to hear any snippet of gossip about gold prospectors in the area. But to no avail, as it seemed that if anyone knew anything they were keeping it to themselves.

The next morning which was day fourteen, we had a very leisurely breakfast then purchased fresh supplies ready for our return journey. As the weather was very hot we rode slowly for the next couple of days as we wanted to let our horses recover from their ordeal of the past weeks. Thankfully due to Roberts care and attention they quickly recovered and were soon back to their old selves. As we still had a couple of day's holiday left, Robert, suggested that we make a detour and spend a night at the Nolan's place near Kandas. Obviously I jumped at the chance of returning there, as the prospect of having dinner cooked by Anna Nolan, was too good to miss. Luckily the detour we choose soon brought us in sight of our destination and we were not to be disappointed as our hosts greeted us like long lost friends. Our over night stay was a feast of good food and great entertainment and as before it was two very reluctant travellers that left their homestead and returned to Newcastle.

All too soon we were back at work in the mines and the summer of eighteen forty-two, was the hottest I can ever recall during my stay in the colony. Tragically the heat wave as usual brought about the curse of Australia [bush fires], these fires once started were very hard to extinguish. This year they even reached the outskirts of the town. The situation was so serious that every able bodied man in Newcastle was called out to try and stop the conflagration. I went with the rest of the miners to the raging fire on the northern outskirts of the town. The plan was to clear large areas of trees and scrub to create a fire break. The heat of the fire was intense and the smoke suffocating as we toiled to stop the fire engulfing the town. At my suggestion we cleared large areas of the bush by letting off a series of controlled explosions, which cleared many trees and created large areas devoid of flammable materials between the town and the bush.

For me the most amazing sight that day was watching the wild animals fleeing from the devastation. I watched as hundreds of different species sort refuge by crossing our firebreak. Running for their lives in all directions were Kangaroos, Koala bears, Bandicoots, Possums and many other animals, including snakes and reptiles of every description all desperately trying to reach safety. Instinct had somehow told them to make for the open country away from the bush; I suppose that this instinct was the result of many such incidents in the past centuries.

After nearly a week of anxiety, we were overjoyed to find that our strategy of clearing firebreaks had proved successful, as fortunately the fire did not reach the town but gradually burnt itself out. But news from other townships and homesteads in the area was not so good and over the next few weeks many settlers and their convict workers came into Newcastle with terrible stories of their hardships. The continuous drought that effected most of the colony for the past few years, allied to the heat wave that summer, was to cause tremendous problems to the livestock with many of them dying from lack of food and water.

Fortunately the next autumn and winter were very wet and the long drought was finally broken. My work in the mines was as usual very hectic and so it was always a great pleasure to have my weekly meeting with Robert, in which we discussed our plans for the following spring. After our last two trips we felt we had gained plenty of experience of bush life and on our next prospecting trip we were determined to ensure nothing would go wrong. Our main concerns were rumours that Bushrangers, as escaped prisoners were called, were committing many outrages in the outlying townships, mostly in the Mudgee area and so we both purchased carbines with plenty of ammunition and also took with us two large hunting dogs for further protection. That year we had to wait until late November, before we could get time off for what was to prove to be our last journey together into the Australian bush.

I now look back on my adventures with Robert Evans with immense nostalgia; Robert was always cheerful, full of humour and optimism, in fact a true friend and a great companion. He has promised that one day he will return from Australia and visit us in Springfort; I sincerely hope he keeps his promise because I would dearly like to meet him again.

The twenty eighth of November, eighteen forty-three, was a very warm day when we left Newcastle and started our ride north. For this trip we had decided to hire four horses, as we wanted to live mostly under canvas and as a result we needed to carry extra supplies. Past experience had taught us that we should travel in very short stages in order to conserve our animal's energy especially during the heat of the day. As a consequence we did not arrive in Singleton our first objective until very late on the third day. Luckily the landlord of the public house remembered us from our previous visits, and after we had unsaddled and stabled the horses we were treated to an enormous dinner. Later we had a very convivial evening with some shepherds, and drovers, their main conversation was the terror the Bushrangers were inflicting on the local population. The next morning after purchasing fresh supplies, we left Singleton on a long ride to the Cudegong River. Due to the extreme heat each morning we started out on our ride very early, always resting the horses at midday. This routine was we found ideal because of the heat of the Australian summer especially when camping. On our journey Robert explained to me that during the preceding year he had spent his time researching rock formations and geology and he was hopeful that we would be more successful on this trip.

By day six, we had arrived at Mudgee tired and hungry as our supplies were now running low. Here in Mudgee thankfully we found the town very much as normal, with everyone telling us that the terrifying rumours about Bushranger's atrocities were exaggerated. At the time because of the sparse population in the outback there was obviously no regular newspapers in circulation and because of this rumour and speculation were rife. As the heat wave showed no sign of ending we decided to rest up for the day and then headed out of town for our next destination the River Cudgegong.

On day eight, with our pack horses loaded with fresh foodstuffs we followed the trail towards Gulagong, but then made a detour and that afternoon we were once again splashing along the river bed of the Cudgegong looking for a suitable camping site. As the river bank was shaded by many large trees it was not long before we found an ideal site. While I fed and watered the horses and prepared the evening meal, Robert started panning for gold but once again he was disappointed.

Days nine, and ten, saw us still making our way slowly along the Cudgegong, each day following the same pattern. After three days of disappointment we decided to head for the local town of Gulagong, hoping to find a decent hot meal and a comfortable bed for the night. Also worryingly each day the heat of the day was intense and consequently the horses were beginning to suffer, not to mention the fact that by now I was becoming very dispirited. At this time I thought we should call it a day and take a slow ride back to Newcastle, but

Robert would not hear of it, he was certain our luck would change so reluctantly I agreed to carry on for two more days.

Day twelve was to be the day that changed both of our lives. We had left Gulagong very early and we were soon back following the course of the river. At midday we stopped for our usual break and while I had a snooze, Robert went off panning in the river. He later recalled that inwardly he had lost all hope of finding gold, but as he began to swill the muddy water around in his pan he thought he saw the telltale glint of metal. To his utter amazement his first pan that afternoon yielded a quarter of an ounce of gold, at that time equivalent to a week's wages for the average workman. As the realisation of what he had found sank in he threw down his pan and let out a cry of euphoria. His shouting woke me from my slumber and I rushed to see what the excitement was all about. It was the greatest surprise I have ever had; when I looked into the pan and saw the glint of gold. As we sat on the river bank, we both stared in disbelief at the glinting metal in the pan. Then rushing back to our campsite I grabbed my pan and rushed to help Robert in his quest. We were both tired and very hungry when darkness fell that evening and were compelled to stop panning. By nightfall we calculated that we had panned about five ounces of raw gold; and that night we both dreamed of untold wealth and prosperity.

On days thirteen, fourteen and fifteen we worked non-stop in the blazing heat. During those few days our small pile of gold gradually increased and by day fifteen we had a substantial haul. But unfortunately we were now running out of supplies especially fodder for the horses. So after talking it over we decided that I should ride into Gulagong to obtain replenishments, whilst Robert carried on with the panning.

On day sixteen, after buying the supplies I spent the night in a public house and rode back to the campsite early the next morning. Robert by then was extremely tired and he informed me that he thought we had extracted all the gold from the riverbed in that area. So we both reluctantly decided it was time for us to return to Newcastle. During our ride back through the bush with our new found wealth, we decided that with the threat of Bushrangers extra care must be taken. So each night we shared sentry duty; two hours sleep, then two hours keeping watch. This policy paid immediate dividends because on the third night of our return journey Robert had just finished his watch and was about to turn in, when in the far distance he heard the clatter of horse's hoofs on stony ground and he then heard the sound of muffled voices.

Both our dogs sensing the danger rushed off to confront the approaching strangers. Realising that we must be ready for all eventualities, we quickly loaded our carbines and made sure they were readily available. The approaching men were cursing and swearing at our dogs and when they got to our camp they threatened to shoot both of them if we did not call them off. Obviously we soon complied with their wishes, as we could tell from their manner that it was not an idle threat. As was the usual custom in the colony night, or day, we immediately put the pots on the fire to make tea. They both sat down by the fire and lit their pipes. The tea was soon made and at my suggestion I prepared supper.

After a long silence the older of the two, who was called Sam, asked us what we were doing in the area. Robert, who was always plausible, informed them we were looking for a grass run for the small cattle herd we were proposing to purchase, but as we could not find anything suitable in this vicinity we were returning to our jobs as miners in Newcastle. Robert's explanation seemed to satisfy our guests who told us they were running out of supplies and they wanted to know if we knew of any homesteads in the local area. From their threatening demeanour we both realised that these were two of the infamous Bushrangers we were dealing with. In the circumstances it seemed prudent to offer them the supplies they needed, hoping against hope they would let us proceed. They gratefully accepted our offer and by daybreak they were on their way. But worrying we were now running low on supplies but our great secret was still intact.

After a long hazardous ride we arrived late that night at the Nolan homestead, knowing that we could be assured of good food and a comfortable bed for the night. After our flirtation with danger and loss of supplies we were both pleased to have the good supper that our kind hosts provided for us. When we left Jim Nolan and his wife Anna the next morning little did I realise that I sadly would never see them again. Robert has I know kept in contact with them and has from time to time returned to see them. But after purchasing sufficient supplies we were soon on our way. The rest of our ride back to Newcastle went very smoothly and we reached the town just in time to celebrate the Christmas festivities.

Our immediate problem was what to do with our new found wealth, as any hint of our discovery we knew would spread like wild fire. Also at that time the colonies population consisted of ninety percent convicts, some of whom were very dangerous. We knew that our lives would be in danger if our secret ever got out. After many discussions and a lot of arguments, we eventually agreed that

I would take my share with me and make my long planned return journey to Ireland. Robert explained that his plan was to quietly leave his employment in Newcastle and return to the Cudgegong River and pan for gold.

After the Christmas celebrations I returned to work in the mines, with my hopes and prayers now centred on my one great ambition of returning home to Ireland. Little did I know it would be another two years long before I would be able to book my passage. During the next few months my health worryingly began to deteriorate. It started with coughing fits and gradually got worse and I then began to have trouble breathing. The many years of breathing dust and foul air in the mines and tunnels had it seems unfortunately taken their toll on my lungs. Luckily my boss and now good friend James Scully paid for my passage to Sydney with a letter of introduction to his personal physician. After a long and detailed examination he confirmed that my mining days were over and he suggested that I should look for an alternative form of employment. This news I relayed to Mr Scully on my return and we discussed what course of action should be taken. His wise advice was to get away from the town of Newcastle, to somewhere where the air was not polluted and recuperate. When my health eventually improved he said, I should fulfil my ambition and return home to my native land and if that day ever comes he added surprisingly, we should return together, as his wife's health was failing and she was pining for the old country.

Fortunately after leaving Newcastle, my health soon improved and by chance I met Brian Murphy, a fellow Cork man, from Buttevant. Brian informed me that he ran a spread near Maitland in the wonderful Hunter Valley and he was at present looking for workers. This was very fortunate as now that my health had improved we agreed that it would be in both our interests if I went to work for him. Obviously it helped that we had a lot in common as we both came from the same background and knew many of the same people especially the girls.

The following eighteen months were really enjoyable, as it has you know, always been a joy for me to work in the countryside. From time to time Robert Hughes came to visit, but although he had left the mines and was now prospecting he had never struck gold again. Although I enjoyed working for Brian, as the months passed I became very restless, particularly as I still had in my possession my share of the gold from the Cudgegong River.

So in November eighteen forty-six, I said my sad goodbyes to Brian, and his family and left Maitland and headed back to Newcastle on the first stage of my long journey home. The ride along the Hunter River had always fascinated me and as this was to be my last chance to enjoy it I did the journey in easy stages. As I rode along its winding course in the early summer I realised that I was seeing it at its finest. But all too soon I returned to the noise and bustle of Newcastle, but this time I knew I would not be staying long.

After finding accommodation I went to the public house that my former mining colleagues frequented to have a farewell drink. As we sat there reminiscing, to my great surprise Robert Hughes pushed his way through the crowded bar. All our many trials and tribulations together were forgotten that night and I am sad to a say that we both got horribly drunk. The next morning feeling like death after my excesses of the previous evening I set out for Mr Scully's office. When I arrived on this occasion I was taken directly to see him, as it appeared he was expecting me. I quickly realised that he had been told by one of the miners that I was in town and intending to see him. Obviously he knew the reason for my visit and had totalled up the amount of money I had on my account. The sum of money I had available he assured me was quite sufficient for a passage back to Ireland.

As we sat there discussing my return home, he suddenly said he was taking me to lunch as we had a lot to discuss. Over lunch he informed me that his poor wife had recently died and as a consequence he had nothing left to keep him in Australia. He had he said, found a buyer for his business and he was now determined to return home to his family in Ireland. In later conversations on board ship, he told me that he had two sons that he adored but tragically both had died at a young age. But what surprised me the most that day was that he insisted that I accompany him on his return journey. I was speechless for a few moments as I contemplated what he had said, but I quickly realised that with his many connections my passage home was now assured. Thanking him for his kind offer we agreed that it was best if he made the arrangements for our departure. The reason being that as a highly respected member of the business community for many years, he was certain that with the vast number of contacts he had it should be easy for us to get a passage back to a port in England. In conclusion he finished by telling me confidentially that the sale of his various business ventures should be completed by the end of the year and after that there was nothing left to keep him in Australia. After lunch, because James was in no hurry to return to the mines, we spent the rest of the day together. Unfortunately, he said he had heard rumours that the potato crop had completely failed in Europe. We both knew from past experience that if

113

these rumours were in fact true the Irish people, with their total dependence on the potato could be heading for disaster. As we parted that night James said he would keep me informed on any developments, then before we parted I bought one last beer and we drank a toast to our safe return to Ireland.

James was a man of his word and over the coming weeks organised our passage on a large cargo ship called "The Rodney," he had also obtained the required authorisation for me to leave the colony. In early January after a hectic Christmas for both of us we boarded a small coaling ship for the short journey to Sydney. On our arrival in Sydney we headed straight to the docks in search of "The Rodney," The ship we were told was due to leave the next day bound for Liverpool, calling on route at Melbourne and Cape Town with a cargo of the finest Australian wool. That night we had our last dinner in Australia and early next morning in great humour we boarded "The Rodney." Once onboard we were shown to our luxurious cabins, for me the contrast was amazing, as the memory of my passage on the transportation ship still gave me nightmares. I will always be indebted to James for his kindness and generosity in purchasing such first class accommodation for me, for although the journey was long and tedious, the captain and his crew were extremely attentive for the whole voyage.

On the morning of the tenth of January eighteen forty-seven, we sailed out of Sydney Harbour and for the first time since my arrest. I felt I was free from the tyranny that had falsely imprisoned me. After leaving Sydney, James and I soon became friendly with a second officer John Meredith. John, although still a young man was a former Royal Navy officer with a vast amount of sailing experience. In our first conversation with him, he remarked that we must be wary of the many hours of boredom we were about to endure. To help us overcome this problem he recommended that each day we should calculate the distance we had travelled and plot our position on the map. We both agreed that this was a good idea and for the rest of our voyage to England we charted our course home on the maps he gave us. Our first port of call was Melbourne, which was reached in three days; here a further cargo of wool was loaded. At the same time our supplies of water, and fresh food was replenished in readiness for our long voyage to Cape Town in South Africa. Soon we were departing Melbourne and sailing out into the Bass Straight bound for the Southern Ocean. We were told by John, that it was a distance of five thousand eight hundred and twenty miles to Cape Town, across some of the most treacherous seas known to man.

By the end of January, we had reached the dreaded Southern Ocean, and the ship was soon being battered by heavy waves, these waves pounded "The Rodney", from all sides and sometimes threatened to break over the poop deck. Both James and I were sick for days on end, but according to our friend John Meredith, we were fortunate because being high summer, the storms were not as violent as he had predicted. As the days passed and the stormy winds abated both of us began to feel better. It was wonderful to at last to be able to leave the cabin and stroll on deck. On occasions we were thrilled to see "The Rodney" run in amongst a school of whales and frequently different specimens of dolphin were to be found swimming under the bough of the ship.

Unfortunately as sickness had confined us to our cabins for nearly a week, we had not kept up to date with the ships progress. John, our mentor updated our maps and confirmed what I thought, that we had been making excellent progress. He told us that many of the crew were unfortunately suffering with deep cuts across the palms of their hands. Also another ailment the sailors suffered from at this time was salt-water sores that formed on their wrists, caused by the continuous use of oilskins during the stormy weather. The constant tugging on the ropes and hauling on the kicking wheels for days on end obviously gave their injuries no respite. Every sailor without exception suffered agonies from these twin related causes. Fortunately for the crew one our fellow passengers was a doctor and he managed to alleviate much of their suffering.

As we sailed east, the stormy seas gradually subsided and the voyage became more enjoyable and by travelling first class we were given the best of everything that was available. It was a totally different experience to the terrible treatment I had endured on the transportation ship and so I tried to enjoy every minute of it. On board ship boredom was a constant factor, but I had bought with me a number of books to read and with the ships own small library there was plenty of reading material available. Also there was always my friend and companion James to converse with; we would spend hours in conversation mainly talking about his past life. Although he was very reluctant at first to speak about his very humble beginnings, his story of being transported for stealing a sheep because his family were starving, to eventually becoming a leading businessman in Australia was totally fascinating. On listening to how he overcame every obstacle that confronted him by being tenacious and persevering was an inspiration to me. He is a man that I will always admire and respect for his single minded desire to improve himself against all the odds.

The voyage across the Southern Ocean was completed in thirty-five days and on our arrival in Cape Town we had a brief run ashore. While we stretched our legs after the voyage from Melbourne, the crew carried on board fresh water and supplies for our long voyage to Liverpool but I was astounded to hear that we still had a distance of six thousand five hundred miles to sail before we reached our destination. With this in mind James and I decided to take the Captains advice and explore the town and the local area. Cape Town lies about thirty miles north of the notorious Cape of Good Hope and is enclosed on the land side with a wall of abruptly rising mountains. Behind the bay that Cape Town is situated on, lays Table Mountain, which is over 3,500ft high and two miles in length. Lying to the east and west are Devils Peak, 3,300ft high and Lions Head, at over 2,000ft. Cape Town itself was originally founded by the Dutch and it still retains the look of an Old Dutch town strangely situated in the African continent. Although I had by this time travelled immense distances, being in Cape Town made me realise that previous to this I had only lived in English speaking countries. Apart from hearing foreign voices on my occasional visits to Liverpool docks, it was totally different here in Cape Town where English speakers were in the minority. The original Dutch settlers had a unique language and owned many of the thriving business's in the town. Also many Indians and Arabs thronged the streets of this very cosmopolitan town; the hustle and bustle was a sight to behold.

Fortunately before returning to the ship, I managed to buy some new books and purchase plenty of newspapers for the long journey ahead. Soon our brief stay in Cape Town was over and we returned to our ship that had now finished its preparations for the long voyage to Liverpool. Once she had sailed out of Cape Town harbour "The Rodney" sailed directly north and for the next week she made excellent progress. As we approached the Equator, the heat once again became stifling and the winds decreased in the area the seaman called the "Doldrums." Each day there was virtually no progress to be logged on our maps, as the ship drifted along for nearly a week. When we finally crossed the Equator, the ritual the crew had spent the previous week preparing for, was about to begin.

This antiquated ceremony was enacted by the crew with the part of King Neptune, played by the boson. He was accompanied by his ugly wife, scarcely recognisable as the old sail maker of the ship. Various courtiers accompanied

King Neptune appearing mysteriously from the locker room under the forecastle. They wore rope yarn wigs, wood and cardboard crowns, mitred fins and implements of office all crudely constructed and painted. Able seaman Baker was the barber and for the next twenty minutes the junior apprentice boys and ordinary sailors were hunted throughout the rigging of the ship until they were all finally captured, stripped to their underwear and brought before King Neptune, who ordered them all to be purged, shaved and dunked. Then the cook, who acted in the role of doctor, administered a draught of his own prescription this disgusting brew was forced down the throats of the young initiates. For the next part of the ritual the poor unfortunates were taken before the second officer Mr Seymour who blessed them and then they moved on to the barber who literally cropped their skulls with a totally blunt pair of scissors. Finally the mermaids seduced the initiates; these seamen were hideously attired in wigs, breasts and finny tails. They tossed the poor wretches into a temporary bath that had been constructed by suspending sails from the mast and filling them with seawater.

Having thrown their victims into the makeshift bath the mermaids leapt into the water and then proceeded to half drown them in their enthusiasm. Such was the vigour of their assault that it was finally stopped by the Captain; who then summoned each initiate in turn to his cabin where they received a certificate. It was a brief and hilarious interlude in our long voyage but thankfully our friend John Meredith had warned both of us to keep a low profile as we were sure to be prime targets for King Neptune and his cohorts.

Eventually "The Rodney" picked up the trade winds that blew north of the Equator, and during the following weeks our rate of progress increased as we headed north towards England. Gradually we could feel the temperature falling and the sea becoming rougher. Unfortunately on reaching the Bay of Biscay we encountered heavy rain and severe gales that hindered our progress. Eventually these subsided and we were then able to cross into the Celtic Sea. The remainder of our voyage was across the Irish Sea, finally sailing into the harbour of Liverpool, on the ninth of April, eighteen forty- seven.

My arrival in Liverpool brought back memories of those happy years we had spent working in the city. It also made me suddenly realise that within the week I would finally be reunited with you. The thought of being reunited once again after so many years sent my pulse racing. With this in mind James and I took the opportunity whilst in the dock area to organise our passage to Dublin for the following day. We then booked into a hotel for the night and while James relaxed in a hot warm bath, I made enquiries at the hotel for the whereabouts of a reputable jeweller. The receptionist gave me a couple of names and addresses in the vicinity and I went to the nearest one and discretely sold the gold that I had found in Australia. I was now for the first time in my life a wealthy man, because the sale of the gold combined with the money I had saved amounted to a very tidy sum.

When I returned to the hotel and read the Liverpool newspapers I realised that the rumours of famine in Ireland were in fact true. That night as James and I sat and had our last dinner together before parting, our overriding worry was had we returned in time to help our families. The newspapers were full of stories mainly about the daily arrival in the city of the thousands of starving and emancipated Irish looking for work, or trying to find a berth on a ship that was going to America or Canada. That night for the first time in many years the terrible nightmares returned and I woke up in a cold sweat thankfully realising that I had only been dreaming.

The very next day we were up very early for our short voyage across the Irish Sea, to Kingstown harbour, Dublin. The sight of again seeing my native land both excited us and also filled us with a sense of foreboding, because here at the docks we saw at first hand the plight of the desperate Irish poor trying to escape their homeland. On our arrival in Dublin we were both extremely surprised to learn that a railroad had been constructed south towards the city of Cork. This was extremely good news for both of us, because we could both travel directly by train to the town of Tipperary. Fortunately many of James's family and friends still lived in Tipperary and I could hopefully obtain transport from there to Charleville. So with great excitement the two of us boarded the train, James had obviously never seen a locomotive before and although I had worked on the construction of the Liverpool to Manchester railroad, I had never actually travelled as a passenger before. It was a thrilling experience and we were both in awe at the speed we travelled at; a journey that would normally take a whole day was completed in only three hours.

But although we marvelled at the wonders of the railroad on the train journey south, we soon saw the scale of the destitution caused by the famine. Our hearts bled for the poor unfortunates that besieged each town we passed, begging for money to feed their families. Everywhere cabins and houses lay empty and the fields were devoid of any vegetation, both James and I could not believe this was the same country that we had left. Upon reaching Tipperary Station, we said our sad farewells and promised to keep in touch, it was a terrible wrench for me leaving James Scully that day as over the past months we had become very close friends and I realised that I owed him a great deal.

Fortunately that afternoon I managed to arrange a seat on a stage coach that stopped at Charleville. Upon reaching my hometown I was appalled at the scenes that greeted me, but sad as I was, my overriding priority was to return to Springfort. With this in mind I went to Foleys stables and hired a pony and trap to carry me and my luggage back home.

CHAPTER FIVE

I was a very relieved individual when I left home to return to the railroad after Easter, knowing that Catherine and my three sons now had Owen to look after them. On my return to the construction site the first person I met was my cousin James Stephens, who was by now totally depressed and angry at the suffering the poor people were continuing to endure. His whole demeanour changed when he heard that my brother had somehow made it back to Ireland. That evening he insisted that we should have a couple of drinks to celebrate Owens's return. Strangely when we parted that night little did we both realise the notoriety that James would have gained by the time we met again. In the coming months he was to leave the construction site and embark on his crusade for an Ireland free from corruption and outside interference.

Unfortunately due to a brief spell of fine weather I was extremely busy on the railroad as we were trying to make up for the recent delays due to bad weather. Because of this it was nearly a month before I had a chance to return home. I eventually managed to get time off and rushed back to Springfort to be reunited with my family. That Saturday as I walked up the lane I was pleasantly surprised to see the immense amount of work that Owen had already completed. Catherine was obviously delighted to have me home and was full of praise for my brother.

I could sense that Owens presence had lifted her spirits as she was once again her old carefree self. Also I could tell that my three sons worshipped him as he always tended to spoil them. Little did I realise how much our lives were to change because of his tremendous help both physically, and financially.

Let me now explain; that night after dinner myself and Owen would have the most important discussion of our lives. It was obvious to both of us that I should carry on as long as possible working on the railroad because my wages were still needed to purchase food. But Owen told me he had wanted, with my approval to radically change the way we farmed at Springfort and he said he now had sufficient funds to implement these ideas.

What he proposed, would over a period of years gradually change the farm from growing cereals to concentrating all our efforts into rearing cattle. At first I was very sceptical, but when I listened to his explanations I realised that his idea was sound. He had obviously given much thought and planning to what he proposed because his final argument alarmed and frightened me. In the coming years he explained, Ireland and the rest of Europe would be flooded by cheap imports of grain from North America. In consequence this would drive down the price we received at market for our produce. This, he said, was the main reason for what he had suggested. In reply I can remember saying, "Even if you are correct in your assumption, the cost of what you are proposing is way beyond our means." It was at this moment that Owen, made me solemnly promise to keep his secret about what he was about to tell me, then he finally revealed the secret of his gold find in Australia. In great excitement he explained that after selling his share of the gold, together with the money he had saved working in the coalmines, he was now in the position to make the changes he proposed. Hearing this unbelievable news I realised that at last all my financial worries were behind me and this realisation obviously lifted a great burden from my shoulders.

We both agreed that we must now proceed with caution, because as any sudden show of wealth at this austere time would quickly be noticed. It was decided that it was better if I carried on as normal with my work on the railroad, whilst he worked at Springfort as the farm had been neglected during my long absence.

So late on the Sunday afternoon I reluctantly said my goodbyes and started my walk back to the construction site. On this occasion I had a spring in my step as I had at last great hopes for the future. Sadly my happy disposition did not last very long, because as I passed through the first town on my journey that evening, I was once again confronted by the full horror of the Famine. It was indeed pitiful to see the plight of the poor people young and old scratching for something to eat, or in many instances begging the authorities to be allowed to enter the local workhouse. The scenes that I witnessed during those times filled my heart with sorrow and I had this deep feeling of anger at the way the people of Ireland were being treated. Unfortunately many of the landed gentry were still taking advantage of the catastrophe by still evicting the tenant farmers who failed to pay the rent. These hard working farmers were now turned out on the road and were now living with their families in any shelter they could find.

As the situation in Ireland continued to deteriorate I began to understand why my cousin James Stephens had become so angry and frustrated by the total lack of any compassion by the government and their lackeys for the hundreds of thousands of people who now faced starvation and certain death. As the crisis continued during the following years, my political opinion changed, because I realised that the only realistic hope for the Irish nation was the repeal of The Union and Irish government sitting in a Parliament in Dublin.

Fortunately for me as the construction of the railroad had now progressed towards its final destination, the City of Cork, one of the stations on its route was my home town Charleville. So the rapid progress we made that summer, by working very long hours, for six days a week, was ultimately very beneficial to me as it considerably shortened the distance of my journey home each Saturday. Also by leaving very early every Monday morning, I was able to reach the site for the start of my shift. Moreover my previous railroad experience was increasingly being utilised by the management. After the departure of James Stephens, we were introduced to his successor Michael Beamish, an engineer who like me had worked on railroad construction in England. At first I found Michael a very difficult person to get on with because of his overbearing attitude towards us navvies. But he quickly realised that I was not a person he could browbeat and gradually our relationship although never very friendly was at least cordial.

As soon as we finished work on a Saturday during that summer, I quickly put my jacket on and was away down the road heading for home. Unlike many of my fellow navvies Saturdays never came quickly enough, as I was always itching to get back home to Springfort. On reaching home, I would always question Catherine and Owen about our crops and any problems they were having. Later when my wife and children had retired to bed, Owen and I would talk long into the night making our plans for the future. As we talked I became increasingly aware that he was a totally different person from the young man I had known before he was transported. He had obviously gone through a terrible experience, but thankfully he had used his time in Australia to his advantage.

In the next couple of years we were to greatly benefit from the immense amount of knowledge he had gained whilst working on Brian Murphy's cattle station. Although we had previously agreed to slowly implement the changes, Owens enthusiasm and commitment were infectious and I was also becoming increasingly impatient for change. After many late night discussions, we eventually agreed that Owen would go to market in the autumn and purchase a couple of head of cattle to start our new venture.

Thankfully the potato blight was not as prevalent that year, but sadly due to the previous two disastrous harvests there had again been a serious shortage of potato seed in the spring. This lack of seed meant that although the crop was free of disease, the amount of potatoes dug at harvest time was again insufficient to feed the starving people. Fortunately with the wages I earned from working on the railroad, we had been able to buy extra seed and this had enabled us to have a bumper crop. But we were the lucky ones, because as Christmas approached more and more of our friends and neighbours became disillusioned and were intending to emigrate in the New Year. Catherine as always did what she could for the needy during the Festive period, but sadly our help was a drop in the ocean during those troubled times.

The winter of eighteen forty seven- forty eight, was without doubt the most distressing period in nineteenth century Ireland. For most of the people it was like living through a never ending nightmare. The newspapers were full of reports of farmers and their families who had just upped and left and headed for Dublin or Cork harbours hoping for a better life by emigrating to England, America or even Australia, as it now seemed to everyone that Ireland was cursed and the horror of the famine would never cease. Apart from the tragedy of thousands dying of hunger, once again terrible diseases spread rapidly through the country adding to the death toll. Sadly the authorities seemed quite oblivious to the situation and did very little to help.

But let me now return to the momentous political events of the summer of eighteen forty- eight. During April of that year, I noticed a significant increase in military personnel in the towns and villages. As if the country did not have enough problems to contend with there were strong rumours that an armed insurrection was imminent. The group of radicals called themselves "The Young Irelander's," had after many months of acrimonious arguments split from Daniel O'Connell's Repeal Party. As previously stated one of their first acts after the split was to start publishing their own newspaper called "The Nation." This newspaper was until the government shut it down, publishing many inflammatory articles that ultimately called for an armed insurrection. The most prolific writer for "The Nation," at that time was the young firebrand John Mitchell, who was in fact arrested and subsequently tried, on the twenty sixth of May eighteen forty-eight and sentenced to fourteen years transportation.

After the trial, the government fearing that there might be a rescue attempt made by Mitchells friends, hurriedly took him in chains under heavy escort to Dublin Bay. At the dockside he was marched onto the waiting steamer "The Shearwater." Once onboard, the ship immediately set sail bound for Queenstown Harbour. On his arrival at Queenstown he was taken under heavy military escort and incarcerated on the dreaded Spike Island. After a few days he together with his only possessions, a small bundle of clothing was ferried out to awaiting ship that then sailed to Bermuda.

With the arrest of John Mitchell, other Young Irelanders were also arrested and tried but they were all subsequently acquitted. Then a series of events took place, which in retrospect given the appalling situation of the country and its people now seemed totally absurd. On the twenty fourth of July, the government had suspended the Habeas- Corpus act, which meant that anyone who they suspected could now be arrested and be imprisoned without trial. On hearing this news the leadership of the Young Irelanders fearing arrest, immediately left Dublin and headed for the remoter areas of Ireland. Most of them went to County Tipperary, where beset by many delays and the total indecision of their leader William Smith O'Brien, allied with the complete apathy of the local parish priest very little was actually achieved. The only military engagement that was briefly enacted was at the house of the Widow McCormack, near Ballingarry. From the reports I read at the time it seems that the rebels had set up a barricade on the Balligarry road. This barricade was intended to ambush a body of policemen that was marching from the town of Thurles. On seeing the barricade and the large number of rebels in attendance, the police took cover in a nearby house. This house belonged to the Widow McCormack, who it would appear was not at home, but her five children all under ten were. The police under the command of Sub-Inspector Trant burst into the house and started to break up the furniture making ready to put the house in a state of defence. O'Brian bravely went to parley with the police in the hope that they would surrender, but Trant declined his offer. As O' Brien, returned to rejoin the rebels, stones were thrown; the police then fired a volley and continued to fire on the rebels until they were eventually relieved by large numbers of reinforcements. The rebel leaders seeing all was lost ordered the remaining rebels to disperse.

William Smith O'Brien, Thomas Frances Meagher, Terence McManus, and John Martin, the ring leaders of the abortive rising were soon captured and sentenced to death. But for once the authorities were lenient and on appeal their sentences were commuted and they were all eventually transported to Australia.

I read the news of the uprising with incredulity, as I could not comprehend the reasoning behind it. It should have been plainly obvious that with the majority of their fellow country men dying from disease and starvation, that there would not be grass root support for an insurrection. The only thought on everybody's mind was how to stay alive and as I have said before, the only other thought on most peoples mind was to emigrate, because most of them realised they could not survive another winter. The real tragedy was that the uprising gave the government in London another excuse to ignore the pain and suffering of the Irish nation.

As the events of the summer of eighteen forty-eight, unfolded, I was surprised when I was ordered to report to Mr Watts the chief engineer of the railroad at his office at Limerick Junction. On my arrival at, I was immediately shown into his office where he sat together with two strangers. After introductions were made, the two strangers started to interrogate me at length regarding my cousin James Stephens. They kept asking me over and over again when did you last see him. To which I kept replying at Eastertide, around the time he had finished working on the railroad. After they had interrogated me for over an hour, they finally realised that I was telling the truth, but before leaving I asked them the reason why they were so interested in my cousin. They said did I not realise that James Stephens had been one of the leaders of the failed armed insurrection. When I said that this was a great surprise to me, they informed me that not only was he one of the ringleaders but he had foolishly lost his life manning the barricades at Ballingarry. The news of James's death was a terrible shock, as I always thought of him as not only a cousin, but also a dear friend and colleague.

In the following months the military presence in the country was scaled back as the perceived threat of an uprising had now diminished. Sadly most of the population had no idea about what had happened and within months the whole affair was soon forgotten as the people struggled to stay alive.

Fortunately at harvest time that year I was able to get two weeks unpaid leave which enabled me to help Owen gather in most of our crops. The weather was perfect that August so all of us, including my three young sons worked in the fields from dawn to dusk. As you can imagine after a days harvesting we all slept very soundly during the hours of darkness. But my sleep was rudely interrupted at dawn on the morning of fifteenth of August, when Catherine woke me saying she thought there was someone knocking on the door. Before I opened the door I enquired who it was who was calling at this time of the morning, I then heard a gentleman's voice ask, could he come in and have a brief word with me as he had a message from James Stephens. Obviously I was very startled to hear someone mention the name of my dead cousin, so I cautiously allowed the stranger to enter the house. The poor man was totally emaciated and had obviously not eaten for days. On seeing his condition I immediately sat him down at the table whilst Catherine hastily prepared breakfast for him. While his meal was being prepared he informed us that his name was Michael Doheny.,

I knew at once who he was because the military had been searching for him for weeks. Michael had been one of the prime movers of the recent insurrection and a reward of three hundred pounds was offered for his capture. By this time Owen had been woken by the commotion and I had to explain to him who our visitor was.

On hearing my explanation Owen, suddenly became very nervous and started to closely question our strange visitor. "How had you found your way to our door and how do we know we can trust you," he asked in a very agitated tone. The stranger immediately rushed out into the yard and started frantically waving in the direction of the roadside hedge. After a few moments hesitation I suddenly saw a man emerge from the undergrowth and slowly walk towards us. To my great astonishment I realised that this dirty and dishevelled person was my cousin James Stephens who was supposed to be dead. At first I thought that I was seeing a ghost, but when we shook hands and we hugged each other I realised that I was not dreaming. Both men were obviously starving hungry and soon devoured the meal that Catherine had prepared for them. After they finished eating realising that they were both exhausted from their ordeal and in no condition to talk, it was agreed that we would leave all explanations until later. Catherine quickly made them comfortable in our bed and they were soon both sound asleep. Owen then suggested that to avoid any suspicion it would be advisable to behave normally, because as he rightly said with his previous conviction and transportation the consequences for him were dire if we were caught harbouring enemies of the state. Both Catherine and I agreed with his suggestion, so after warning the children not to say a word about our guests to anyone, we all returned to the harvesting.

After dinner that evening with our sons safely tucked up in their beds, Catherine, Owen and I sat and listened spellbound to our illustrious guest's dramatic story. Firstly James explained that he had been badly wounded by a gun shot whilst defending the barricade at Ballingarry, he was wounded so badly that the doctor that attended him thought he would not survive. On hearing the doctor's prognosis many of his friends assumed the worst and rumours soon started to circulate of his sad demise. Fortunately these rumours were premature and he soon recovered from his wounds, but he thought it was prudent not to dispel the story of his tragic death.

On his recovery he had eventually met up with Michael Doheny in Knockmoledown mountain region. Michael had managed to elude the military forces hunting for him and had been hiding out in the mountains for weeks after the failed insurrection. On meeting up with Stephens it was decided that their best hope of reaching France and freedom was to link up with their influential friends that lived in Cork City. After leaving the safety of the mountains they had had many escapades and near misses, but had somehow managed to avoid capture. But every attempt they made to reach Cork City had been foiled, as all crossings of the River Lee were heavily guarded. They were now trying to get to the town of Dunmanway where they hoped to get help from known sympathisers, but the Government forces were also still heavily patrolling that area.

As we discussed their plight that night, I asked them to explain to me why with the people of Ireland dying in their thousands did they go ahead with the insurrection? To their credit they both agreed that in hindsight what they had attempted had been lunacy. To which I replied that if and when another rising is ever contemplated the whole country must be organised and made ready. My cousin nodded in agreement at my words and promised to heed my advice. Before going to bed they told us that they would much appreciate our hospitality for one more day as they were still feeling exhausted. The next evening James Stephens surprised me because he spent the whole evening entertaining my three sons with stories and magical tricks, he later confessed that it was his ambition to eventually have a large family, because of his love of children. But sadly it was never to be, for although he was to marry his long suffering wife Jane, his life long crusade to free Ireland ultimately brought years of poverty and depravation for both of them.

Before dawn the next morning Catherine prepared a large breakfast for our guests and also gave them some food for their journey. Then after many handshakes and our blessings they were gone. Strangely in the light of subsequent events, this is the first time I have ever told this story.

Months went by without any news of the fugitives, but with the terrible winter weather that followed, their visit was soon forgotten as like everyone in Ireland our priority was keeping dry, warm and fed. I carried on with my working in the appalling weather on the railroad, but many days work was lost due to snowfall and the heavy rains that followed. Fortunately Owen concentrated on making much needed improvements to the farm. We knew that we had to build a better shelter for our cattle if we were going to increase our small herd. So that winter although as I have said the weather was appalling, Owen worked tirelessly on this task. I was still managing to make my way home on most Saturday evenings and tried to help him when the weather permitted. As I have previously mentioned, I had almost forgotten the visit of my cousin and his friend but all this was to change when I received a letter in late October. On opening the letter I was very surprised to find it was from my cousin's friend, Michael Doheny. This letter I have always treasured as I feel its author was one of this country's greatest patriots and here is the text of it in full.

Dear Patrick and Catherine,

After leaving your very hospitable household, James and I wandered far to the southwest into the remotest parts of County Kerry and after many adventures, we eventually received help, {I will not divulge the persons name for obvious reasons or give any indication of their whereabouts}. James, then accompanied a lady to Cork dressed as her ladies maid and managed to escape by ship to France, where he immediately made his way to Paris. Once in Paris he soon met up with fellow revolutionaries and although he knows the dangers he talks non stop about returning to Ireland. He assures everyone that when he returns he will start an insurrection that will overthrow the government and give Ireland its freedom.

After we parted the weather became excessively wet and very cold and the biggest obstacle on my route was the crossing of the river that enters Kenmare Bay. It was impossible to cross the bridge into the town of Kenmare because of the military check points that guarded it. My guide had managed to provide me with a horse, but when we reached a ford and tried to cross the horse hesitated and then tried to back away. After much cajoling we eventually managed to force the poor animal into the river and he carried me directly across to the other side. The owner of the horse now instructed me to send him back across the river saying that he would go back of its own accord. Once again I led him into the river, but when the exhausted beast was halfway across the strong current carried him struggling down river. We both ran along the riverbank hoping the horse could somehow swim to safety. But the heavy rains had turned the river into a torrent and as I ran I could hear the ominous sound of cascading water. The last I saw of the horse was when he was carried over the precipice into the raging waterfall where I was certain he was dashed to pieces.

Obviously my guide could not now cross the river to join me, so once again I was on my own but this was now an entirely different situation because without my guide I had no idea how to proceed. All I knew was that I must keep away from the towns of Kenmare and Killarney because they were garrisoned by the military. But I had been told that the majority of the population in County Kerry would where possible be welcoming. So that morning I reluctantly waved goodbye to my guide and started to walk in a westerly direction. The drover's path I followed carried me between two large mountains that were almost obscured by the low clouds and the driving rain. As I trudged along soaked through to the skin, I somehow knew that at least my safety was assured because only fools would venture out on such a day. Late that afternoon, after many weary miles I eventually arrived in the Black Valley, this tiny village consisted of a few small derelict cabins that were mainly devoid of inhabitants. But at the end of the valley I came across a very poor dwelling that had smoke coming from it's the chimney. By now I was totally exhausted and desperately in need of food, so in desperation I knocked on the door. The lady of the house immediately invited me in and sat me down on a pile of old sacking. Within minutes my host had supplied me with a scalding hot potato and a delicious cup of buttermilk. As my eyes became accustomed to the light, I realised that the cabin was in the filthiest state. It soon became obvious that the cattle shared the cabin with the family as the floor was covered in cow dung. These droppings had not been removed for days, but the half naked children who lived there sat on it as if it was an expensive carpet. The housewife immediately proceeded with the help of two little girls to remove the filth.

As the rain had now stopped I went out for a short walk, and on my return the owner of the house, a giant of a man had returned home. He immediately made me welcome and supper was prepared which consisted of some of the finest trout I had ever eaten. After the meal a rude bed of hay was made up for me and being very tired I slept soundly that night. The next morning my host provided a large breakfast and then with his son as my guide I carried on with my journey in the direction of Gagarneybara with the main object of getting in contact with my lady friend at Dunmanaway. So at a meeting point in a wooded area at a place called Coolmartin, my guide managed to get a message to my friend in Dunmanaway. I had to use the utmost caution as the police authorities were making simultaneous searches for me in every area of the county. This was immediately apparent as it seemed that every house in the vicinity had been searched. My lady friend who in the last three weeks had made strenuous efforts to find me and had gone to the Kenmare area for that purpose, was continuously harassed and was arrested three or four times. On one of these occasions the poor girl was stripped nearly naked as they searched her for any incriminating documents. She eventually decided that trying to meet me would be a big mistake, so she sent me a note telling me to disguise myself as a peasant and to proceed directly towards Cork City. The note continued by telling me to be at Cookstown at six o'clock that very evening where I would meet three men who would accompany me by a safe route to Cork.

By the time I received this information it was nearly four o'clock and the distance to Cookstown, was nearly seventeen miles. So with the help of my guide and his friend, I dressed myself in the clothes that had been worn by the lowest Cork peasant. Then we were very fortunate to obtain a car that was driven by a young servant boy. The road we travelled on that night was knee deep in mud and our progress was so slow that we eventually arrived in Cookstown at eleven o'clock that evening but found no trace of the three messengers.

Nothing remained for it but to try and get to Cork City by our own means, so we drove on to the city with the boy eventually becoming so tired that I put him in the car to sleep, and drove the horses myself. Fortunately no one gave us a second look so we passed through the city unnoticed. It was nearly dawn when we finally arrived at the house of the gentleman who had undertaken to get me out of the country. After introductions I was shown to a bedroom where everything had been prepared for me. I stayed with those two wonderful families for over three weeks, but finally on the twenty ninth of September eighteen forty-eight after over twelve months on the run I walked on board the Bristol package boat named "The Deventer," just as she was losing her cables. The next few minutes were fraught with the utmost suspense, whilst I hid on the foredeck of the ship amongst the cattle, covered with rags and dirt. My eyes were fixed on the detectives who stood at the cabin entrance and scrutinised every passenger as they boarded. But suddenly the ships bell rang and much to my relief the detectives stepped back on shore.

I could see in the distance one of my friends who had watched my movements that morning, give a discreet wave. Then the "The Deventer" slipped her cables and we were soon in the river. The Bristol package then worryingly made a short stop at The Passage, but this appeared to be only a formality because she then chugged on through Queenstown Harbour and out into the sea. As she cleared the harbour I turned back to take one last look at the sight of my beloved Country wondering if I would every return.

At nightfall I managed to find a berth and after a surprisingly good nights sleep I made my way on deck to see the shores of England looming ahead. The steam packet then sailed up the Bristol Channel to the River Avon where we were delayed waiting for the tide to turn. Night had fallen when we eventually reached Bristol and by waiting for the right moment, I managed to slip away from the boat with ease. Now my problem was finding accommodation. Obviously this was not easy as I looked and felt like a tramp. Eventually I found an inn and after ordering a glass of ale and paying for it with a gold sovereign a bed was soon made available for me.

As the next day was Sunday I had no trouble boarding a train to London and a few hours later I arrived at Paddington Station. Once in London my costume attracted an enormous amount of attention. My Irish peasant apparel especially attracted the attention of the gangs of youths who roamed the city. I was particularly harassed when I got to Oxford Street, the harassment became so bad that I grabbed one of them and handed him over to a policeman. The other hooligans then disappeared and I made my way to Museum Street and then to the house of a Mr. Parker, an old acquaintance of mine. Mr Parker initially did not recognise me, but when he realised who I was went into a rage and told me I should immediately leave his house and never return. After so many trials and tribulations this rejection was hard to bare and in utter despair I walked away completely at a loss as what to do next. I must have walked the streets of London for hours racking my brains trying to find a solution to my problem.

Suddenly it came to me, in previous years I had lodged with a woman who lived in Marylebone. Luckily my wanderings had brought me near to her house and so within minutes I was knocking on her door. On seeing me she nearly fainted and quickly hurried me out into the street as she said her house was being watched continuously by detectives. Luckily she knew of an Irish woman who lived nearby who might help me, realising that I had no alternative I agreed to go there. On our arrival the poor woman on seeing my condition received me with tears. It would appear that her son and daughter-in-law had spent the day with her and were about to return home, to their house in the suburbs on the Surrey side of the city. Their suggestion was that I should return with them to their home, to this I readily agreed. On hearing my reply the young man immediately ordered a coach and we were soon on our way. When we arrived at their house I was quickly ushered in via the back door, because I looked completely out of place still dressed in my Irish peasant's clothes. Once inside my hosts immediately prepared a wonderful hot bath and I had my first shave in weeks. My old clothes were then replaced with a clean linen shirt and a woollen suit. That evening after the best dinner I had eaten for many months I felt that at last freedom was at hand.

On waking the next day we had a long discussion regarding how I should make my escape to France. It was finally agreed that I should dress as a cleric and wear a wig to further alter my appearance and then I would catch the boat train that evening. So after a substantial meal I donned my disguise and said my goodbyes to the young lady that had made me so welcome. Her husband insisted on coming with me, when I made my way back to the city and at eight-thirty that evening I boarded the express train from London Bridge Station bound for Dover harbour. My good fortune continued, because I was able to walk onto the mail packet unmolested and by two o'clock the next morning I set foot in France, at last free from all anxiety and worry.

I had landed in Boulogne and after a rest and large breakfast I caught the ten o'clock train to Paris. On my arrival I boarded an omnibus to the Hotel Louvre in the Rue St. Thomas where I knew some of my friends were staying. That evening I dined with these friends and some of my fellow passengers who had travelled overnight from London. In total our party consisted of twelve and after a wonderful meal we all relaxed together in the lounge. Eventually the conversation turned to Ireland and the recent events that had taken place, free at last to speak my mind and obviously slightly intoxicated the comments I made were obviously very controversial. It was soon apparent that one old gentleman had taken deep offence at what I had said, because he rose from his chair and angrily shouted that my views sounded like comments which would be uttered by that rebel Doheny. With this both my friend and I went into fits of laughter, much to the annoyance of the old gentleman who could not understand the reason for our mirth. Eventually the conversation again returned to the subject of Ireland. It was then I expressed my opinion that English, paupers in Ireland, should be transported back to Liverpool, the same way the Irish paupers in Liverpool and other cities were being returned to Dublin. To this he replied that there would be no peace in Ireland until the Mitchell's and Doheny's of this world were hanged by the neck. He then said that in his opinion Doheny would soon be apprehended and that sentence carried out. After these last remarks and his prophecy that I would soon be hanged both my friend and I laughed till tears were running down our faces. Then announcing that I was the terrible Michael Doheny I removed my wig to the utter astonishment of those assembled.

As I am about to depart for America I thought you would like to hear the story of my escape that would not have been possible without your help and the help of many others, once again Many Thanks for your hospitality.'

Your obedient servant. Michael Doheny.

Postscript. Enclosed is a short message from James. 'He is extremely busy at the moment so please excuse the brevity of his letter.'

Note from James Stephens.
My Dear Patrick,

I would like to thank you and your wife for the help you gave me in my hour of need. After many trials and tribulations I have arrived in Paris. At present I am employed as an English teacher but hope soon to return to Ireland and continue my work.

Yours as ever, God bless you and your family. James Stephens.

CHAPTER SIX

Ireland's great hunger continued all through the terrible winter of eighteen forty-nine with no sign of any improvement. We had now endured four of the worst years in Ireland's troubled history. The devastation was now complete, not a town or village had escaped disease and starvation, with hundreds and hundreds of houses and cabins lying empty as their inhabitants had either perished or fled the country. From this period I have kept in my journal a cutting from the Cork Gazette dated twenty fifth of November, eighteen forty-nine, which paints a horrific and very poignant picture of the country during those terrible years. The gentleman who wrote the letter to the newspaper was from the nearby town of Macroom and it reads as follows:

Dear Sirs,

We are only at the termination of a frightful famine or that to all appearances at the commencement of a worse one. Good God are we going to witness the dreadful scenes that have only just passed over us, or are we going to behold our poor fellow creatures moving like mere shadows through the streets, falling on the high roads from hunger and starvation and dropping down at our very doorsteps. Are our exemplary clergymen and liberal gentlemen, to place their lives in jeopardy as they have done before in visiting the sick cabins of the poor man, extending with their own hands relief and endeavouring to afford consolation before the soul had taken its departure from the entirely starved and emaciated person? I now also want to draw attention to the disgraceful practice that was carried out during the period of awful distress, when nothing should dissuade people from relieving the destitute, the practice of poselytism, a new accompaniment of the famine the duties that devolved from the priests were indeed as laborious in as much as they had to combat against famine, disease and death on the one hand and on the other hand against those proztelizators, justly termed soul jobbers in every locality where this dreadful system worked the proselytize school consisted of a dozen or so of the poorest children of that place, a bible master, or mistress who dispensed knowledge to the hungry stomachs.

The pottage pot was superintended and conducted by female proselytizer and its contents distributed every day after five or six hours of lecturing. Charitable donations were lavished in purchasing bibles, paying the master and mistress so much per week and as a matter of course adding a little to their own private funds. It is not melancholy to know that all this was in operation when famine and disease desolated the land. Now another year of famine is upon us and I ask myself what will be done about those two scourges of the poor the proselytizer and the corn merchant. I can tell you they will wait for another opportunity and this will surely be at hand, in the mean time public opinion should be brought to bear on them; their names should be published in the national press, as individuals such as these are so base and despicable to an extent unmatched in any country known to man.

So another winter arrived this was to be undoubtedly the worst in my lifetime, this time there was to be very little Government help so the people of Ireland starved and those that could emigrate left the country for good. Thousands upon thousands had already gone and now it was the turn of the small gentleman farmer and shopkeepers from the town to depart for foreign shores. The terrible scourge of immigration, especially amongst the young leaving is still with us today, many a family member and also friends have I seen leave never to return. Will our heartache never end?

You're obedient servant John Grady.

The questions this letter raised should have been addressed by the authorities, but it was totally ignored and no action was ever taken. In the years to come the people of Ireland would never forgive or forget the terrible injustices of those times. This would inevitably lead to the trouble and strife that occurred in the years following the end of the famine.

But to continue with my story, the railroad construction had slowly moved towards Mallow. Strangely when the rail line reached Charleville the land owner Colonel Harrison would not allow the line to pass through his estate. The problem was ultimately solved when the line bypassed his estate on its southern perimeter. This is why the station was built nearly two miles from the town. The section from Charlevile to Mallow was fortunately relatively straight forward and on St. Patrick's Day, eighteen forty-nine Mallow station saw its first train. This train had covered the one hundred and twenty mile journey from Dublin, in the incredible time of five hours. But on reaching Mallow more problems arose when the engineers realised that a huge ten arch viaduct must be built before the line could continue to Cork City, its ultimate destination. This viaduct was needed to cross the River Blackwater and its construction was to delay our progress for many months. But the owners of the railroad were determined that we must complete the line before the end of the year. Unfortunately this meant that I worked seven days every week that summer apart from one weekend in late August.

The pressure that we were under was reminiscent of my time on the Liverpool to Manchester railroad. But trains were now running from Mallow to Charleville, so I got home very quickly on the one weekend that I was allowed off. As I have said the work was extremely strenuous during that period, but we eventually reached the temporary terminus at Blackpool. This station is located one mile north of Cork City and the inaugural train journey left Blackpool station for Dublin, at seven forty five on Monday the twenty ninth of October eighteen forty-nine. The time to Dublin for that train was seven hours which in at that time was amazing, as the same journey on a stage coach could take at least eighteen hours. But over six years were to elapse before the 1,355-yard tunnel needed to extend the railway into Glenmore Station, Cork City was completed.

During the years of eighteen forty-nine, to eighteen fifty-two, the farm gradually became more profitable, mainly due to all the hard work and planning that we had received from Owen. It was during this period that he started to fully implement his theories that we had discussed when he had returned home. With his financial backing we were able to slowly change our farming methods from mainly arable into grazing land. Curiously in later years the railroad helped to increase our profitability as the cattle we reared could be transported by rail for export directly to England, but at that time we had no way of knowing this. Owens foresight and business brain would ultimately bring us a level of prosperity that we had always hoped and prayed for.

I continued to work for the railway construction company until I finally resigned in the summer of eighteen fifty-two. During those last years I had worked on the excavation of the tunnel from the Blackpool terminus to Glenmore station. Here once again the knowledge I had gained during my time spent in England was invaluable and I was much in demand until the tunnelling itself was complete. But although we were still working long hours, I now had the convenience of the train for my journey to and from Charlevile. This enabled me to now return home every weekend, but leaving my wife and family early each Monday morning became ever harder to endure. After those enjoyable weekends at home working in the fresh air of the country, the thought of returning to the noise and dust of the tunnelling became a nightmare for me. Although I longed to leave, I somehow managed to keep working until the end of May, eighteen fifty two. On my last day I must confess that I was very drunk when I finally said my farewells to all my work colleagues. By this time I was now forty six years old and was determined never to work for an employer again. I realised that I was very fortunate to have been employed during that period when many of my neighbours and friends had died or left the country. But I felt it was now time for me to concentrate on improving and if possible expanding our farm.

Ever since his return from Australia my brother Owen had been a tower of strength for us and now that I was finally back home my head was full of plans for our future. But in life nothing ever works out the way that you hope and plan for and my ambition to expand our farm with Owens help would never to be realised. My homecoming was at first all I could wish for, Catherine and my three sons welcomed the fact that I was now permanently around. Also for the first time in years we had a wonderful harvest. But all this was over shadowed by my intuition that all was not well with Owen. Weeks went by before I plucked up courage and asked him if he had any problems as he seemed very restless and distant. In reply Owen informed me that he intended to emigrate to America. When I asked him why he had made this decision, he explained that there were two reasons why he had come back from Australia; the first was to marry his fiancée Maureen Kelly. The news of her death, had, he said broken his heart because she had been the only girl he had ever loved. The other reason he had returned was to see me again and now that he had helped us survive the Famine and hopefully prosper he felt it was time for a new challenge.

He told me that he had heard of a gold rush in California and thought that he would go there prospecting. I was obviously shocked at this decision, but I understood his reasoning and had to reluctantly respect his wishes. No words can express the deep feeling of emptiness that I felt when I heard his explanation. But Catherine and I thanked him from the bottom of our hearts for all his hard work and financial assistance, because without his support we would never have been able to hold on to the tenancy during the last turbulent years.

He decided that he would leave for America after the harvest was gathered, in the autumn of eighteen fifty three. As I have said fortunately that year the harvest was the best in living memory and the cattle we reared and sold at the October Market fetched record prices. Catherine was pleased because it was the first time for ages that we allowed ourselves the luxury of buying some new clothes and some small presents for our sons. But the only dark cloud that had hung over us that summer was Owens, determination to leave Ireland once more. Although he had definitely decided to leave I knew from his demeanour that this decision was made with a heavy heart, as he reluctantly started to make enquiries about a passage to America before the coming winter.

By a strange coincidence in late September he received a letter from Australia. We were working out in the fields when the postman arrived that morning, Catherine on seeing that the letter was addressed to Owen and from Australia, realised that it was important so she immediately rushed out of the house looking for us. My first reaction was one of blind panic when I saw her running across the fields calling our names. Thankfully on this occasion my instincts were wrong, as the letter had good news for Owen. With great excitement he read out its contents, it was he said from his old friend Robert Hughes and it told of large finds of gold that had recently been found in the New South Wales territory. In his letter Robert suggested that Owen should rejoin him in Australia and the two of them could then go prospecting for gold together. As it transpired this was the opportunity Owen had been dreaming of.

Within days he had written back to his friend thanking him for his kind offer and telling him that he would be returning to Australia as soon as was possible. With his decision now made Owen quickly made his arrangements for the arduous journey. From his previous experiences he explained nothing could be left to chance and the ship that he would sail on would be the best available. With this in mind he travelled by train to Dublin and booked his passage and on the return journey he stopped off in Tipperary to visit his old friend James Scully. James was shocked to hear that he was returning to Australia and urged him to remain in Ireland but to no avail.

When he returned to Springfort he had bought presents for all of us in Dublin. Our three sons received gifts that were beyond their wildest dreams and Catherine was given a cloak made of the finest material. I received Charles Dickens latest novel Barnaby Rudge which I think is one of Dickens finest books. Although his leaving was a devastating blow to me, in later years I came to realise how upset my wife had been at his departure. His unstinting work and affable nature during my long absences she would often recall had pulled her through the most difficult period of her life.

The preparations for his departure reminded me of the emigrants leaving Ireland before the mass exodus of the famine. A special mass was said on his behalf in Charleville, which was attended by all of our relatives and close friends. At this service the Parish Priest blessed Owen and wished him God speed and then we all prayed for his safe passage. During the following week two priests came to the house to say the Stations. Having the Stations said in your home was an age old tradition and was seen as a great privilege. Fortunately we had cleared all the furniture from the house and bought plenty of refreshments because the house was full to bursting point for this wonderful occasion. After the Stations were said everyone clambered to say their confessions and then the two priests said mass. As I recall, it was a lovely sunny autumn day and after the service the party started. We were lucky to have Michael O'Shea, the local fife player and his brother John playing the fiddle. Those two fine musicians soon had the crowd up dancing. During the evening after having a few drinks, Catherine begged me and Owen to dance the Kerry reel that our mother had taught us in year's gone bye. I must tell you that I was soon out of breath and had to stop, but Owen, danced like a man possessed and when he finished the crowd roared their approval.

That night brought back memories of the many wonderful evenings of music and laughter that had taken place at Springfort before the recent catastrophe had engulfed us all. But this was an occasion where we forgot about those problems and danced and sang until the early hours of the morning.

Gradually our friends and family started to drift away and on leaving they all said their final farewells to Owen. When the last of our guests had departed Owen, broke down and confessed that he was again beginning to lose his resolve and was having second thoughts about the long and treacherous voyage he was about to endure. But instead of trying to convince him that it was in his best interests to stay in Ireland, I insisted he went to bed, whilst we wearily cleared some of the mess. Catherine and I then tried to get some sleep as we knew that the next day would be extremely tiring and emotional. On waking that morning Owen had regained his resolve and seemed more determined than ever to return to Australia and very reluctantly I helped him pack his bags.

Before leaving, Catherine cooked a special breakfast for us all, fresh bread was baked and this was accompanied by large slices of ham, with traditional butter milk and on this occasion a hot cup of tea. After breakfast we all boarded the wagon I had hired, and drove to Charleville Station, where we caught the

139

train to Cork City. Although both Owen and I were clearly upset, for Catherine and our three sons today's rail journey was the highlight of their year. You had to be with us that morning to witness the great excitement on their faces when the train left the station. The locomotive quickly picked up speed and we were soon flying along through the countryside. For my family the speed that we were now travelling at was far beyond their comprehension as they had never travelled so fast in their lives, I could tell that Catherine was so excited on the journey that morning that she had forgotten the reason why we were going to Cork. As we travelled along the railroad I gave a running commentary about the places that we passed and also explained about the difficulties we had encountered when the line was being constructed. We soon reached Mallow and after a short stop we crossed the huge viaduct that I had helped to build across the River Blackwater.

Then we were on the final section of the line, passing by Mourne Abbey we soon reached the outskirts of Cork City. The final part of our journey was through the long tunnel that had caused us who had toiled on it so much trouble. Although Owens thoughts were obviously elsewhere, he was highly impressed by this feat of engineering that we had accomplished. As someone who had first hand knowledge of tunnelling, he expressed a great deal of interest in my explanations about the problems we had encountered on its construction.

My wife and family were very excited as this was their first visit to Cork City. The noise and the hustle and bustle of the crowds frightened them at first, but they soon overcame this as Owen again showered them with presents. He then left us as he had unfinished business to attend to. Later that evening we found lodgings for the night, Catherine and my three boys were all very tired after their exciting day. But before going to sleep two of my sons James and William vowed that they would become train drivers when they grew up.

With my family safely tucked up in bed, I stayed up late into the night drinking and chatting with Owen for both of us this would prove to be our last ever evening together. That night we discussed all of our shared experiences especially whilst in England. Owen in particular reminisced about the night that I came to his rescue when he was attacked by the Ganger whilst we were working on the canal in Shropshire. He said, he still remembers the look of fear on the bullies face when I sent him crashing to the floor. This incident and many others he recalled, but unlike Owen I had forgotten most of them. Before finally going to bed I once again expressed my heartfelt thanks for all his help.

When he replied he had tears of emotion running down his face, he was he said, leaving the family that he loved and cared for. After saying these words he produced a bag full of gold sovereigns and insisted that I take them to safeguard our future. I knew from his expression that I must take this gift, because to refuse would have been seen as a huge insult.

In the morning we all made our way to Queenstown harbour and on our arrival I marvelled at the way Owens demeanour completely changed. Gone was the country boy image he liked to portray in Charleville and now I saw the real Owen, very business like and professional. He immediately hired a skiff to take us all out to "The Endurance" the vessel that was about to take him to Australia. Climbing onboard Owen urged us all to join him, at first I declined as I have always disliked ships. But when I realised that my wife and sons were itching to go me reluctantly agreed... With much laughter and great difficulty the five of us negotiated our way onto the ships deck. Once onboard "The Endurance" we were fortunate because one of the crew gave us a tour of the vessel.

In the dim and distant past I had travelled on various ships to and from England, but this vessel that was incidentally on its maiden voyage was entirely different. Our guide proudly boasted that "The Endurance" given favourable conditions could break the record for the fastest voyage to Australia. As we toured the ship you can imagine the look of wonderment on the faces of my family. Because it was a new vessel everything was obviously gleaming and the crew in their smart uniforms looked very professional. We were taken to see Owens cabin which he assured us was although to our eyes quiet cramped, was a paradise compared to the hell hole he had to endure on the convict ship. While we sat chatting in his cabin a member of the crew kindly brought us hot drinks and biscuits for the boys. But the moment had now arrived that I had been dreading. All my life I have hated having to saying goodbyes and this occasion was obviously even worse as I was saying it to my brother that I loved. I knew from the look on Owens face that he was having the same emotions, because tears were running down his face as he kissed Catherine and shook my hand. For our sons it was a great adventure when they climbed back down the rigging and returned to the harbour in the waiting skiff. Their laughter and gaiety were somehow infectious and cheered both of us on that sad day.

The next morning on our return journey to Charleville it did not seem appropriate to mourn the sad departure of my brother. because Catherine and the boy's were still very excited by the events of the last couple of days and in the circumstances it would have been wrong for me to spoil the biggest adventure of their young lives. Also my wife having never travelled further than the town of Mallow, the journey by train to Cork City and the sights and sounds she witnessed were never forgotten and she would reminisce about them until the day she died. But although I outwardly kept up a happy appearance, inwardly my mind was in turmoil. For months after Owens departure I was in a state of shock, but gradually I came to realise that he was only one of millions who had left our troubled country hoping to find a better life. In looking back who could blame them because for most their only future was one of desperate hunger followed by eviction and life on the road or death by disease in one of the notorious work houses.

For us in Springfort the next couple of years were relatively prosperous, because I was fortunate to have the benefit of the money Owen had left us. This had enabled me to end tillage and totally concentrate on arable farming. His funds had allowed me to increase my small herd of cattle and also build winter quarters for them. These changes to the farm were ultimately to pay dividends in the years to come. But sadly for many, conditions were still appalling and the number of evictions showed no sign of abating. It was calculated that over one hundred thousand tenants were evicted between the year's eighteen forty- eight and forty- nine. It was plain to everyone that something drastic was required as the Irish politicians sitting comfortably in Westminster were unable, or unwilling to do anything to help their long suffering countrymen. But what followed would ultimately change politics in Ireland forever and is still indirectly influencing our politicians to this day.

The new organisation that ultimately changed everything was The Irish Tenants League, under the leadership of Mr. Gavin Owen. This Irish Tenants League was to be the forerunner of numerous other similar organisations that were to fight for tenants rights for the next forty years. Fortunately for us in the Charleville area as I have previously said the local landowner William Wrixon-Beecher was a compassionate man and where possible tried to keep down the burden of rent rises for his tenants. Other local landowners did not so understand and in the nearby town land of Killmallock, the land agent was notorious for evicting his tenants for the slightest reason. As week by week the numbers of evictions increased, the mood of the people gradually changed from one of total despair into a feeling of anger and defiance. This defiance was to bring a return to the secret societies that had flourished before the Famine and serious disturbances were once again a feature of everyday life in Ireland. These secret organisations wrought terrible retributions on anybody who rented land where tenants had been evicted and also against the landlord who threw people onto the roads.

To illustrate what was happening, I have retained another cutting from a newspaper of that time,

This is from the Cork Gazette dated the tenth of October eighteen fifty- three:

Murder of Major Mahon.

'We have to record another bloody deed as a result of the agragarian war, which is still being waged in all its horrors between Irishmen, for the soil of Ireland. The murder of Major Mahon at Killmacthorn did for the establishment of the tenant's rights, the murderous clearance by the landlords and the bloody clearances of landlords wrought by peasants alike proclaimed the necessity of new laws to put an end to such criminal mutual exterminations. Today we hear of the havoc caused by landlords of West Carberry, the next day we are called upon to report the havoc caused by the peasants of Roscommon. God knows where this is all going to end. Major Mahon, whose murder is the latest stain upon Ireland, was returning home about six thirty last Monday evening from a meeting of the Board of Governors of the Roscommon Union, when he was shot dead by an assassin about four miles from his home at Stokestown, according to our information two peasants were involved in the murder, both fired their guns, one missed completely but the other gunman's shot proved fatal as he hit the Major in the chest.*

Major Mahon was formally in the Ninth Dragoons, but he succeeded to the inheritance of the late Lord Harland's estate about two years ago. It is said that local people despised him for two reasons, the first was his refusal to continue with the corn acre system and the second was his clearance of what he deemed was the surplus population on his estate. He subsequently chartered two vessels and shipped his evicted tenants off to America. One of the ships tragically sank on route with the loss of all hands. Obviously the news that many of their family and friends had died in such harrowing circumstances was a factor in the murder of Major Mahon. These and other stories about the terrible occurrences we read in horror.'

As the number of outrages continued to rise the authorities reverted to their age old solution, which was to flood the country with soldiers and militia. Ireland once again became almost a police state, with the governments totally reliant on

informers for their information. Sadly everyone became very wary as you could not be sure who was listening to your conversation. I was particularly worried because of what had happened in the past to my brother Owen and told my three sons to keep their own council and stay out of trouble.

During this time, after many years of inaction the Independent Irish members of Parliament in Westminster at last formed an organisation to fight for tenants rights. This grouping was called The Catholic Defence League, and its timing could not have been better. Because when the government in London lost its overall majority in eighteen fifty-three, an election was subsequently called. After a hard fought contest the eventual winners were the Conservatives. But much to their dismay they did not win enough seats to command an overall majority in Parliament. This situation immediately raised expectations in Ireland, as the newspapers speculated that the Irish Independent members would now hold the balance of power. With skilful use of this position it should it was thought, enable them to demand concessions from the new Conservative government.

Unfortunately these expectations were soon dashed when two members of the Irish Party, William Keogh and John Sadlier were offered posts in the new government. Much to the consternation of their colleagues and everyone who had voted for them the two men readily accepted. This in effect led to the break up of the Catholic Defence League and its reverberations were to be felt in Ireland for the next ten years. In a few short months it quickly became apparent that both William Keogh and John Sadlier were two very unsavoury characters. Sadlier was the instigator of a gigantic financial swindle which was eventually uncovered in eighteen fifty-six. This fraud involved securities that he had personally forged over a number of years. Sadly this was to lead to the collapse of the Tipperary Joint Stockholders Bank and the ruination of thousands of small Irish farmer, who had accounts with that Bank. Subsequently Sadlier, committed suicide in London, before he could be brought to trial. Keogh later became a judge but in the preceding years by a strange coincidence he also committed suicide.

But at home as I have previously stated the change in our farming methods had gradually increased our income and the other major factor in the improvement to our living standard was the increased help I was receiving from my sons. My eldest son Michael was now sixteen years old and in my long absences had learned a great deal from his uncle Owen. We were also very fortunate because his two brothers James, now fourteen and William, who was twelve, had also benefited

144

from their uncles tuition. The four of us together with my wife Catherine were now a formidable team and at harvest time we were very much in demand. But although our life was thankfully improving, for the majority of the Irish people the only option left was still emigration. This emigration was to increase when stories of enormous gold finds in Australia began started to circulate.

In the summer of eighteen fifty-three, a National School was finally opened in Charleville, which William, much to his resentment was obliged to attend for his first formal schooling. At first he very much hated losing his freedom and having to attend school five days a week. Our three sons had spasmodically attended the hedge school and with Catherine's help could read and write. But obviously William, being only twelve at the time the new school opened was the only one of our sons who had to attend until the leaving age of fourteen. Fortunately William was a bright lad and had no trouble with his school work but he had to endure a great deal of ribbing from his brothers. During the two years he attended school he was always very busy especially in term times when he was always up very early to do his chores before leaving for school. The strange thing was that in the winter months, both his brothers became interested in what he was being taught. In later years both of them admitted that they had learned a great deal from William and had secretly wished they could have had a formal education. Michael in particular owed much of his future success in life to the knowledge he gained in those years from his younger brother.

According to my farm journal, which I was still managing to keep up to date, we had an exceptionally good year in eighteen fifty- four, cattle prices were very competitive and so the livestock we sold at the Buttervant Market that October fortunately fetched a good price. All of Owens perseverance and hard work was at last coming to fruition, but sadly he was not around to enjoy the fruits of his labour.

As was traditional my wife Catherine, on returning from the Buttevant Market each year immediately began to make her plans for the Christmas Festival. Both my sons and I knew that this was the time to keep out of her way as the house would be cleaned then painted and woe betide anyone who brought in dirty boots or caused a mess. Christmas was always the highlight of my wife's year and in years of plenty she delighted in entertaining and feeding the needy in our Townland. During our celebrations that Christmas I was overjoyed to receive the following letter from Owen, not knowing that it would be our final correspondence from him.

145

Dear Patrick and Catherine,

I arrived in Melbourne, on fourteenth April eighteen fifty-four, after a long and terrible voyage. For most of the journey the weather had been atrocious. Endless days of gale force winds and heavy seas, so it was obviously a joy to finally disembark in the city of Melbourne. On landing it took me a few days to adjust to walking on land again after months of being at sea. But it was very heartening for me that Robert Hughes was waiting at the quayside; he explained that he had been waiting patiently for two weeks for my ship to arrive.

Melbourne at this time is heaving with gold seekers from every part of the globe and so after living in Ireland for the past five years the hustle and bustle of a large town took a while to get used to. Our priorities were to obtain all the supplies and equipment we needed, but in doing so I was amazed at the cost of everything. It quickly became apparent why it is so extremely expensive, this is because the shopkeepers know that the gold seekers will pay any price as they are desperate to move on to the gold fields. Luckily for us it was autumn when I arrived, as you well know that the seasons here are opposite to yours in Ireland. Because of the extreme temperatures in the summer months travelling is difficult, but the autumn weather this year is perfect.

As we rode out of Melbourne, Robert told me that gold had been found inland at a place called Ballarat. But unfortunately it seemed that the whole world had heard the same story because the road was teeming with thousands of hopeful souls. Every person we talked to told us the same story about the vast wealth they understood would be easily accessible, all that was needed they said was to dig a large hole and gold nuggets would be found in huge quantities.

Robert and I pushed on towards Ballarat, trying to avoid the main roads where possible. Our plan was to keep our own council but also to keep our ears open for any news on the latest gold finds by doing this we were fortunate to hear wild stories about large nuggets of gold that had been found in an area nicknamed by the locals Eureka Lead. On hearing theses rumours, when we arrived at the gold fields we asked for directions to the Eureka Lead. That evening after we had pitched our tent and fed the horses, we headed to the local hotel for a drink and also to hear the latest gossip. Luckily for us one of the drinkers there informed us that he was one of a group of diggers called The Kilkenny Boys, who were mining in the vicinity. As we chatted he said that they were short handed and suggested that we could join them in their quest.

The next morning Robert and I went in search of The Kilkenny Boys stake and when we eventually found them I was greatly surprised to meet a very old friend of ours James O'Shea. You may remember James, as we had both worked with him years ago on the Liverpool to Manchester railroad. Obviously we had a long chat about old times and what he had had been doing in the intervening years. It would appear that he had worked on railroads the world over and was working on a new construction in Australia, when the Gold Rush began. The thought of finally making his fortune had made him leave his job and like thousands of others he had headed to the goldfields. With his previous mining experience he had gathered about him a group of men from his home town of Kilkenny. He then asked me what I had been doing since we last met; I replied that this story could wait until another time because it would take me hours to tell the tale. The only thing I told him on that occasion was how you had worked on the Dublin-Cork, railroad but were now happily back with your family farming near Charleville.

When the conversation returned to the job at hand, James told us that they had just started to sink a new shaft that he calculated would have to go down to a depth of at least one hundred and twenty feet. This was because the gold in that area runs in veins or gutter. These veins are channels, or ancient water courses which are now buried at various depths between eighty and a hundred and twenty feet in the clay. These ancient watercourses are very unpredictable and no one could calculate in which direction they travelled. Sinking a shaft was he confessed a calculated gamble, but he said that we were welcome to join his gang and take our chances. After chatting to James O'Shea, both Robert and I agreed we would take up his offer for a couple of months, hoping against hope that we would all be successful in our endeavours.

On returning to our camp site we packed up our equipment and removed it to a site near the Kilkenny Boys stake. The very next day we got started, but how I suffered for those first few days, because after spending the past months at sea I was obviously not used to the manual work, but that discomfort quickly passed and I soon found myself enjoying the banter and the friendship of my new colleagues. For a few short weeks I revelled in the work, as we made rapid progress digging the deep shaft. Unfortunately those happy days abruptly ended and I quickly learned that the miners had many grievances; which were usually caused by the Australian Colonial Government Officers and the corruption of their local agents. Sadly it would appear that I could not get away even in Australia, from the grasping and evil money grabbers that caused so many of the problems that beset Ireland.

147

The Colonial Government had its base about a mile outside of the town of Ballarat. This base consisted of a timber courthouse and rows of military tents that were used as offices. The officer in charge when we arrived was Commissioner Read, and it soon became apparent why he was hated by every miner in the goldfields. Mr. Read who I was told was a small man in stature, but had big ideas and had recently replaced a Mr. John Clowe at the beginning of April. Mr Clowe had his faults I was told, but he was a man that at least listened to the men's grievances. The new appointment I was informed had upset the miners because Mr Read did not have any previous experience and his lack of knowledge had quickly alienated every gold seeker in the Ballarat area. This distrust was to quickly turn to anger because of his high handed attitude and the uncompromising way that he carried out his orders from his superiors.

The government in London, on hearing of the gold rush had apparently appointed a new governor for The State of Victoria; his name was Sir Charles Hoffman. Hoffman's orders from London were to strictly control the Goldfields and ensure every miner paid a license fee. To carry out their wishes Hoffman, on landing in Australia, immediately sent his friend Mr Read as Commissioner with orders to collect every penny that was due to the government on pain of dismissal. On his arrival at Ballarat, Read was not made aware that his two immediate official associates John Deans, the police magistrate and Mr Milne, the senior sergeant of the police were the two most notoriously corrupt men at that time in Ballarat

All the problems that the gold seekers faced were discussed each evening after our days work had finished. Every miner at Ballarat it seemed knew that Mr Deans was hand in glove with a man called Bentley, an ex-convict who kept the local hostelry called 'The Eureka Hotel.' This friendship was ultimately the main reason for the trouble that would occur in the near future. But although I knew that the situation was deteriorating and the tension was rising in the camp, I was determined to ignore everything and concentrate on finding the gold that I had come so far to find. During the next couple of months Robert kept begging me to leave Ballarat, as he thought that the dangerous situation could quickly escalate and the miners would be dragged into a confrontation with the government officials. This knowledge he explained came from his long experience in the colony, there were no benefits in us staying and waiting for the inevitable armed confrontation. How I wished I had listened to his advice, as his warnings were to quickly bare fruition.

With the tension rising, large meetings were called to protest about the local injustices and the widespread dissatisfaction that was felt by the gold seekers. It soon became obvious that only a tiny spark was needed to set off a confrontation with the authorities. The tone of these meetings became increasingly belligerent; as many of the gold seekers had pawned everything they owned to journey to the goldfields and were in no position to pay the license fee. As I write this letter, I realise Roberts is right and we have decided to move on in October as we now have a great dislike of Ballarat and all its corruption. I must confess that each night I lay awake for hours wondering why I ever left Springfort and all my family and friends. Sadly I realise what a terrible mistake I have made and as soon as I am able, you can be assured I will be returning home.
In closing, I hope that Catherine and the boys are all keeping well. Robert sends his best wishes and promises to send me back to Ireland a rich man.
Your loving brother, Owen.

Owens letter cheered us up immensely that Christmas, but it was in February, as I recall when the post arrived and much to our consternation this time the letter from Australia, was not from Owen, but his friend Robert Hughes. It was with great trepidation that I opened the letter. On seeing the look of anxiety on my face my family all stopped what they were doing and gathered around to listen as I read out its contents.

Dear Patrick,

I am most distressed in writing to you at this time knowing how close you were to your brother. It is with great sadness that I have to inform you of his most tragic death on the third of December eighteen fifty-four, when he was mortally wounded by Colonial troops at the local town of Ballarat, after a short and bloody battle. As you know from Owens letter trouble had been brewing for months and I had wanted us to leave this area. For some unknown reason Owen was convinced that we would strike it lucky here. In Owens letter to you he explained that the diggers were very angry because of the license tax being imposed on them by the Governments agents. There was also an unbelievable amount of corruption occurring, which was also inflaming the situation and before long the frustration of the diggers reached boiling point and when one of their number was murdered and the culprits were freed without a trial, the simmering tinderbox that was the Ballarat goldfields exploded.

149

The Government officials then panicked and instead of negotiating with the miner's leaders they immediately sent for troop reinforcements. As soon as they heard this dramatic news the diggers began to arm themselves. From that time on the situation began to get out of hand, as it quickly became apparent that amongst our number were men that had previous military experience in conflicts the world over. These fighting men were elected as our leaders and it was decided after a long discussion that we would fight if necessary. Tragically, without anyone's knowledge some the hotheads amongst us on seeing the column of troop reinforcements took it upon themselves to immediately attack it.

On the preceding day there had been a mass meeting of over ten thousand diggers, at this meeting an Irishman called Phillip Lalor was elected to head a delegation which would endeavour to meet the Commissioner and try to resolve our grievances. Once again I begged Owen to leave Ballarat as I knew from my previous experiences that the colonial government would never back down especially after their forces had come under attack. Owen agreed I was right but he felt he owed it to the rest of our gang not to leave and he was still very optimistic that we would soon strike gold. Anyway after the mass meeting it was decided that we should erect a stockade, it was also agreed that Frederick Vann, an Italian who claimed to have had a long and distinguished military career should be our Commander in Chief. On his appointment he immediately began to organise and drill the men. It also became apparent that more arms ammunition and food were urgently needed and so foraging parties were sent out with orders to obtain any supplies that could be had.

Obviously as soon the diggers began to make these preparations the government spies in our camp quickly made the authorities aware of our activities. Whilst all these things were happening another Council of War was called and at this meeting the main speaker was Phillip Lalor and by a unanimous vote he was elected Commander in Chief, superseding Frederick Vann. The main reason for this was that the majority of the miners that now wanted to stand and fight were Irishmen and Lalor was a man they admired and trusted. At conclusion of the meeting the leaders went back to the stockade, but Philip Lalor leapt up on to a tree stump and gave the following rousing address to his men, "It is my duty now to swear you in and for you all to take the oath to be faithful to the Southern Cross. Here I with all your attention, the man who after this solemn oath does not stand by our Standard am a coward at heart. I also call upon the persons who do not intend to take the oath to leave this meeting at once."

At the conclusion of his address various groups of miners were ordered to stand to attention around the flagstaff. These men including your brother Owen were now heavily armed and ready to fight and full of valour they recited after Lalor the following oath. "We swear by the Southern Cross, to stand by each other and to fight to defend our liberties."

On seeing all this happen at first hand, I decided that with or without Owen, it was time for me to leave. This decision will haunt me for the rest of my life because I should have dragged Owen away from the danger he faced, but to my everlasting regret I left Ballarat early next morning after saying farewell to Owen and my fellow miners. The date that I rode away from Eureka Lead was the second of December and as I left the goldfields, I witnessed columns of diggers marching towards the stockade that was now the headquarters of the miners. These reinforcements on their arrival were immediately organised into groups and drilled and each man then had his rifle inspected and was given twenty rounds of ammunition. On seeing these military preparations my heart was full of dread, but I still hoped against hope that a compromise would be achieved.

Once I left the goldfields I rode endlessly for many days, trying to convince myself that I had made the right decision. After a week of hard riding, I found myself in a small town not far from my home in Sydney. Realising that my horse needed a rest after my long journey and also that my supplies were running low I decided to stop for the night at the local hostelry. After making sure my horse was fed and watered, I walked to the hotel, relishing the thought of sleeping in a comfortable bed for the first time in months. As I entered the hotel the clerk on the desk was in conversation with some other travellers and when I finally got his attention he asked me if I had heard the sensational news that a pitched battle had taken place between government forces and miners in the goldfields at a town called Ballarat. In reply I said that I had been riding through the bush for the past week and had not heard any news whatsoever. Well, he replied, the tragic events that occurred are the only topic that people are talking about and then he went onto to relate the whole terrible story. As I have already stated, when I rode away from the Goldfields feelings were running high but I had hopes that a compromise would be agreed.

But knowing the way the authorities in Australia worked I should have known better because on the Sunday after I left, the troops attacked. Their assault on the miners stockade began at dawn without any prior warning. The attack had surprised the miners and after a brief struggle they were completely routed leaving

151

over thirty dead. It was widely reported late that many of the unsuspecting miners were brutally massacred in their sleep.

That night I hardly slept a wink wondering what course of action I should take, but by morning I knew that I must return to Ballarat. So after a hurried breakfast, I hired a fresh mount and after purchasing sufficient supplies, I headed back to the goldfields knowing I would not rest until I knew if Owen was safe. On my return journey I was somehow convinced that Owen was too clever to have been caught in a trap, and I was sure he had escaped the carnage.

When I reached the vicinity of Ballarat I came across many miners who were leaving the area. They were all deeply shocked by the cowardly attack on them by the military and were leaving to seek their fortune elsewhere. On enquiring about the casualties I was advised to contact Father Joseph, the Catholic priest who attended the miners. Eventually after many hours of searching I found Father Joseph, the poor man had not slept since the battle and was still in a state of shock.

With no doctors willing to attend the injured for fear of reprisals, he and a couple of helpers were looking after the many wounded miners. Sadly when I enquired about Owen he became very animated and I sensed that something was terribly wrong. On realising who I was he insisted we leave the building, obviously I agreed and followed him out. Once we were outside he laid his hand on my shoulder and with tears running down his face he informed me that you're loving brother had been killed trying to defend the stockade. The surviving diggers testified that he had shown great courage during the assault and he was one of those that had sounded the alarm at the start of the attack.

On realising that they were being attacked many of the defenders had fled in panic, but a few including Owen had tried to stand and fight. Their resistance although brave had proved futile as the stockade was soon completely overrun by the superior government forces. Many of the miners leaders had then gone on the run and the government had offered rewards for their capture. When I asked about the dead, he replied that they had been buried the very next day with all the diggers giving them a tremendous send off. Father Joseph then went onto tell me that after the funerals the men marched down the main road past the government buildings still showing their defiance in the face of the tremendous provocation that they had to endure. With great reluctance I returned to the tent that Owen and I had shared together and carefully packed his few remaining possessions. These items I intend to return to you in person.

I am now back in Sydney and when I have settled my affairs here my intention is to leave Australia for ever. Each night I lay awake blaming myself for your brother's demise because without my urging, your brother would never have returned to this godforsaken country.

Obviously my thoughts and prayers are with you at this terrible time.

With all my sympathies kindest regards,

Robert Hughes.

By the time I had finished reading Roberts letter we were all crying, Catherine was inconsolable as she had grown very close to Owen, and had appreciated all his kindness and the help he had given us. The news broke the hearts of my three sons, because Owen had acted as a father to them during my long absences when they were growing up. His influence on them during their formative years had obviously left an enduring impression because whenever his name is mentioned there are always tears in their eyes.

That evening I remember walking around the farm in a state of shock not knowing what I should do. Suddenly Catherine suggested that as it was impossible for me to travel to Australia as I was proposing, we should ask our Parish Priest to say a Requiem Mass in Owens honour During the coming weeks while we were making the necessary arrangements for the mass Catherine insisted that I write to James Scully Owens old friend and former boss who lived in Tipperary. Within days Mr Scully replied and in his letter he suggested that a small monument should be erected at his expense at our local cemetery. With this in mind he said that he would be coming to Charleville the following week. He was as good as his word and on the following Monday I met him in town.

It was obviously a very sad occasion as we were both totally devastated by Owens death. For a few brief moments I could not think of anything to say but Mr Scully soon put me at ease and invited me to have breakfast at his hotel. As we sat and ate our meal it was soon apparent that he had looked upon Owen as not only an old friend but more like a brother. I agreed with his sentiments when he said that as we did not have Owens remains he felt that at least there should be a permanent memorial in his honour. With this in mind we both went to the local undertakers and after selecting the wording I thought was appropriate Mr Scully insisted on paying the bill. With our business finished I insisted that he should accompany me back to Springfort and see for himself the legacy of Owens foresight and hard work Although his visit was brief it was very obvious why Owen held James in such high regard because he had a wonderful personality and a marvellous sense of humour. Before he left us that day both Catherine and I thanked him for his generosity and made him promise to return for the Requiem Mass.

It was surprising and very heartening for us to see the vast crowds including James Scully that attended the Mass and the blessing of Owens memorial stone. It was very apparent from the conversations I had that day, that my brother had always been liked and respected in the Charleville area. Many of the older generation recalled how he was unlawfully arrested and transported and cursed those who had now taken his life. The shock of Owens violent end has remained with me to this day and each year I have a mass said on the anniversary of his death.

CHAPTER SEVEN

At the time of receiving the news of Owens's death, our circumstances were at last improving and that winter I had been busy making plans for the coming year. But the loss of my brother was like a dagger to my heart and there was now a tremendous emptiness in my life. To fill this void for the first and only time during our marriage I started drinking. Each afternoon I slipped away to Charleville and every night I returned home roaring drunk. Sadly poor Catherine had a wretched time trying to cope with my drunkenness and violent moods. My three sons were left with the burden of running the farm and were bewildered by my actions. As my depression deepened my drinking increased and on many occasions I never even made it home. On many occasions I woke up in a doorway or a field, shaking with the cold and with the only thought in my head being where could I buy my next drink.

As my condition worsened, I began to lose all self respect and shamelessly began begging for money to satisfy my craving. Fortunately for me my eldest son Michael, unbeknown to his mother was determined to rescue me from my stupidity. One morning in early April as I was wandering through Charleville, searching for a scrap to eat, Michael and my other son James suddenly pounced on me and threw me into the back of our cart. Then riding as fast as they could they rushed me back to Springfort. Once back at the farm, they carried me to the edge of our duck pond and dropped me in. The freezing cold water soon brought me to my senses, but they would not let me out until I agreed to listen to what they had to tell me. I could see from their expressions that they meant business and reluctantly I promised to hear what they had to say.

On hearing the commotion Catherine suddenly appeared at the scene and was shocked to see the condition I was in. She immediately brought me into the house and made me eat the first decent meal I had eaten in weeks. Then she stripped me of the stinking rags I was wearing and ordered me to go to bed. Once in the luxury of my own bed I realised how tired I was after weeks of sleeping rough. But sadly when I woke up I found my whole body shaking and I was craving a drink. Somehow I rose from the bed and dressed myself, thinking that I could slip out of the house without being noticed. My hopes were quickly dashed, because Michael, knowing that I would take this course of action had organised one of my family to keep guard on me. James was on duty on this

155

occasion and on hearing me dressing informed his brothers, who came rushing in to give him support. On seeing the three of them standing there I realised that it was impossible for me to sneak out. Thankfully although my whole body was aching for a glass of whisky the determination of my sons that night started me on the rode to recovery.

Many weeks of agony were to follow before the demons finally left me and throughout that time I was never left on my own for one moment. But what finally brought me to my senses was the stern lecture that I received from my wife. In our long marriage this was the only time that I can honestly say that she threatened to throw me out. Firstly, she argued how would Owen react if he was alive and secondly what was the reason for my stupidity. We had been more fortunate than most families in Ireland during the Famine and were now reaping the benefits of Owens forward planning. She went onto say we were now on the verge of achieving everything we had worked for, but it would appear that I was determined to destroy our lives. Her final and most compelling argument was the example I was setting to our three young sons, she said my actions had made me the laughing stock of the Parish. Our sons especially William, who was still at school had been the subject of a tremendous amount of ridicule and now only left the farm when necessary. This situation could not she said carry on. The answer was simple either I stopped drinking completely or I should leave now and never return.

I could tell from her expression that she meant every word that she had spoken and by the time she had finished her whole body was shaking with emotion. For a few moments I stood in silence, shocked by her words that although harsh were true. When I eventually replied, I said "I was sorry for the disgrace I had brought on the family and that I would try to keep away from the drink," I quickly realised that my words were inadequate and only my pledge of total abstinence would satisfy her. This pledge, she insisted must be made in front of the Parish Priest, knowing full well that once made there would be no going back. Looking back now at this low point in my life, I can only thank God that my wife and our three sons showed me the error of my ways. Within the week I made my firm pledge on the Bible in the presence of our Priest, never to touch hard liquor again. That promise I have proudly kept until this day.

That following summer I tried hard to make amends for my indiscretions by working from dawn to dusk, only leaving the farm to attend mass on Sundays. The first few Sundays were hard to bear as my drunken behaviour had obviously been a talking point for many of the congregation. But as the weeks passed with the help of Catherine and my sons our lives returned to normality. The only problem that I found hard to confront was the fact that Owen had left his mark everywhere I went on the farm. In those years after his return from Australia, the prodigious amount of effort he had obviously carried out was everywhere to be seen. New ditches had been dug to improve the drainage, hedges were improved to segregate the fields and most important of all was the building of the cattle shed. This building was to become very important to us in later years when it was used for milking and producing our dairy products.

After our busy harvest and the traditional October Market, I began to think about what I could do in the long winter months. Michael my eldest son as previously stated had been given no formal education and he was now determined to rectify this. At first I helped him in his endeavours, but such was his determination to improve his knowledge he quickly absorbed all I could teach him. Luckily the curate of our local church Father Cullen volunteered to help him and during the following year he made rapid strides. Reading became his obsession and ultimately it was to be the main reason he longed to travel and see the world. For a young man living in a small town with limited prospects, his imagination must have run riot when he read stories and newspaper articles about pioneers in America and the brave British soldiers fighting the Russians in the Crimea. Having had exactly the same feelings when I was his age I knew that given the opportunity he would one day leave Ireland.

When I realised that Michael, no longer needed my help, I started to caste around for something else to occupy my spare time, Catherine encouraged me to fill this void in my life by once again taking an active interest in the problems that were confronting Ireland, both locally and nationally. On a national level the problems of Ireland were to be at the forefront of political debate in the Houses of Parliament in London for the next thirty years. The main reason for this was that for long periods the Irish Members held the balance of power between the Liberal and the Conservative parties. At first as we have seen after the election in eighteen fifty-two, when the Tory Party did not have an overall majority they had offered cabinet posts to two newly elected Irish Independent Members of Parliament. This act of treachery immediately caused a rift amongst the Irish Members that was to last for many years, but as we will see the balance of power was to gradually shift, firstly under the leadership of Isaac Butt and subsequently his successor Charles Stewart Parnell.

But what occurred politically in the aftermath of the Famine, was the question I wanted answered. Although we were very fortunate in our parish that our livelihoods were gradually returning to normal, in many of the poorer regions of the country, it was reported that large estates were now totally devoid of people. The inhabitants had either died of starvation, or emigrated to far off countries. Their landlords many of whom were from the English aristocracy, had been declared bankrupt or sold their estates for a fraction of their true value. The London Financial houses that now held the deeds for these vast empty areas were desperate to find purchasers. In their desperation they sent their agents to Ireland with instructions to value the land. It was often said that geologists were also part of these survey teams; their orders were to locate if possible any trace of mineral wealth. The hope was that any such find would make a sale more viable.

Irish politics during this period were at their lowest ebb, the death of Daniel O'Connell and the arrest and transportation of many of the Young Irelanders had left a void that was to last for many years. As we have seen the election of eighteen fifty-two had raised everyone's expectations, but the shenanigans of the Irish Members of Parliament in the subsequent years quickly disillusioned the electorate. All through that decade I found that there was a total indifference amongst the people for politics and politicians. This situation I soon realised was exactly what the authorities wanted, a cowed disillusioned population would they knew be easy to manipulate and would cause the minimum of fuss.

As I sat by the fireside that winter my thoughts returned to the long discussions that I had with my cousin the young firebrand James Stephens, whilst we worked together constructing the Dublin to Cork railroad. His argument was that politics would never achieve the freedom from outside influences that Ireland required. Only when Ireland became an independent Nation with its own elected parliament would the long overdue radical changes take place that would improve the lives for everyone. This ideal he prophesied could only be achieved by an armed struggle, but as we have seen his first involvement in an armed insurrection had ended in total humiliation.

Over the coming months the more I thought about his solution, the more I realised that he was right, but sadly at this period his views had little if any support.

The situation in Europe at this time was entirely different, with turmoil and insurrections in many countries. In Paris, the workers and peasants had manned the barricades in eighteen fifty-one, in a popular resistance movement that opposed the government of Louis- Napoleon. It was reported in the newspapers that a number of Irish refugees were amongst these revolutionaries. This fact was confirmed to me when after many years of silence; I received the following letter from James Stephens, dated the fourth of November eighteen fifty-four.

Dear Patrick,

As you can see from the postmark I am still residing in Paris and although it is hard for me to earn a living I somehow survive. At present there are a number of us fellow patriots living here in exile, waiting for our opportunity to return home when the time is right. Whilst here I have recruited amongst others, two excellent lieutenants, Michael Doheny, whom you know and have helped and John O'Mahony, who is an excellent organiser and will surely be an asset to our cause. John and I are in constant contact with the French revolutionary groups in the city and during the recent fighting we fought alongside them. As a result of these contacts I have been able to study the methods that are employed by the secret societies in France to ensure that their security is not compromised. You can be assured that the lessons I am at present observing hopefully will one day in the near future be put to good use. But as I have said to you repeatedly in the past, although I wish and pray for freedom for the Irish Nation, my main ambition is as you know that the Irish land should be given to its rightful owners the Irish people, unless this happens, Irish independence is ultimately not worth the trouble and sacrifice of obtaining it.

Whilst on this subject I would appreciate your opinion of the current political situation in Ireland. Is there any mass dissatisfaction amongst the people against the authorities that could be exploited? This is the questions that you can obviously answer for me, as I desperately need to know if I can achieve my desire to create an organisation that will rid Ireland of its oppressors.

But enough of politics how are you and your lovely wife, I often think of the help and hospitality you gave Michael and I when the government forces were trying to apprehend us. It can be very lonely in a foreign land and I am desperate to come home to see my father, and my one remaining sister. With this in mind I have decided to return to Ireland in the near future and you can be assured that I will come and visit you.

God be with you all. Your cousin James.

That very evening I wrote a letter in reply, thanking him for his kind words, but warning him that the people were cowed and downtrodden and in no mood for insurrection. The Famine, I wrote had left the majority of the remaining population preoccupied with one thought and that was how to feed themselves. Those terrible times had left scars that would take generations to heal and any ambitions he had for Ireland was I assured him wishful thinking.

Fortunately for us at Sprinfort the next few summers were very good to us and our lives began to return to normal once again. On Saturday nights, Catherine would invite our neighbours and friends to the house and usually a musician or two would come along. Once the music started the dancing always followed, then everyone in the house would sing or recite a verse. The older people in the crowd could remember the songs handed down from generation to generation. These were mainly sang or recited in the Gaelic tongue and told stories of famous Celtic warriors who had battled in vain against the various nations that had invaded Ireland over the centuries. Those songs have always stirred a strong sense of Patriotism in me and made me long for an end to Irelands never ending problems.

My thoughts now turn to one unforgettable Saturday summer evening, when a visitor arrived at our house for the first of his many visits. This new arrival was our new curate to the Charleville Parish and he was a man who would eventually help change the face of Ireland for ever. This new young man was Thomas Croke, whose uncle was our parish priest for many years. When Thomas arrived that evening our friends and neighbours were in awe of him at first, but when he joined in with the music and dancing, they soon realised that he had come to relax and enjoy himself. My only worry that evening was what would be his reaction if he was asked to sing for us. Well my worries were unfounded because he sang a traditional Celtic air in his own inimitable style. The news of his participation at our party that night quickly spread throughout the Charleville area and he was soon inundated with invitations. From that very evening Thomas, and I became firm friends and this friendship was to go along way in helping me get over the loss of my brother. He had I knew lost his own brother William who was our curate during the Famine years. William had worked tirelessly helping the sick and dying, day in and day out in without any regard for his own health. Tragically this devotion to his parishioners was to lead to him catching the famine fever at the very young age of twenty seven. So it is ironic that our life long friendship was to develop because of our common grief at losing a brother.

In later years Thomas, then Archbishop Croke of Cashel was to fulfil a promise he made to me when he blessed a new monument in Holy Cross Cemetery, Charleville, in honour of his sadly departed brother. This monument in the form of a tall headstone has a marble tablet inset bearing the following inscription:

"This marble marks the grave in which are deposited the mortal remains of Rev. William Croke, the nephew and curate of Rev. Thomas Croke, P.P., of Charleville. His career though brief was remarkable for the exercise of those qualities which endeared him to a people whom he zealously and faithfully served and who in return admired and loved him. He was an enlightened, laborious and pious clergyman. sterling, uncompromising patriot, a friend to the poor and an enemy to oppression. He died on the fifth of February, eighteen forty-eight, in the twenty seventh year of his age. May he rest in peace, Amen."

But although our initial conversations were about our shared family bereavements, we both quickly realised that we shared the same political beliefs. As I have previously stated in the decade after the Famine, the political situation in Ireland had reached an impasse. In looking back it is now very obvious that a vacuum had been created by the Irish politicians in Westminster not fulfilling the promises to the people that had elected them. In retrospect this vacuum would ultimately lead to the creation of a totally different breed of politician. This new breed of politician were in the beginning only rudimentarily agitators for land reform. But as we shall see the vacuum that had been created was also to open up opportunities for the Nationalists, to gain the support of the electorate under the leadership of my cousin James Stephens.

The discussions I had with Thomas Croke during his time as curate of our parish were to further influence my political views and also make me focus my energies in the turbulent years that followed. On his insistence I should always keep a low profile as he was sure that because of my brothers past and also having James Stephens as a cousin my name was obviously known to the authorities. His wise prediction would eventually be vindicated when in later years the local Militia raided the homes of known Nationalists after another failed insurrection. Although I was never an active member of the numerous parties that sprang up in the following thirty years, it was known in Fenian circles that Springfort was a safe haven if the necessity arose. Sadly Thomas Croke soon left Charleville to begin his meteoric rise to fame, but he was never to lose his vision of a better life for the Irish people. Although we were not to meet for many years, his help and compassion would again rescue me from another low point in my life.

With our lives gradually returning to normality Catherine never mentioned those terrible months when the drink took over my life. Consequently with the income increasing due to the rising cattle prices during the eighteen fifties, our farming year regained some of its old familiar pattern. Michael the eldest son was, apart from my brother Owen the hardest working person I have ever come across. Fortunately for me my other two sons looked up to their elder brother and tried to copy him in everything he attempted. With four strong men to feed Catherine now had her hands full cooking as we all had healthy appetites. As they grew up my wife and I would spend hours discussing our son's individual characteristics and hoping against hope that they would not emigrate.

Michael we agreed was definitely the spitting image of her father John McGrath, as a child he had always been very tall for his age and was now around six feet tall. Like his grandfather he was immensely strong and also very handsome with fair hair and piercing blue eyes. At our gatherings on Saturday nights he was obviously the one all the young girls wanted to dance with. But unlike his two brothers, as he grew to manhood he became very ambitious to improve himself. As I have previously said although he had very little formal education, as he got older he would spend hours after work each evening studying. This hard work combined with a natural aptitude, quickly began to reap dividends and by the age of eighteen he had educated himself to an amazingly high standard. I had always hoped and prayed that Michael would eventually take over the running of Springfort, but I reluctantly began to realise that his ambitions lay elsewhere.

James our second son was a typical Casey, short and stocky and always trying to make a penny. Unlike his elder brother who was not really keen on sport James like his Uncle Owen was a fanatical hurly player and practised endlessly. When he was not at the hurly he once again like his Uncle Owen, loved the company of the young girls of the Parish. On more than one occasion during his roving days a local farmer had confronted me about my son's behaviour. On these occasions I would always endeavour to remind the accuser of his own youthful misdemeanours, this was because fortunately, most of them were my contemporaries. Obviously I had to admonish him at times but I knew that I was wasting my time because he was never ever going to change his ways. But I often prayed that he would eventually meet the right girl and settle down in Ireland.

William our youngest was my wife's favourite, he and his mother had similar personalities, both were extremely kind and always willing to help anyone in need. He was the studious one in the family, always to be found with his head in a book. At school he always excelled at arithmetic and in later years we were to entrust him with all of our finances a decision we were never to regret. Unlike our other two sons who were very strong and robust William was always very sickly. All through his life he was to suffer long illnesses especially during the winter months. Any cold or chill he caught would worryingly affect his breathing and usually turned into a bout of pneumonia. But he was very fortunate that his mother was always on hand to nurse him back to health. She would devote all her attention to him, on many occasions to the detriment of her own wellbeing. As a result of this both patient and nurse became even closer, a bond that was never to be broken. All of the potions and poultices that she used to help him overcome his illnesses were ancient remedies and over the years she was to become renowned locally for her medical knowledge and expertise.

Those idyllic years when the five of us were at last able to enjoy the fruits of our endeavours were once again about to come to an abrupt end. We did not realise that a harmless visit by my wife's brother Danny who had returned from America was about to cause us much anguish. Our visitor Danny McGrath had emigrated many years before and both my wife and I did not recognise him at first. His long stay in America had completely changed him physically as he was now very plump and balding. But the most striking changes were his air of authority and his thick American accent.

He had arrived in a hired trap whilst we were haymaking in the summer of eighteen fifty-seven. Catherine, on belatedly realising, who our visitor was, quickly ran out in to the fields to summon us into to meet her long lost brother. After a hastily eaten meal, Danny to give him his due insisted on helping us that afternoon in the fields. That evening when we all returned to the house tired and weary from our exertions we found that Catherine had cooked a special meal in honour of our guest. Over dinner her brother confessed it had been a long while since he had done any physical work and he was completely worn out... He then went on to tell us that he was now working in New York for a detective agency.

After we finished our meal it was obvious that our guest was extremely tired and although we offered him a bed for the night he insisted on returning to his hotel in town. But before leaving he confessed that it had always been his ambition to return to Ireland and see his parents at harvest time, but now that they had died and their farm was no longer in the family this was obviously not possible. He went on to tell us that during his lifetime away from his beloved Ireland he had always dreamt of those wonderful times he had as a boy working in the fields in the summer time. In those far off times he reminisced, the culmination of our endeavours was the drawing in of the hay to make the hayrick that supplied the cattle feed for the winter. On this day all of your neighbours and friends would arrive to help, and when the job was finished the women cooked a feast fit for a king. Then with your hay collected and saved it was now our turn to help each neighbour in turn, until everyone had their hay drawn in. When I told him that in recent years with the revival of rearing livestock the tradition had been revived he was overjoyed.

But as usual, we were at the mercy of the weather but if the present dry weather continued I predicted we would be building our hayrick on the coming Saturday. On hearing this he promised to return every day that week to help us. This was great news for us as we could always do with another helper at this the busiest time of our year.

That night after he had left us we all questioned Catherine about her brother; Michael in particular seemed very interested. Catherine said she could only barely remember him as she was only a child when he left Ireland and apart from the occasional letter her parents had received in the dim and distant past to all intents and purposes she thought he was dead.

The next day Danny was as good as his word and arrived bright and early ready to start work. But this time he came suitably attired in typical Irish farm workers clothes that he had purchased that very morning. As the day promised to be very hot, he had also been very sensible and purchased a large hat, because on the previous afternoon his head had caught the sun due to his baldness. That day my sons questioned him about l his travels and he was only to happy to answer them. It soon became obvious that he was a born storyteller and in the following days he thrilled my boys with stories of his many adventures. In the years since he left Ireland, he told he had travelled across much of North America.

During each meal break that week my sons and I would sit and listen to Danny's, tales. On leaving Ireland he had taken passage to New York; on arriving there he was fortunate to find work as a labourer. But unlike many of his fellow Irishmen who drank all they earned, he saved his money for a year and then started to travel. From New York he made his way up the coast to the large town of Boston. This town had a large Irish community and so he found it very easy to find work. But once again this was labouring and after a few months he decided to move on. Before leaving Boston he had a stroke of luck when he heard that construction workers were being hired for a new railroad being built. This railroad was to run from a small town called Stonington along the coast to South Providence on the outskirts of Boston.

Obviously my curiosity was roused on hearing that he had found work on a railroad construction. He had no idea that I had an extensive knowledge on the subject and so he was astounded when I asked him various technical questions. It quickly became apparent that the two of us had a great deal in common as we discussed our different experiences, but although I had endured some awful weather both in England and Ireland; it was nowhere near the extremes that Danny had witnessed. The freezing temperatures and blinding snowstorms of an American winter were a nightmare that he could not cope with, so when the spring finally arrived he decided to head inland to the town of Chicago.

When his friends in Boston heard that he was proposing to make the long overland journey to Chicago they advised him to purchase the best horse he could afford. At first he laughed at this idea, but when he was told of the distance involved he readily agreed with their suggestion. Over the next few years it was soon quiete apparent to him why the horse was such a prized asset in America and why horse stealing was a hanging offence in many States. By early June with all his preparations now complete he headed inland making for the town of Buffalo. After many days of hard riding he finally reached his destination. In earlier years the town was mainly a trading centre for the fur trade, but the arrival of the Erie Canal in eighteen twenty-two changed everything. This five hundred and twenty four mile waterway went east to the city of New York, thus enabling the wheat growing areas in the Mid West of America to feed the ever growing population of that great metropolis.

But the major attraction of Buffalo was the world famous Niagara Falls and Danny said they are a sight to behold. The volume of water that cascades down s he told us is unbelievable and unlike anything he has ever witnessed.

Although he had only intended to have a brief stop and continue his journey, he soon realised that there was plenty of work available in Buffalo now that the wheat harvest had began. Within a day he had found work loading the canal boats with grain that was being transported east. The work was hard but the pay was good and he was lucky to keep working all that summer. But when the work dried up he continued his journey to Chicago, his route taking him along the shores of Lake Erie. This lake was so large he told us that it was almost an inland sea. He rode along its shores for days until he arrived at his destination. Chicago. Chicago he found was almost identical to the town of Boston, because it also had a large population of Irish immigrants. But once again he was unprepared for the North American winter and he was to soon find that the weather in Chicago was even colder than what he had experienced in Boston.

That first winter he managed to find a few menial jobs, but his hard earned cash soon disappeared and so he had to reluctantly sell his horse to buy food. When spring finally arrived he once again found work labouring. He struggled on for the next couple of years doing any work that came his way, but always harbouring an ambition to improve himself. his chance finally came in the summer of eighteen thirty- eight, when he met an old acquaintance for a drink after work His friend Tommy Murphy, had recently been recruited into the newly formed Chicago Police Department. This force had been formed because crime in the city had got totally out of control. Tommy said that most of the new recruits were Irish and he would recommend him if he was interested. Obviously he realised at once that this was chance he had craved for and within weeks he had been accepted and had embarked on his new career.

At that time he told us Chicago was divided into three districts and he was sent as a rookie officer to Station Two, the most notorious district in the city. For the next ten years he and his fellow officers fought a never ending battle against the criminal gangs that infested their district. But because he was single and unattached, his police work quickly took over his life and this total dedication soon became recognised by his superior officers. Although promotion was slow, he gradually rose through the ranks and he eventually achieved his ultimate ambition when he was promoted to the rank of sergeant.

His promotion enabled him to attain everything he had long dreamed of; a house of his own with a garden to grow vegetables, but most of all and what every Irishman the world over aspires to, financial security. Also by being a senior officer he also became acquainted with his counterparts in the other two other districts in the City.

One of the senior policemen that he came in contact with at this period was a young Scottish gentleman named Allan Pinkerton. At their first meeting Danny thought that Pinkerton was an arrogant upstart, but subsequently the two of them became firm friends. This friendship has somehow endured, but at

166

times has been very fractious mainly because of Pinkerton's drunken behaviour. On many occasions Danny said he had had to intervene and stop his friend from wrecking bars in a drunken rage. Strangely when he was sober Pinkerton was an excellent police officer and was eventually promoted to Deputy Sheriff after solving a series of high profile crimes. As their friendship developed Allan Pinkerton began to confide more and more in Danny. He told him that he was working in secret for clients who had been victims of robbery or other serious crimes and because of his many successes, the remunerations he was receiving for this private work far exceeded his policemen's pay and so he was seriously thinking of leaving the police service and setting up his own detective agency.

Over the following two years they discussed Allan's dilemma on numerous occasions but he finally made his up his mind early in the Spring of eighteen fifty- two, when he resigned from the police force and started up his own National Detective Agency. The expanding railroads all across the Mid West states of America, attracted gangs of desperados all eager to rob them, so many of the railroad companies began to hire Pinkerton's National Detective Agency. They hired him firstly for protection and secondly to track down and arrest the robbers. As his Agencies reputation grew Pinkerton started to expand his workforce and area of influence.

He was obviously now a busy man and so it came as a big surprise when he told Danny that he was opening a branch of his agency in New York and said he wanted him to be his representative there. Allan told him that he had thought long and hard before offering the post to his friend as he knew how much he had grown to enjoy his life in Chicago. But he argued that Danny was now a very experienced policeman and he was certain that he was the man for the job. That night Danny recalls he laid awake for hours thinking about Allan's offer and finally realised that it was too good to refuse. The next few weeks were extremely emotional for him, firstly it was a terrible wrench leaving all his friends and colleagues on the Chicago Police Department and secondly selling the house where he had spent so many happy hours.

On reflection he realised that he needed a new challenge and on arriving in New York with his new boss Allan Pinkerton it quickly became apparent that he had made the right decision. Crime in the city was spiralling out of control and news that Pinkerton's National Detective Agency was opening an office there had made headlines in many of the newspapers. Danny told us that if he thought he needed a new challenge he certainly found it in New York, a city that seemed to grow by the day. The docks were filled with a never ending throng of immigrants that filled the already teeming tenement buildings where crime was an everyday part of life. The deprivation in these areas created the violent gangs that New York was to become notorious for, but as solving crime was what he was paid for the Agency was soon inundated with crimes to solve. Fortunately he was able to hire two former policemen who knew all about the City and its problems. Once again he found that like Chicago most of the police in New York were Irishmen, and his new recruits were no exception. He had then worked solidly for the next few years and gradually expanded the agency, but now that he had the financial means his heart ached to return home to Ireland.

Each day in the fields that week Danny thrilled my sons with stories of the numerous crimes he had solved and the scrapes he had with the many gangsters in New York. At first I was very sceptical and thought that most of his stories were balderdash, but when on the one occasion he removed his shirt because of the heat of the day, I gasped at seeing the many scars that covered his torso. On enquiring about them, he replied nonchalantly that they were all collected in the line of duty. As the week progressed I could not help but notice that my eldest son Michael had become totally infatuated by his long lost uncle. Knowing that he had always expressed a desire to travel, I realised that Danny's stories and his promises of help if he ever wanted to join him in America filled my heart with dread.

By the end of that week of fine weather the hay was ready to be drawn into the yard. This was the day we had all worked so hard for especially Danny, who had a slaved that week on our behalf. Early on the Saturday morning all of our friends and neighbours arrived with their pitchforks in readiness for the long hot day we had in front of us. As was traditional the wives came to help Catherine prepare the food and drink for us men. Just like our American guest this day was always one of the highlights of the year for me, the non stop banter and leg pulling filled the day with laughter and merriment. Then in the twilight on that glorious summer evening when the last load of hay was drawn in from the fields and piled onto the enormous stack everyone cheered and made for the feast that had been prepared. That night although we were all tired from the long day, when the music started the dancing was soon in progress. Danny my brother-in-law was spellbound at seeing and hearing the songs and dancing that he remembered from his youth. Eventually after much persuasion Catherine managed to get him to dance and much to our amusement once started he never sat down for the rest of the evening.

That night Danny was so tired he decided to stay the night with us, but before getting into bed he asked me if he could take Catherine and my three boys to Killarney for a couple of days holiday before he returned home. Obviously both my wife and I were delighted at his suggestion and we readily agreed.

The next morning although I was awake very early, Catherine was already up and about preparing for her trip to Killarney. That Sunday was a red letter day for my family, because when our sons heard that they were off on holiday the excitement was intense. Bags were quickly packed and then we all attended Mass and afterwards we all rushed off to the station. It was strange for me to wave them all goodbye and to suddenly be alone, but I was overjoyed that they were all having a holiday. It was nearly a week before they returned minus Danny, who had gone straight to Queenstown harbour in order to catch a ship sailing to New York. Their holiday had been a huge success and was talked about for months after, as it had been a big adventure for our three sons. Catherine told me later that her brother had spared no expense on ensuring they all enjoyed themselves.

On their arrival in Killarney, under her guidance he had purchased new clothes for all of them, and then he had taken them to their hotel, this was a real luxury for her, because she had never dreamed of ever staying in a hotel. But meal times were a worry because of the amount of cutlery on the table, Danny realising her dilemma quickly instructed her and the boys in how to conduct themselves. Their first meal she said was filled with laughter because the waiter assumed that they were man and wife and that they carried on this pretence at every meal time much to the delight of our sons who thought that it was hilarious.

Each day on her fairy tale week a pony and trap was hired and they would spend the day visiting all the famous sights of the local area, this included Muck Ross Abbey, the remote and beautiful Gap of Dunloe and a boat trip around the Lakes with marvellous views of the Macgillycuddy Reeks, they were also very fortunate because the weather was wonderful allowing them to enjoy picnics from the contents of the large hampers supplied by the hotel. Poor Catherine had never been pampered in this way before and she told me that she thought she was in another world. I promised her that when our sons were old enough, we would have holidays together, but obviously not as lavish as Danny had provided.

On his return to New York Danny wrote and thanked us for our hospitality; this was the start of our corresponding together for the rest of his life. But for me the upsetting result of his visit was the unsettling of our eldest son Michael. It had fuelled Michaels long held ambition to travel and each time Catherine wrote to her cousin he begged his mother to mention that he had made his mind up about emigrating to America. Eventually after much soul searching she complied with her sons wishes and wrote the letter. In reply Danny cautioned Michael, to think carefully before he committed himself as it was a huge step for him to take, and once in America it would be virtually impossible to afford the fare back to Ireland. Both Catherine and I begged him to change his mind but to no avail and when we both realised that his mind was made up and it was futile to stand in his way, we reluctantly allowed him to write his own letter to his uncle confirming his intentions.

Week followed week with no sign of a reply, Christmas came and went with Michael becoming more and more desperate for a decision. Then in early March eighteen fifty-nine the long awaited letter arrived addressed personally to Michael. Danny apologised for the delay in replying, it had been caused by his need to catch up with the many investigations that his agency were pursuing. He went onto say that as it was obvious that his nephew was determined to leave Ireland and join him in New York and he was enclosing sufficient funds to cover the cost. Both Catherine and I were outwardly pleased for him as we did not want him to miss the opportunity he so obviously desired, but in private the two of us were devastated at the thought of losing a son we so loved.

What followed was the all too familiar ritual that has affected every family in Ireland during my lifetime. A mass was said for Michael's safety and wellbeing which was attended by all his friends and neighbours. It was no surprise to me that many of the young girls there were very upset at his departure, as his good looks and easy going nature had captured many of their hearts. But for myself and Catherine the following weeks passed in a flash and soon it was time for Michael's departure. On that unforgettable morning we all travelled by train to Cork City and then walked the rest of the way to Queenstown harbour.

Fortunately for Michael the ships that now crossed the Atlantic had vastly improved and many of them were now were partially driven by steam and thanks to his uncle's generosity he had managed to get a berth on one of these new ships. On reaching Queenstown harbour, Michael said his sad farewells and was quickly taken out to the waiting vessel.

CHAPTER EIGHT

Michael's departure had sadly left another void in our lives, but our work on the farm had to continue especially now that we had a herd of cattle to look after. Apart from losing a son, I had also lost my right hand man and someone who would be hard to replace. Fortunately William had now finished school, but although he was very willing he did not have the strength at his age for any heavy work. Luckily for us his older brother James quickly realised that he must take over Michael's responsibilities. That summer as the weeks progressed he began to live up to my expectations and my nightmares at losing my eldest son began to evaporate. By the age of twenty, James was as strong as an ox and apart from the occasional drunken Saturday night he was the ideal son. William though was the son I secretly admired, as I have said he was a sickly child but his grit and determination to prove himself was an inspiration to us. In the years after he left school he began to fill out and toughen up and this together with his fine business brain made me realise that in time he should be the one to eventually take over the running of the farm.

Sadly after a few good harvests, when the fortunes of the Irish people had at last began to improve, poor weather and falling farm prices would once again lead to the threat of mass starvation. This would be followed by the inevitable forced evictions. But this time things would ultimately be very different as the Land League agitators became better organised and more determined than their predecessors. The change from a docile down trodden population that had somehow survived the Famine, to the decades that followed of an angry violent people seeking radical solutions to their dire problems was a phenomenon that has never been fully understood. But in the following pages I tell the story about my cousin James Sephens, who was very influential in helping this change. He and a multitude of others were to sacrifice everything for the sake of their beloved country and they were to ultimately change forever the course of Ireland's history.

No narrative of my life would be complete without a chapter on the most influential person I have ever met, namely James Stephens. He was a man who you either loved or loathed; there could never be a middle path. Throughout his turbulent life he has always been controversial and he always believed that it was his destiny to be the leader of a successful rising against English rule and the setting up of an Irish Republic. In a previous chapter I explained how at the start of the Famine, James had been instrumental in helping me obtain employment on the construction of the Dublin to Cork railroad. At that time it was virtually impossible to find work and thus his help had enabled me to feed and clothe my family while many other poor souls starved. For this alone I owe him a great deal of gratitude for without this help I know that we would have certainly lost everything.

As you will recall he was then involved in the failed rising by the Young Irelanders in eighteen forty-eight and was assumed to have died in the siege at Ballinagarry, but although badly wounded he had somehow managed to escape from pursuing military forces. He had subsequently met up with Michael Doheny another fleeing rebel and they had taken refuge with us at Springfort whilst on the run from the authorities. After many months of living in danger of betrayal, they had both somehow managed to make a daring escape to France, where James would ultimately spend many futile years in exile. During his first years in Paris he met and was influenced by many of the revolutionaries of the time who had flocked to that city from all over Europe. This was a heady time; change was in the air and with the brief overthrow of Napoleon the Third shockwaves were felt all over Europe.

Michael Doheny his fellow escapee on the other hand had other plans and as soon as possible found a ship to New York. On his arrival he was treated as a hero by the thousands of Irish immigrants that now resided there. After many weeks of being feted by the people of that city he eventually settled down to write about his miraculous escape, in his highly acclaimed book 'The Fenian Track.' Obviously he did not mention by name the people who had helped him, but in later years I am proud to say I received an inscribed copy of his book from him. Eventually Mr Doheny, would become a very influential member of The Clan Na Gael an American organisation that raised funds to support The Land League, agitation in Ireland.

I was still receiving the occasional letter from James Stephens during this period post marked Paris. He always asked the same question, was the country ripe for revolution? Obviously this was difficult for me to answer, but I suggested that he should return and gauge the feeling of the people for himself. In one of his letters he confessed how much he missed his family and friends and had become very homesick. He knew that to return at this time would be extremely dangerous, because although presumed dead he could easily be spotted by a government informer and be arrested.

It was not until the winter of eighteen fifty- five, that he eventually felt it was safe to cross from Paris to London. Once in London he met up with some old friends and then travelled with them to Manchester for the Christmas festivities. With great trepidation in January eighteen fifty-six, he boarded a steamer at Holyhead for the short journey across the Irish Sea. Any worries he had about being recognised and arrested on his arrival back in Ireland were totally dispelled. On his return he unfortunately was struck down by a terrible bout of influenza and was confined to his bed for ten days. Once he had recovered he went directly to his hometown of Kilkenny hoping to see his beloved father and his only surviving sister. Tragically in the years since his escape from Ireland, he had for security reasons not contacted his father or sister and was devastated to be told that both had died of broken hearts when his death was announced in eighteen forty eight.

Overwhelmed by grief and remorse he went to see his local Parish Priest, who, although now a very old man fortunately still remembered him. Obviously the priest was shocked to see him as he had officiated at a funeral supposedly for the dead James Stephens. As they talked that afternoon James told the story of his amazing escape to France, his years in exile and his burning desire to return home. In return the priest explained the tragic circumstances of the deaths firstly of his father, who on hearing of his only sons demise took to his bed and quickly passed away. James's sister was also dead within the year; she had caught cholera whilst helping the poor of the parish.

On leaving the Priest later that evening he spent the night in the local Hotel. The next morning still in a state of shock from the priests revelations he thought long and hard about his future. At first he resolved to return to Paris, but before leaving his home town of Kilkenny he knew he had a duty to visit his mother's family who still lived locally.

This decision was he recalled in later years the turning point of his political career. Because on locating his relations who incidentally were another branch of the Casey family he was overwhelmed by the welcome he received. His aunts and uncles had unfortunately all passed away, but his cousins once they realised who he was were overjoyed at his return. He was to stay with them for over a month and during that period he was able to relax and once again enjoy life amongst friends. The news of the death of his close family had deeply affected him and for a time he recalls, he lapsed into a deep depression. Fortunately that month spent relaxing in the quiet of the

Irish countryside was the tonic he needed and his health both mentally and physically rapidly improved.

While staying with his relations in Kilkenny, some old school friends came to visit and much to his astonishment they told him they had a very interesting grave to show him. At first he refused to go with them, but on reaching the graveyard he realised the reason for the visit. For there before his eyes was a tombstone with his name inscribed on it. With great merriment they explained that to fool the authorities into thinking he had died at Ballinagary in eighteen forty-eight, they had filled a coffin with rocks and had a formal burial service.

This incident really lifted his spirits and he was soon making plans for the epic journey which was to eventually change the course of Irish political thinking. What he had in mind was a walk of three thousand miles that encompassed every part of Ireland. During his travels he was hoping to gauge the scale of dissatisfaction with the Government and their lackeys in Dublin Castle, because his ultimate aim was to reignite the desire for an Independent Irish Nation and he wanted to personally ascertain the people's attitude. He later said that on his travels it soon became clear that the upper and middle classes had no interest whatsoever in Irish Nationhood. But amongst the labourers and small tradesmen in the towns and villages he visited there was a great sense of dissatisfaction and he felt these were the men who could be recruited into an organisation that he wanted to establish. Eventually at the conclusion of his long walk he was very elated by his findings and immediately began to put his radical ideas into practise. This endeavour was, he later recalls, to consume his every waking minute for the next ten years.

Fortunately whilst on his epic journey he found time to surprise us with a visit in July of that year. Obviously it was wonderful for us to see him again after all this time for although we always had differing opinions on many subjects, it was always stimulating for me to hear his thoughts and aspirations for the future. It was even more relevant on this occasion, because having only recently returned from Paris, the hot bed of radical thinking; his pronouncements were I thought, extremely revolutionary. As was usual our long conversations, although heated always ended amicably as we both fundamentally agreed that the people of Ireland were down trodden by the prevailing forces that governed the country. Before leaving he gave me a solemn promise that he would never rest until Ireland was a Republic with its own Parliament in Dublin. His argument was that we had lost all control of our affairs since the day that our politicians were forced to become a minority in the House of Westminster in London.

What grieved him most was at the hour of Irelands greatest catastrophe when millions had either emigrated or died the government in London had stood by and watched it all happen and had barely lifted a finger to help.

Apart from the change in his political views, the change in his appearance had also radically altered. When he arrived Catherine told me later, that she was very embarrassed as she had no idea who this stranger was. She had to pluck up courage before asking him the reason for his visit. James, quickly realising her predicament explained who he was. At the mention of his name she sat him down at the table and sensing that he was very hungry prepared a meal for him. Strangely that afternoon I had finished work early and on nearing the house was surprised to hear Catherine speaking to a man with a foreign accent. On hearing me approaching the house my wife ran out into the yard and told me I would not recognise our illustrious visitor. She was right, because James had changed completely from the young provincial engineer of former years. Gone was the young self effacing individual that I had known instead before me was a stranger dressed in the clothes that reminded me of a travelling actor and speaking with a strange accent. But within minutes of us being reunited the discussions started and hours of friendly argument ensued.

During his brief stay he confessed that it was the first occasion in months that he had allowed himself time to relax, as he knew he was amongst trusted friends. His stories about life in Paris fascinated our sons and they were never to forget his visit and although they were never politically minded they always showed an interest in his later exploits. Undoubtedly the death of his father and sister was still troubling him and in my wife Catherine he found the perfect person to unburden his sorrows to. She bless her soul, was always a good listener and was also very good at dispensing her advice. James, to give him his due would later write thanking her for listening to him and said he would always be eternally grateful for the understanding she had for the guilt he felt.

The following morning I was surprised when he volunteered to help us around the farm, he explained that he needed to have a break from his travels and he asked if he could stay with us for a few days. For us it was a great honour and we readily agreed, but with one condition that he did not go into town as he could be recognised instantly and might be arrested. The time he spent with us that summer will always be remembered, because apart from the subject of Ireland's future, he could converse on every topic imaginable. He in fact used every opportunity during his brief stay to encourage our sons to read the books he carried with him. One of these books was written by the most celebrated English writer of the time, Charles Dickens who was in fact my favourite author. My cousin James was undoubtedly the most intelligent person I have ever known, but unfortunately subsequent events have not portrayed him in a good light.

So after spending seven happy days with us he reluctantly said goodbye, but not before promising to one day return. On his departure Catherine prepared a large bag of provisions for the next long gruelling stage of his journey. His destination he told us was the town of Killarney, where to earn some much needed funds he had obtained a position as a French tutor. The engagement was at an academy called The Miss Morris School that taught the daughters of the wealthy families of the town. Also he hoped to witness the inauguration of Bishop Moriarty, the new Bishop of County Kerry, as he had heard that this man of the cloth was an outspoken critic of the establishment. It was his declared intention he said, to seek an interview with Bishop Moriarty to discus the plight of the poor and ways to prevent the mass eviction of tenants from their homes and farms.

But it was not until May eighteen fifty- eight, that we saw him again. This time it was a very different James Stephens from the relaxed person who had left us all those months a go. Unfortunately his manner had completely changed from the charming urbane cousin I had always known. He was now very assertive and impulsive, with an attitude that now bordered on arrogance. Sadly he now seemed to have a complete contempt for everything and everybody especially the Irish politicians at Westminster. During the brief discussion we had on this his last ever visit to Springfort I tackled him about the apparent change in his attitude as I was anxious to find out the reason for it. He was I reminded him in the home of his cousin and friend who had always stood by him through thick and thin and had always afforded him a welcome in whatever circumstances. There was a long silence, during which I could see that my words had struck home and when he eventually replied he apologised at once for his attitude and he asked to be forgiven for being so arrogant. Obviously I accepted his apology and within minutes we began to argue as usual with the whole episode thankfully forgotten.

As we chatted I could tell that he was very excited and could hardly contain himself but before he imparted his secret to me he made me solemnly promise that what he was about to tell should never be repeated. To enable me to comply with his wishes, I found the family bible and swore an oath that I would keep his secret. For safety sake he suggested we went for a stroll around the farm so even my wife could not hear what he was about to divulge. When we had walked to the point furthest from the house, in a hushed voice he told me about the counties he had visited in the months since his last visit. Apparently he had soon tired of his employment in Killarney and had headed north towards Connemara. Here he found nothing but desolation, the land he said was totally devoid of man and beast. It was soon obvious that his mission in that area was impossible so he headed back to Dublin.

Once back in Dublin he began to contact fellow republicans, some of whom had also returned from exile. James, as impatient as ever quickly gathered his fellow conspirators together and after a series of clandestine meetings they agreed to establish a secret organisation called the Irish Republican Brotherhood. This organisation was formally founded at his lodgings in Lombard Street, Dublin on St Patrick's Day the seventeenth of March eighteen fifty-eight. The society he told me was dedicated to the establishment of an Independent Democratic Republic and to my astonishment he announced that he had been elected Chief Organizer.

Then in a solemn voice he promised that one day he James Stephens would be elected the first leader of an Irish Republic. But sadly he confided in me that this could only come about by armed insurrection, as the authorities would never allow it to happen democratically. His prediction was to prove prophetic in the following years as Ireland lurched from one crisis to another. I knew that what he had told me that afternoon was treason and if the authorities became aware of his intentions he would face the gallows.

After his startling revelation I was lost for words and unusually so was James. We both sat there for what seemed hours contemplating the future before my cousin suggested we made our way back to the house. As we strolled home across the fields that afternoon I asked him about his immediate plans. He would he said leave very early the next morning heading for the town of Skibbereen in West Cork, to meet a literary society there called 'The Phoenix Association.' He had heard glowing reports from his associates regarding the leaders of this organisation, many of whom were later to become thorns in the side of the government. The most famous of these were Jeremiah O'Donovan Rossa and his associates Morty Monahan and Brian Dillon. James expressed the hope that this Skibbereen group could be persuaded to join forces with his organisation, thus giving him a foothold in the West of Ireland. Although 'The Phoenix Society' professed to be a literary society he knew that this was merely a front for a group of radical thinkers who had ultimately the same hopes and aspirations as his organisation.

But before arriving back at the house he let me into one last secret, he said that in order to confuse the authorities he had adopted the pseudonym of Mr Shooks. In the next few years much to my cousin's delight, the name Mr Shooks would become notorious throughout Ireland. Also his secret organisation was to expand at a tremendous pace eventually having a branch in every town in the country. Although I never became an active member myself, James knew that I could always be called upon to help in an emergency. But in the light of what had happened in the past to my brother I made James, promise that he would never try and enrol my two sons.

He left at the at the crack of dawn weighed down with provisions that Catherine had provided for his journey, sadly this was to be the last time I ever saw him. Apart from telling my wife Catherine, I have kept my cousins conversation a secret until this day.

In the coming months rumours started to circulate about a secret underground organisation that was busy recruiting young men all over Ireland. After every Sunday mass that summer the only topic of our conversations was the latest activities of this clandestine group. If you could believe what you heard it would appear that these recruits were already drilling and arming themselves in readiness for an imminent armed insurrection. Our Parish Priest, although sympathetic to the Nationalist cause, had been instructed by the Bishop to condemn this Secret Society, an instruction he was duty bound to carry out but it was obvious to most of his congregation that the young men of Charleville simply ignored their priest's advice. All the while I continuously scanned the newspapers for news of James Stephens, or Shooks, but it was not until the government officers swooped on 'The Phoenix Society' in Skibbereen on September the tenth eighteen fifty eight and simultaneously made arrests in Mac room and Kilkenny of O'Donovan Rossa and his associates that the scale of this new secret society became apparent.

At the subsequent trial of 'The Phoenix Society' it was revealed that an informer called Goulah, who was working for the local stipendiary magistrate named Fitzmaurice, had apparently infiltrated the organisation. Fitzmaurice had been sent by the authorities in Dublin to investigate The Phoenix Society and where appropriate take action. From correspondence I later had with Stephens, the statement which had been read out in court by the informer Goulah, stating that he had attended a meeting at the Priests Leap on the border between Cork and Kerry was a complete fabrication. The informer's statement had also the court that he had seen military drilling actually taking place. Some of the men drilling were members of the Phoenix Society from Skibbereen who now stood before the court. The informer then went onto say that at this meeting he was told that the aim of the Society was the taking up of arms against the government. James went onto write that the perjurer then claimed that he was told that a large number of fully armed Irish Americans would be landing in Ireland before Christmas. At the same time a large force of French army volunteers would arrive to link up with the Americans. The arrival of these two armed allies was to be the signal for an uprising that would defeat The Crowns forces. After their victory Ireland would at last be declared a Republic. Finally Goulah stated that one of the Irish rebels, who went by the name of Shooks, was now making the final arrangements for the landing of the American and French forces.

The mention of the name Shooks at the trial really caused him a great deal of heartache and the knowledge that an informer had penetrated the organisation to such an extent really caught him off guard. The trial before a jury packed with government sympathisers was quickly over and all the defendants were found guilty. After many lengthy conversations with their attorney a Mr McCarthy Downing, they were eventually persuaded to plead guilty. Their decision was treated favourably by the judge who gave them only a year in jail if they promised to be on good behaviour in the future.

Subsequently Stephens said in his letter that he was leaving Ireland for America, the main object of his visit was to hopefully raise funds for his organisation. We have he said, renamed ourselves 'The Fenians' after the mythical band of Celtic warriors called Fianna, who centuries before had also fought to free Ireland from its oppressors. In closing he said he was very reluctant to leave Ireland at this time but as usual he was chronically short of funds. He had he said sent emissaries to sympathisers in New York but they had not been very successful.

He arrived in the United States for the first time on the thirteenth of October eighteen fifty- eight, his first impressions he recalled later was of a shambolic organisation more interested in picnics and parties than raising awareness of the problems faced by the starving and evicted kinsmen still left in their homeland.

Very depressed by what he found, he nevertheless decided to press on with his mission. That winter was the most frustrating time of his life and a lesser man would have quit. But Stephens was as always the supreme optimist and carried on meeting people and preaching his ideas for an Irish Republic freed from tyranny by an armed rebellion with him as its leader. In the spring of eighteen fifty-nine, sad but not disillusioned he returned to Ireland, in his pocket was the results of all his labours the paltry sum he had managed to collect was only six hundred pounds, but once back in Dublin he was soon addressing meetings his head full of new ideas and plans for the future. In later years his contemporaries would all agree that although he was a vain and overbearing person, his capacity for hard work and organising were without parallel in Irish history. He was to build in a few short years virtually single handed an organisation that would eventually become nationwide, and in doing so incorporate many of the secret societies such as the Whiteboys and Ribbonmen, that still very prevalent all over rural Ireland.

Once he had organised The Fenians into an effective force he set about making the detailed plans required to mount a successful armed rising. The next step he made was to establish a constant line of communication with America. The person he proposed for this onerous task was John O' Leary, a man who he both admired and trusted. But this proposal was bitterly opposed by the other senior members of the Brotherhood and John O'Leary himself; was not very keen on the idea. After much debate eventually Stephens, as usual got his way and O'Leary was immediately dispatched to America. His orders were to concentrate on raising as much money for the cause as possible. Also Stephens insisted that from now on all communications from America must only be directed for his attention.

On his arrival in New York, O'Leary worked tirelessly with his American counterparts and he was very fortunate that by this time the Fenian Brotherhood in America had three extremely able leaders, their names were John O' Mahoney, Michael Doheny and General Michael Corcoran. Now that he had at last a very capable agent looking after his organisations interests in America, Stephens was able to concentrate all his considerable energies into substantially increasing the membership of his clandestine grouping in Ireland. Once again he was very fortunate to have as his able lieutenant Thomas Clark Luby, who together with numerous other active members soon recruited thousands of new adherents for the fast expanding Fenian Movement.

This momentum that Stephens, tremendous drive and energy built up was to reach its climax in the year eighteen sixty one. Terence Bellew McManus one of the leaders of the Young Irelanders uprising in eighteen forty-eight, had died in San Francisco. It was decided by the Fenian Brotherhood that they would transport his coffin by railroad across the United States. Large crowds of Irish Americans flocked to see the coffin as it passed through numerous towns and cities on its journey. When the coffin eventually arrived in New York it was taken to Saint Patrick's Cathedral to lie in state; once again thousands of mourners came to pay their last respects to one of their heroes before the body was shipped back for burial in Ireland.

James Stephens was determined that once the coffin arrived in Ireland he would personally make all the arrangements for the funeral. But as soon as the body reached Dublin his problems began, firstly the Archbishop of Ireland would not allow the coffin into his Cathedral. The next problem was that the Archbishop forbade any of his priests to officiate at the funeral. Stephens was not to be thwarted and with help of a sympathetic priest named Patrick Lavelle he overcame this problem. With everything now in place the stage was set for what was to prove a spectacular propaganda success for Stephens and The Fenians. The date of the funeral was set for tenth of November eighteen sixty- one and the day's events are still talked about until this day.

On that morning the weather was freezing cold and the streets of Dublin were deep in slush from the heavy snow that had fallen during the night. But the inclement weather did not deter the people of Dublin as it was later estimated that a crowd of over thirty thousand mourners lined the streets. In was an event superbly orchestrated by Stephens, horsemen dressed mainly in black and carrying batons kept the vast crowds in order. An official delegation had arrived from America including Michael Doheny and John O'Mahoney two of the deceased's old comrades in arms. At the graveside one of the Americans gave a formal funeral oration by torchlight and then the radical priest Patrick Laveller spoke the following eulogy "I am proud to see the people of Ireland and of Dublin are not dead and that they have hope and that though the prophet be dead the spirit he evoked will outlive him and even in the present generation raise his country from degradation to the glory of a nation." At the conclusion of his oration his words were greeted by cheers and clapping that seemed to deeply embarrass him.

From the time of the McManus funeral The Fenian organisation really began to flourish and in early eighteen sixty- two, Stephens accompanied by his close friend Thomas Clark Luby, embarked on an organising tour of Ireland. These tours were to become a regular event during the following years and they were to give him enormous satisfaction because they were usually a great success and he was always at his best when he was organising and recruiting new members. In the summer of eighteen sixty two in an attempt to raise funds in Ireland as they were still desperately short of money, he decided to start his own newspaper, "The Irish People" with John O'Leary, (now back from America) as editor and O'Donovan Rossa as his business manager. The Irish People, although not the financial success that he had hoped, did provide a platform from which he could constantly expand his ideas for the future government of Ireland. In numerous articles he reminded the Irish people of the political freedom that The Fenian Brotherhood enjoyed in the United States. How was it he wrote, that the immigrant Irish in America had more freedom to express their opinion about the way Ireland was governed than the poor oppressed people who remained at home. Things would have to change, he went onto write, the people must be heard and their grievances listened to he warned the authorities or trouble would undoubtedly ensue.

At that time he had high hopes of much needed supplies of arms and equipment arriving from The United States, but all thoughts of receiving help from America were dashed with the start of their Civil War.

With the outbreak of the American Civil War many Irish Americans soon joined the conflict, fighting for both sides North and South. Obviously during the following four years of bloody carnage they were to gain a unique experience of modern warfare. For Stephens and the Fenian Brotherhood, the hope was that they would use this expertise in the liberation of the Old Country when the conflict eventually finished. But he knew that they needed organising and so in eighteen sixty-four, he decided to return to America. This visit was to be a great personal triumph, coming as it did at the conclusion of the Civil War. He went on a successful tour of the victorious Union Armies recruiting many of his fellow countrymen into The Fenian Brotherhood. On returning to New York he boasted that there were now one hundred thousand highly trained military men ready to fight to free Ireland. In a letter he wrote to me at the end of that year he said that we are bound for action next year. "I ask you in the name of God, to believe that no others, after us can bring the cause to the test of battle and that our battle must be entered at some time in the coming year."

With the ending of the Civil War the Fenians in the United States, did indeed become more aware of the possibility of an armed rising in Ireland and much to Stephens, pleasure supplies of money increased considerably. At the same time a number of envoys were sent over from America to try and ascertain if the organisation in Ireland was indeed ready for action. In March eighteen sixty five, Colonel T. J. Kelly arrived in Dublin on a fact finding mission. On his arrival he was met by Stephens and his lieutenants. They took him on a whistle stop tour of their organisation around Dublin, and the surrounding towns and tried hard to impress their illustrious guest. Their efforts proved fruitful, because he was very impressed by what he had seen. On his return to America he immediately reported back to The Brotherhood in New York, that everyone in Ireland was now ready for action. Furthermore he was heartened to conclude that over half the occupying military were now Fenian minded.

The person directly responsible for the recruiting of British soldiers and the local Irish militia was a young member of Stephen, organisation, a firebrand called John Devoy. Devoy in addition to the success he had achieved in recruiting thousands for the cause also managed to bring over from England seventeen deserters from the British Army to work in Dublin as drillmasters. In a few years under the leadership of Stephens, together with dynamic young zealots like Devoy, the organisation had expanded rapidly all over Ireland. Using any means whatsoever but normally under the cover of football matches, drilling proceeded at a furious pace. At the beginning of eighteen sixty-five, Stephens boasted that he had nearly eighty-five thousand men organised, the only problem was the lack of rifles. In America, O' Mahoney issued a final call for funds and in the month of August alone he raised over thirty thousand dollars for the cause.

At the end of August the country held its breath as it was very evident that something drastic was about to happen. Stephens later recalled that he was certain that his hour had arrived and it was now time to rid Ireland of the oppressor. But on the twelfth of September the Government struck, 'The Irish People' newspaper was suppressed and its office was seized. Its editorial staff Thomas Luby, John O'Leary, and Jeremiah O'Donovan Rossa were immediately arrested and all telegraphic communication with Southern Ireland was suspended. Although Stephens had always urged his followers to be careful with security at all times, the authorities had two agents highly placed in the organisation feeding them with information. At the time of the arrests in Dublin, Stephens had somehow managed to avoid capture but on the morning of the eleventh of November the house in Sandy mount, near Dublin where he was hiding was surrounded by police and he and his colleagues were arrested. All hope of a rising now quickly evaporated and the Americans who had come over to help fled the country.

With the arrest of the Chief Organiser the secret military council of the Fenians now met and elected General Millen an American as its temporary commander. At this meeting they discussed ways of freeing Stephens from Richmond Prison and Devoy was instructed to make an attempt.

Captain Thomas Kelly and John Devoy masterminded his sensational escape from prison with the aid of two warders named Byrne and Breslin who were both sworn Fenians. It was Breslin who let Stephens out of his cell in the middle of a stormy night on the twenty fourth of November, eighteen sixty-five. Then with Byrnes help he brought him to where the escape party were waiting with a rope ladder this was then thrown over the outer wall. With the help of the two Fenian warders Stephens quickly scaled the wall and disappeared into the city of Dublin. The authorities immediately offered a reward of one thousand pounds for his capture but fortunately he was never betrayed.

For Stephens this disappointingly would prove to be the highpoint of his political career, because whilst in hiding that winter in Dublin, he made the fateful decision to call off the rising. This decision was to ultimately cost him the leadership of the organisation he had so painstakingly set up. More arrests were made that winter including the capture of John Devoy and his associates. But Stephens although much sought after, was once again smuggled out of the country this time with the help of the dashing Colonel Kelly. Kelly managed to arrange a passage for him on a collier bound for Scotland, which somehow avoided the stringent search parties at Kingstown harbour. But once at sea the collier was caught in a terrible storm that raged for over twenty four hours. When the storm finally abated the collier managed to dock in Arbroath on the east coast of Scotland. Obviously Stephens, was very relieved at landing safely and after a nights rest they caught a train to London.

Both Kelly and Stephens realised they could now relax as they knew the authorities would not be looking for them in London and so they spent the night in a hotel. The next day they travelled across town to London Bridge Station where they caught the boat train to Paris, en route for America. Tragically this was to be the start of more than thirty years in exile for James Stephens from the country he so loved and fought for.

During those hectic few years unsurprisingly I only received a couple of hastily written notes from my cousin. From its outset I had been an avid reader of his newspaper The Irish People but worried that the inflammatory articles that appeared daily would soon attract the attention of the authorities in Dublin Castle. Obviously I had seen the Fenians secretly drilling and preparing locally and was aware that trouble was brewing. Deep down I knew from past experience that the government would be watching the situation carefully and so I was not at all surprised when the Fenian leaders were arrested. For this reason I had forbidden my sons to join the Brotherhood, explaining to them that we might be useful again in the future as a safe house. I went on to explain to them that I had promised James Stephens that I would never become outwardly involved politically in his organisation because I could compromise myself with the authorities.

It was a surprise then when in March eighteen sixty-six, I received the following letter from my cousin, sent from New York.

Dear Patrick,

You have obviously heard of my dramatic escape from Richmond Jail, Fortunately I somehow managed to reside undetected in Kildare Street, in the centre of Dublin for many months. Whilst residing there I had numerous discussions about the rising, but I held the view that not enough rifles and ammunition were available to mount a successful armed insurrection. I also became aware that a damaging split had occurred amongst our supporters in America. This split made it imperative for me to go to the United States in order to reassert my authority on the organisation there. Sadly on arriving in New York I was deeply dismayed to find that the split between the two factions was too deep to reconcile. The main faction led by Colonel John Roberts, was now in the ascendancy and was determined much against my will to invade Canada. But I found to my horror that their preparations were now at a very advanced stage and could not be stopped It was only now that I have come to realise that the men of action here have now taken over the Brotherhood and they will not be deterred from their course. Although I beg and pray that any action against the invader must take place in Ireland, I am certain that any attack upon Canada would be a total disaster to our cause.

185

My problems here multiply by the day and as I sit here writing this letter my thoughts return to the wonderful week I spent with you and your family and I wonder in private why I set out on this journey which has caused me to lose everything including any hope of ever returning to my beloved Ireland.

Please give my blessing to your wife Catherine and your sons,
Yours sincerely James.

This was the only time in my life that I ever heard Stephens have regrets at the crusade he had started on.

The year of eighteen sixty-six would prove to be Stephens last as Head Centre of The Brotherhood. At a series of meetings held in his lodgings in New York that started in early December, he argued again and again for a postponement of the rising. His argument as always was that the organisation had a serious lack of military resources in Ireland. But subsequently much to his chagrin he was accused of cowardice, then after much rancour he was deposed and the leadership passed to Colonel Thomas Kelly. Having deposed Stephens, the next step taken by the new leadership was to cross the Atlantic and begin the rising in Ireland. Much to his credit, Stephens wrote at once on their behalf to the leaders of his organisation in Dublin, explaining that he was in bad health and feared that he was not long for this world. Consequently he urged them that in his absence to rise up should Colonel Kelly give the order.

What subsequently occurred in eighteen sixty-seven, was the complete disaster that Stephens had sadly prophesied. Government informers had infiltrated into the leadership of The Brotherhood in Ireland and an informer named John Joseph Corydon had made the authorities aware of the organisations plans. Once again through a series of raids, many of the leaders were arrested before the rising even began. What followed were a few sporadic incidents but they were soon crushed. Many of those arrested were to get long harsh prison sentences and were eventually to become a thorn in the government's side, these desperate men included amongst their number Michael Davitt, of whom we will hear much about later.

On concluding the story about my cousin James Stephens, I am very sorry to write that he was to spend the most of his life in extreme poverty scratching a living in Paris. Sadly he was always short of funds but from time to time some of his old comrades visited him bringing with them donations they had collected from well-wishers. With the collapse of the rising in eighteen sixty-seven, a splinter group of The Fenians began to resort to extreme measures, including a dynamite campaign against targets on the main land of Britain, Stephens denounced in the strongest possible way all forms of extremism, and assassinations of government officials.

We still received the occasional letter from him on his return to exile in Paris where he eventually married, but sadly marriage would only add to his financial problems. Catherine and I would agonise about his money problems and on occasions I managed to organise a collection on his behalf amongst his supporters in the Charleville district. On receiving these donations Stephen, always wrote thanking us for our kindness and explained how much he and his wife appreciated our friendship in his hour of need.

With the failure of the rising membership of the Fenian party dwindled with most of its leaders either in prison or in exile. But as their influence waned Charles Parnell's star was in the ascendancy because in The House of Commons in Westminster, he had managed to thrust the problems of Ireland to the forefront of the political agenda. Also with the direct action being taken by The Land League, under the dynamic leadership of Michael Davitt many of the grievances of us tenant farmers were now being debated in Parliament for the first time. It seemed ironic after years of total neglect many Members of Parliament were now complaining that Irelands, problems were taking up most of the available time.

Subsequently although the influence of the Fenians and Stephens appeared to wane his legacy still remains with us until this day. His idea for a cultural revival has found its outlet with the formation of the Gaelic Association, with the emphasis on the playing of Gaelic football and hurling and his hope of a revival of the Celtic language the legacy and aspirations of the man remain with us.

He was to finally return to Ireland from exile on the twenty fifth of September eighteen ninety-one, after making a solemn pledge to the government that he would never again play an active part in politics. By a strange coincidence on the same ship was that other great Irish patriot of the nineteenth century Charles Parnell. It was only the personal intersession of Parnell, that had allowed James Stephens to return but although they were fellow passengers ironically they never met. Tragically for Parnell and the country he fought so hard for this was to be his last journey to Ireland for he was to die soon after. On his return James was as usual strapped for cash, but this time his prayers were to be answered. Many of his old friends and compatriots now rallied to his support and a fund was set up and sufficient monies were collected to buy a house for him and his long suffering wife, this would enable them to live in comfort to the end of their days.

Unfortunately their comfortable life together was not to last, because on fourteenth of November eighteen ninety-two, after a short illness Mrs Stephens died. The poor woman was only fifty-two years, but after years of poverty and stress her body was worn out. James is still much admired today and is often called by his old name The Fenian Chief, or as he prefers The Phoenix. Even now after all his years in the wilderness he still predicts that one day his dream of an Irish Republic will rise out of the ashes like the mythical Phoenix. Looking back over the nineteenth century the irony is that the three great Irish Patriots, O'Connell, Parnell, and Stephens were never the same force after they had been imprisoned. For some unknown reason arrest and incarceration had affected their confidence and judgement.

I still receive the odd letter from him but I find it hard to reply because my eyesight has rapidly deteriorated and any thoughts I had of going to visit him in Dublin must now be forgotten. But my lasting memory of my cousin was as a friend, who helped me and my family obtain employment that allowed me to feed and cloth my family in our hour of need.

In concluding my story about Stephens I hope that all the sacrifices he made during his lifetime for Ireland and its people will never be forgotten and the flame that he lit although at times virtually extinguished will burn forever.

CHAPTER NINE

Although in the previous chapter I have written in great detail about my cousin James Stephens, for the ordinary people of Ireland this latest botched insurrection once again meant that we were subjected to virtual military occupation with thousands of troops and militia flooding into every area of the country. As we have seen Stephens had tried to persuade the firebrands in his organisation to postpone the rising but to no avail and in the following narrative gleaned from newspapers at the time I will give my account of what happened next.

By the year of eighteen sixty-six it was obvious that Dublin Castle, the centre of administration in Ireland, was seriously alarmed that an armed rebellion was about to engulf them. There were constant reports of men drilling and organising all over the country and rumours that highly trained veterans of The American Civil War had arrived in Ireland to lead the rebels. These worries were to become a reality in the first few months of eighteen sixty-seven. The Fenian Brotherhood had actively been recruiting in England and was particularly active in the North, especially in Liverpool and Manchester with their large immigrant populations. These Fenian activists had decided to raid Chester Castle hoping to obtain much-needed rifles and ammunition which would then be taken directly to Dublin on the steamships that crossed the Irish Sea from Holyhead in Wales.

The raid was planned for February the eleventh and early that morning it was noticed that strangers had started to arrive in the town in large numbers. These men, many of whom were labourers had come by train from towns all over the north east of England. By early afternoon it was said there were over a thousand Irishmen waiting for the signal to occupy Chester Castle. But the organiser of the attack Captain John McCafferty had learned in advance that the authorities had been made aware of his plans and so at the eleventh hour he managed to call off the raid. The guard at Chester Castle had been strengthened and a detachment of elite soldiers were on their way by express train from London to thwart any attempted attack. With considerable speed McCafferty and his agents got the message to their compatriots to abort the project. It was later reported that the local police force found large quantities of arms and ammunition dumped in the vicinity of Chester railway station.

Forewarned by their English counterparts the Dublin police arrested dozens of Irish labourers as they fled by steamer from England. Most of them had given up their jobs in England and had arrived back in Ireland penniless. McCafferty was himself, arrested but gave an alias of William Jackson, but unfortunately when searched by detectives a ring was found in the lining of his jacket inscribed "Erin I love thee and thy patriots," Presented to Captain John McCafferty, IRB by the Detroit Circle of the Fenian Brotherhood as a token of our esteem. It was not known at this time but one of McCaffertys own men had been giving the authorities information for months; this man John Joseph Corydon was a well-trusted Fenian, who had penetrated the organisation on behalf of the British authorities.

When the debacle at Chester Castle became known the remaining leaders of the organisation in Ireland sent urgent messages to every district of the country postponing the rising. Then at a meeting of the top military leaders of The Fenian Brotherhood in London a new date, the fifth of March was agreed. But tragically once again this information was given to the government by Corydon, who had travelled to England with a senior figure in the New York IRB named General Massey. Massey had arrived in London with orders to link up with the fellow conspirators and then immediately begin the insurrection. After this crucial meeting in the military leadership he hurried back to Ireland and began to make urgent preparations for the start of the rising. On the evening of the fourth of March when General Massey stepped off a train at Limerick Junction he was tapped on the shoulder by a detective. It was only when he was arrested that he realised that his friend and confident was the traitor Corydon. A man of disrepute Corydon had betrayed him along with all the Fenian plans. It later transpired that he had been giving information to the authorities since September eighteen sixty-six.

Unaware of the disaster that had engulfed its high command, the Irish Republican Army was on the march in Dublin, Cork, Tipperary, Clare, and Limerick. There were two successful attacks on barracks on the outskirts of Dublin, firstly at the town of Stepaside and then at Glen Cullen. Cheered on by their success the rebels by now a force of around several hundred attacked a strong force of police at the town of Taillight south of the City, but it was reported that on this occasion the police were organised and when they opened fire the rebels fled leaving their dying and badly wounded colleagues where they fell. Worse was to follow at the town of Drogheda when forty policemen armed with the new Lee Enfield quick firing rifles routed a body of over one thousand Fenians.

Much nearer to home at the local town of Kilmallock the barracks were attacked by a group of rebels with Colonel Dunn, a resident of Charleville as their leader. It was later reported in the newspaper that fifteen police in the barracks had come under attack from a determined band of Fenians, led by a captain wearing a dark green uniform and a slouch hat with a large feather in it. The attackers were driven off after a three hour gun battle in which at least two rebels died. The report also went on to say that one of the constables had kept a note book beside him and during the intervals between firing had written the names of any of the attackers he recognised. Elsewhere in County Cork the Fenians had one of their few successes when two thousand rebels led by J.F.O' Brien and William Mackey captured the police barracks at Ballyknocknane. The same armed band then successfully carried out sabotage on the Great Southern Railway, tearing up rails, destroying points and cutting telegraph wires they also managed to derail the Dublin express without causing any injury to the passengers.

Also in County Cork a band of well-organised rebels captured a coastguard station at Knockadoon and made off with the arms they found there. On the morning of the sixth of March there was a brief gun battle in Tipperary at a place called Ballyhurst, a force of Fenians, under the command of an Irish-American officer T.F. Bourke had assembled at the site of an Old Danish earthwork. But before Bourke could organise his men they were attacked by a military column. In the ensuing gun battle the better trained and armed soldiers fired a volley and the rebels fled in total disorder, Bourke himself was soon captured and when searched he was found to have a copy of the Fenian oath which read, "In the presence of Almighty God Solemnly I swear that I will not bear arms against, or by word or act give information, aid or comfort to the enemies of the Irish Republic, until regularly relieved of this obligation. So help me God."

Various actions continued around the country, but it was soon obvious that with the arrest of the military leadership the rising was doomed to failure. The last dramatic action was fought out in Kilclooney Wood in County Tipperary, when the three leaders of the successful raid at the coastguard station at Knockadoon were surprised by a military column. After a running fight through the woods that lasted the whole day one rebel Peter O'Neil Crowley was killed and his friends Thomas McClure and Patrick Kelly were eventually arrested. Back in Charleville, Colonel Dunn the leader of the party that carried out the attack against barracks in Killmallock was arrested and after a brief trial he was freed on condition that he returns to his native America. The local men

191

who had been identified and incarcerated were not so fortunate, because after a brief trial their sentences were both long and severe. Thankfully for us my two sons had reluctantly taken my advice and had not become members of the IRB and although they were never to acknowledge that my advice was sound, they were both shocked and horrified when they heard of the treatment that was inflicted on the Fenian prisoners. While the sporadic actions continued it was reported daily that the military were arresting suspects and Martial Law was in force in many areas including the district around Charleville.

Unfortunately The Fenian Brotherhood in America had not been made aware of the disaster that had occurred in Ireland, so consequently in April of that fateful year a privateer that they had fitted out set sail bound for the coast of Ireland. On board were thirty eight officers all holding commissions in the Irish Republican Army. In the hold of the ship packed in piano cases, sewing machine cases and wine casks all labelled for Cuba, were about five thousand modern breech-loading and repeating rifles and one and a half million rounds of ammunition. In fact all equipment that a successful rising would have required. In late May, the privateer now rechristened the "Erin's Hope" slipped unnoticed into Sligo Bay; there to meet it was Richard O'Sullivan Burke, the Fenian armaments organiser. After weeks of patiently waiting for the arrival of The Erin's Hope, he was obliged to row out to the ship with the sad news that there was not the slightest hope of getting any help from the people of Sligo. This must have been a shattering blow to the ships company but after coming so far they were reluctant to give up. So they left Sligo Bay and sailed south along the coast looking for a suitable landing site.

Eventually they were to sail as far as Dungarvan, County Wexford, but by then it was the beginning of June and their provisions were running low. Obviously they were now becoming desperate and after many debates it was decided to land a few of the officers and then sail the ship back to New York. A Waterford fisherman named Whelan had come alongside the "Erin's Hope" and agreed to land two of the officers. But stupidly twenty-eight of them jumped aboard his small fishing boat. Whelan fearful that his boat would capsize landed them all in three feet of water off the coast. The sight of the twenty eight desperate men wading ashore obviously caused a stir in the local community and within hours word of their landing had reached the ears of the militia. This led to a thorough search of the area and the poor unfortunates still soaked to the skin were all arrested within twenty four hours.

Sporadic incidents continued to be reported throughout the summer of that year but the event that was to make the greatest impact on public opinion in Ireland for the rest of my life actually happened in Manchester, England. Unknown to the English authorities, the Headquarters of the Fenian organisation was now based in London, as it was thought that they would be safer there. In London, under the noses of the security forces they audaciously held a convention in the summer of eighteen sixty seven. At this meeting Captain T.J. Kelly was elected Chief Executive. Kelly was by now well known as a senior member of The Brotherhood and was being hunted by the police in England and Ireland but with the traitor Corydon now exposed; the organisation could maintain a much more effective level of security.

The most dramatic event of that year actually began on the eleventh of September, when police arrested two men who were acting suspiciously in a shop doorway in the centre of Manchester. At the time of their arrest the two men gave their names as Wright and Williams. But within hours their real names were known to the police. By chance the two men arrested were none other than Captain Kelly and another high ranking Fenian named Captain Deasy the commander in Cork City on the night the rising began in March. A week later the most serious Fenian action for many years was fought on the streets of Manchester.

It was later reported that an unescorted prison van carrying Kelly and Deasy in handcuffs from the police court to Bellevue Gaol, was surrounded by thirty armed Irishmen as it passed under a railway arch. Some of the armed gang forced the terrified police on the outside of the van to lie down on the ground thus ensuring that they and any of the bystanders could not intervene. Whilst the others immediately started to batter open the locked van endeavouring to rescue Kelly and Deasy. Inside the van with the two Fenians, were some other prisoners and Police Sergeant Brett. Called upon by the Fenians to unlock the door and surrender Brett refused, so a Fenian named Peter Rice fired a bullet at the door hoping that it would smash the lock, but tragically the bullet mortally wounded the hapless Sergeant. While the poor man lay dying one of the women prisoners in the van searched his pockets and found the keys and passed them out through the ventilator. Within minutes Kelly and Deasy, still in handcuffs had been released from their cells and were down from the van. Still handcuffed they jumped over a wall and then ran across the railway lines and to this day they have never been recaptured.

What happened next has added to our deep sense of injustice and will be remembered for years to come by the people of Ireland. After the tragic murder of Sergeant Brett the authorities began to arrest every Irishman that they could find. The identity procedure the police then used was so flawed that it was actually very surprising that of the five men charged, four actually had been involved in one way or another in the rescue attempt. One of the five men charged was named Maguire a Royal Marine home on leave at the time of his arrest and who had never been at or near the scene of the crime, the others were Edward Condon, William Allen, Phillip Larkin and Michael O Brien. At the trial the counsel for the prosecution insisted that William Allen had fired the fatal shot. In fact this was not true, as we now know Peter Rice had fired the gun and he along with Kelly and Deasy had managed to escape to America. The trial itself was a forgone conclusion and Allen, Larkin, O'Brien and Condon, together with the unfortunate Maguire were all sentenced to death by hanging.

At the end of the trial all the accused denied firing the fatal shot, and each one said in turn how much they regretted the death of Sergeant Brett. Much to the irritation of the authorities they all also made nationalistic speeches from the dock. In his speech Condon made the most famous remark of all, when he said, "I have nothing to retract or take back" he declared, "I can only say God save Ireland" and then as the London Times reporter in court wrote before the Fenians were led away they all declared in unison, "God Save Ireland."

After much deliberation by the judiciary, it was later recognised with huge embarrassment that in Maguire's case there had been a terrible miscarriage of justice. Fortunately he was eventually given a free pardon, but obviously this decision cast doubt on the evidence given against the other defendants. As an American, Condon was in fact reprieved, but only after intense diplomatic pressure by the United States Embassy. Its intervention on behalf of O'Brien who was also American was unsuccessful as he had been released by the British authorities in eighteen sixty-six on condition he returned o home.

The final chapter of this terrible year was the public hanging of Allen, Larkin, and O'Brien on a foggy morning on the twenty fourth of November eighteen sixty-seven. The executions caused a sensation in Ireland, especially when it was reported that both Larkin and O'Brien suffered terrible agony as a result of bungling by the hangman.

The hurried trial and the subsequent hangings were to have serious consequences for Anglo Irish relations during the next twenty years; because although most of the leaders of the Fenians Party were now in exile, their legacy still remained and as we will see they were to have a profound effect on the future politics of Ireland. As a consequence of what was seen as pure revenge, the Irish people now had an immense amount of sympathy for the Fenians and their cause. It was universally perceived that these men had only been executed because they were Irish patriots. At Masses and services all over Ireland for many weeks following the executions, priests prayed for the souls of the three men who soon became known as the Manchester Martyrs. One of the biggest of the Requiem Masses that winter was one I managed to attend at the Cathedral in Cork City, where a congregation of thousands heard the Bishop pray for the repose of the souls of these three brave Irishmen.

These executions were the first carried out on Irish patriots since the execution of Thomas Emmet in the previous century. Within days a song written by an Irish Republican sympathiser named T.D. Sullivan, with the words " God save Ireland !" cried the heroes, "God save Ireland!" say we all, had became the National Anthem of the Irish people and to this day is sung before closing time in every public house in the land. After the successful escape of Kelly and Deasy in Manchester, another rescue attempt was made to release a prominent Fenian, Richard O'Sullivan Bourke, from Clerkenwell Prison in London where he was awaiting trial. This rescue attempt was to go desperately wrong, when on the afternoon of the twelfth of December eighteen sixty-seven, a policeman disturbed two men who had placed a barrel against the wall of the Prison. One of the men on seeing the policeman approaching lit the fuse attached the barrel and then started to run away. The ensuing huge explosion wrecked the prison wall and totally destroyed a number of houses in the vicinity and damaged many others in the area. Altogether twelve Londoners tragically died as a result of this horrific act and over thirty were badly injured many of the poor souls losing their limbs.

This terrible atrocity in the heart of the capital of the Empire came as a tremendous shock to the British Government and created panic across the length and breadth of the country. As panic slowly subsided, public opinion in England started to focus on the Irish problem and one politician in particular had been thinking long and hard about this thorny issue. This man was William Ewart Gladstone, who finally became Prime Minister in eighteen sixty-eight. As we will see Gladstone although very reluctant at times did eventually enact laws that enabled us and our fellow tenant farmers to purchase the land we farmed.

That winter and early spring Ireland was once again under the control of the military, arrests were carried out on any person thought to have Fenian sympathies. But Thank God life slowly returned to normal and instead of politics dominating the news; for once it was the weather and the good farm prices. One of the consequences of the comparatively steady improvement in our standard of living was the huge drop in the number of poor souls being forcibly evicted from their farms; the actual number of evictions had thankfully dropped that year to the lowest on record. This in turn led to a reduction in the number of young people emigrating; this factor alone seemed to give us all a feeling of hope for the future.

All the upheaval caused by the failed rising and its aftermath would eventually lead to an immense change in the political climate in Ireland. The overriding concern for all of us tenant farmers was and always has been, fixture of tenure, as I have previously stated evictions had fallen but we did not know for how long this situation would last. The loss of our livelihood was bad enough, but as tenants there was no compensation for any improvements that we had made to the land during your tenure and so this obviously meant that many years of backbreaking toil could be lost at the whim of the landowner or his agent. Land agitation and a greater say in the affairs of Ireland, leading ultimately to a call for Home Rule were to dominate politics both in Ireland and the House of Parliament in London for the rest of my lifetime.

Three new laws on voting helped pave the way for the upsurge in the changes that were about to take place in the forthcoming elections. The first of these laws was passed in the year eighteen sixty- seven, this crucial new legislation increased the number of people who were eligible to vote. Then in eighteen seventy-two the secret ballot was introduced, this law was to go a long way in stopping open intimidation of voters by landlords or others with vested interests. In hindsight this legislation would ultimately strengthen the ability of us tenant farmers to express our desire at the ballot box for a better life. The last important law change was introduced in eighteen eighty-four when the vote was given to agricultural workers, this was to treble the number of Irish voters.

With these changes the Irish Party in the House of Commons, first under the leadership of Isaac Butt and then subsequently under the dynamic stewardship of Charles Stewart Parnell, was to ultimately propel the Irish question into the forefront of British politics for decades to come.

CHAPTER TEN

As previously stated with the leadership of the Irish Republican Brotherhood, either in prison or exile the authorities hoped that the Irish people would gradually return to their senses and reject all forms of militancy. But times had changed and the government was about to find that over the next decade compromises must be made as the political situation in both England and Ireland was about to change for ever.

As mentioned in the previous chapters Isaac Butt was in fact the founder of the first effective Irish Parliamentary Party in Westminster. He promised before being elected that he would be able to coerce the Irish members to speak as one voice in the House of Commons on Irish matters.

Butt had risen to prominence as a young barrister who had famously defended the Young Irelanders, William Smith O'Brien and Thomas Meagre after the abortive rising in eighteen forty-eight. He had also defended some of the prominent Fenians who went on trial in eighteen sixty-five. The interesting thing about Isaac Butt was that not only was he a senior figure in the organisation calling for tenants rights, he was also one of the leading figures in the movement calling for an amnesty for all Irish nationalists now held in prisons in both Ireland and England. Not content with his involvement in these two causes, he had also become active in the Home Government Association. The genius of Butt was that he was able to pull these three movements together to form the first co-ordinated organisation calling for Home Rule for Ireland.

This would result ultimately in the now famous election victory in Kerry in eighteen seventy-two when for the first time a Home Ruler, by the name of Blennerhassett was elected to Parliament. His election was achieved against a background of tremendous opposition, which even included the hierarchy of the Catholic Church. As a result of this electoral victory a conference was called and in eighteen seventy-four The Irish Home Rule League was founded. Subsequently at the General Election a few weeks later, fifty-nine Home Rulers were elected. This all seemed to bode well for the future as at long last it would appear the people of Ireland would have a party that was going to air their grievances in the Parliament at Westminster.

Sadly once again our hopes were dashed as unfortunately the party under Butt's Leadership in the House of Commons was to prove very ineffectual. This was because only about twenty five of its members consistently worked together. Butt himself was by this time in terrible debt and he had to work extremely long hours as a barrister in order to satisfy his creditors. Unfortunately this situation meant that he was in effect only a part time leader. In the election of eighteen seventy-four, a small number of Fenians had been elected as Home Rulers, one of whom was the firebrand Joe Biggar. These Fenian members of Butts parliamentary party became more and more restless at the lack of progress that was being made. This frustration would ultimately lead Biggar, to practise a technique of obstructing the business in the House of Commons by reading long extracts from previous Acts of Parliament. His aim was specifically to delay the passage of a bill to grant the Government special powers in Ireland.

Then on the now fateful night of the twenty second of April eighteen seventy-four, Biggar spoke for over four hours non-stop against this coercion bill. As he rambled on that historic night, a new member entered the House of Commons. Unknown by virtually anyone in the chamber at that time, this man would soon replace Isaac Butt as the leader of the Irish Party. Ultimately in a few short months his name would be on everyone's lips and he would eventually be named the Uncrowned King of Ireland. This recently elected Member of Parliament for County Meath was an Irish aristocrat and a Protestant, educated at Cambridge University, his name Charles Stewart Parnell.

Parnell was to make his maiden speech four days later when he objected to a remark made by a former Chancellor of the Exchequer, who had said "Ireland is but a geographical fragment of the British Isles," to which Mr Parnell had famously replied, "Ireland was not a geographical fragment but a Nation."

In eighteen sixty-seven, William Ewart Gladstone as we have seen was elected as Liberal Prime Minister for the first time. After the recent tragedies at Manchester and Clerkenwell, he realised that he had to address the age old problems of Ireland. From the time of his first ministry until his retirement in eighteen ninety-two, although criticised by both English and Irish politicians, overall I think he was the first Prime Minster that actually achieved improvements for us tenant farmers. The first of many measures that his government was to pass for the improvement of the Irish people was the Act of Disestablishment of the Church of Ireland. In my view this was long over due.

The most vital issue that Gladstone addressed was the introduction of his first Land Bill, this was to be the first of many very important measures he would introduce in the next twenty or so years. This Bill introduced in eighteen seventy, had as its main aim the provision that henceforth any landlord who wanted to evict a tenant for any reason would have to pay a sum of money to that tenant in compensation for any improvements he had made to the farm during his tenure. Although at first glance this looked like a giant step forward for us tenant farmers, it soon was pointed out by the Irish Members of Parliament in Westminster that the tenant farmers did not want compensation for eviction, but total freedom from the terrible threat of losing their farms and livelihood. Public opinion in Ireland soon swung in favour of the Irish Party on this matter, as it was quickly noted that a landlord could pay compensation to his sitting tenant and then evict him. He could then increase the rent to any new tenant. Or alternatively he could immediately raise the rent of the sitting tenant as an insurance against any loss he might incur in the future and then if he eventually saw fit could still evict him and his family. Finally if the landlord was determined to get rid of his tenant, he could raise the rent by an amount that the tenant could not possibly afford and provided that it was not at a level that the Law Courts defined as exorbitant, he was then within his rights to evict the tenant without any compensation whatsoever.

It seemed to me at the time that what the law needed to establish was what is a fair rent? Once this was established; the law should then protect the tenant farmers from eviction as long as he paid his rent. But at the time most of the Irish farming community did react in a positive manner to Gladstone's policies, as it seemed for the first time that a British Government was at last showing an interest in the problems that had beset the Irish people throughout this century. Against this background of optimism, Isaac Butt presided over the first meeting of the Home Government Association held in Dublin in September eighteen seventy.

Unfortunately there was downright hostility between the remnants of the Fenians and the Irish Parliamentary Party. During this period I also read with great interest about the wide section of Irish opinion that had now been mobilised for the campaign to release the Fenian prisoners still serving long sentences of penal servitude in British prisons for their involvement in the failed insurrection. The main driving force behind the agitation for an amnesty was obviously the Fenian party, which was still a powerful underground movement in Ireland and was still receiving substantial funds from its sympathisers in America.

The senior organiser of the Amnesty Movement was John Nolan and under his auspices this organisation brought to the attention of the public in both England and Ireland the atrocious treatment that was being inflicted on the Fenian prisoners by the British authorities. It focused particularly on the appalling treatment suffered by O'Donovan Rossa, who after throwing the contents of his slops bucket at a Prison Governor, had been sentenced to thirty five days in solitary confinement. For the duration of thirty five days he was manacled with his hands tied together behind his back. The only exception to this was at meal times, when they allowed him to have his hands manacled in the front. He was to say later when asked how he had remained sane during this terrible ordeal that he had spent his days reading and had somehow managed to turn the pages over with his teeth. His ordeal although dreadful, was in fact not as bad as that of Michael Davitt who was incarcerated in the hell-hole called Dartmoor Prison.

Davitt as a young boy of twelve had lost an arm in a factory accident in Lancashire and later as a young man had joined the Fenian party. He was actually in Chester on the day of the aborted attempt to raid Chester Castle for arms. Although he had managed to evade capture on that day, the police eventually arrested him and in eighteen- seventy he was wrongly sentenced to fifteen years penal servitude in Dartmoor Prison for allegedly being involved in an assassination plot. On his arrival at Dartmoor, the authorities realised that because of his physical handicap, he could not work on the gangs mining stones. Instead the brutal regime at the prison had him harnessed to a cart like an animal and for many years he was made to drag stones from the quarry.

After many months of campaigning, the government was ultimately obliged to set up a commission of an enquiry. This enquiry would eventually confirm in its findings, that excessive punishment had been inflicted on the Fenian prisoners by the prison authorities. But all the while John Nolan kept up the pressure and was busy organising mass meetings on behalf of the Amnesty Campaign. At one such meeting at Cabra it was reported, that over two hundred thousand people were in attendance. Realising that he had the authorities worried by the tremendous support that his campaign was having, the next idea Nolan had was to enter O'Donovan Rossa as a Parliamentary candidate for the upcoming by election in Tipperary whilst he was still in prison. When the result was announced, it was no surprise at all that O'Donovan Rossa now thought of in Ireland as a martyr was duly elected in a landslide victory. But he was soon unseated by the authorities, the reason they gave for disqualifying him was that he was a convicted felon.

The Amnesty Movement was to have other major successes at this time, especially when in January eighteen seventy, my cousin John Sarsfield Casey along with ten other Fenians, were released by the British government. They had been transported to penal settlements in Australia, after the aborted rising in eighteen fifty-seven. John Nolan and his associates were on hand when the steamer carrying the released prisoners finally docked in Dublin Harbour. Once ashore mass celebrations swept the city and the returning Fenians were feted like heroes wherever they went. During that week they attended a Pantomime at the Theatre Royal Dublin and when they were shown to their seats, the entire audience rose as one and set up a deafening round of cheering which lasted for several minutes. My cousin John later recalled that he watched in astonishment as people stood on their seats cheering and clapping. He then told me that as the noise gradually abated the orchestra quickly realising the mood of the audience started to play our new unofficial national anthem, "God Save Ireland" at this the audience all stood to attention and sang.

The returning Fenians were mobbed wherever they went and when the train bringing John Sarsfield Casey and his fellow rebels arrived in Cork City, the Cork Herald reported that a line of police with fixed bayonets could not hold back the vast throng of well wishers that had come to welcome their hero's home. Two men from Cork City, Eugene Lombard and Morgan McSweeny, were carried shoulder high by the crowds back to their homes at Coal Quay. When the connecting train eventually brought my cousin John back to Galtee station, I was there to greet him together with hundreds of family, friends and many local Fenian sympathisers. Unfortunately it was not until the following day that I eventually managed to hold a conversation with him. We discussed many subjects that day but when he described the terrible experiences he had endured, it reminded me of the conversations I had with my brother Owen, who had also witnessed the terrible treatment that was handed out by the sadistic prison guards in Australia. On leaving Galtee that evening we shook hands and I wished him well, but I made him also give me a solemn promise that he would never again return to the colony where my brother had been so tragically murdered.

Sadly the other Fenians, still languishing in British prisons were not so lucky; Michael Davitt in particular was to serve another seven terrible years before his release. During that time he began to formulate the ideas that he would later to become famous for. His far sighted plans for challenging the ownership of the land and tenants rights were the foundation of the struggle he embarked upon immediately upon his release. Davitt would eventually become one of the foremost leaders of the movement that obtained major reforms for the tenant farmers in Ireland. But all this was in the future, meanwhile tensions were still rising between the Amnesty Movement and the Tenants Rights Association and it was only the diplomatic skills of Isaac Butt that managed to bring the two organisations together.

While all this was happening in Ireland and at the House of Commons in London, back home in Springfort by the spring of eighteen seventy-two, I was now sixty six and finally beginning to feel my age. The many years of hard work on the railroads and our struggle during the Famine years was finally catching up on me and so with Catherine's encouragement I decided to hand over the running of Springfort to my two sons that were still at home. Our eldest son Michael you may recall had emigrated to America with the assistance of Catherine's brother who worked in the New York. On arriving in America, he was very fortunate that his Uncle Danny had managed to use his connections and obtain employment for him with the New York Police Force. When I read the letters he regularly wrote to us, it would appear that he had made the right decision, but at the time I had been very much opposed to him leaving Ireland. I had been proved wrong in my assumption because once he had joined the police force he had gone from strength to strength and it was not long before he reached the rank of Sergeant. Our only regret was that he was now married with two small daughters and my wife Catherine knew she would never see her grandchildren. Although he sent us photographs at Christmas this only increased my wife's sadness.

So with Michael in America it was left to our two remaining sons William and James to take over the reins from me. All that now remained for us to do was to inform the Land Agent, Mr Grogan, of my decision at the next Gale Day. Gale Day was always on market day in October, when it was normal for the tenant farmers to pay their rent from the proceeds of their harvest. The land agent had known the boys for many years and as always was most helpful, but the only problem was the lease could only be in one person's name. His advice to us was to leave the lease in my name and on my death he promised to ensure that the title would pass to my son. In the long conversation I had with Mr Grogan, he told me that there was growing pressure on the Government to sort out the land question and he thought that given time things could change. Obviously in hindsight, he was to be proved right, but no one then knew of the pain and heartache that would have to follow before things did eventually change for the better.

Having radically changed our farming methods to take advantage of the rising demand for livestock we had obviously reduced our dependence on the growing of crops. This change had added benefits for us because it had also drastically lightened our workload as tillage was very labour intensive. Fortunately livestock prices had increased and the change had been very beneficial as they had increased our income. At the time of deciding to become more involved in rearing livestock, I had advised both my sons to acquire as much knowledge as possible about cattle rearing. Over the years the expertise they gained was to save us a small fortune in veterinary bills. Also their services were always in demand amongst our friends and neighbours. From this time on I gradually stepped back and left them to their own devices. At first I confess I found it hard but gradually life for me became easier and there was now time for me to visit some of my old cronies in town and I was relieved at last from the constant worry of running the farm.

During the next couple of years, life for us became quiet comfortable and the first year that our sons were in charge was the most profitable we ever had at Springfort, a fact that they obviously delighted in reminding me about. For them the chance to rile me gave them great pleasure after all the ribbing that I had given them in the past. As usual Catherine sided with her sons and I pretended to be hurt by their banter.

The following summer after the hay was saved, both Catherine and I decided to have the holiday we had promised ourselves since we were first married but could never afford. We had been advised that Ballybunion in County Kerry was the place we should visit and so after what seemed like weeks of preparation, we finally boarded the train at Charleville Station bound for Killarney. Once in Killarney we caught the connecting train for Tralee and finally arrived at our destination Ballybunion. By the time we found the guest house that our friends had recommended Catherine was like a young girl again. It was for her a dream come true and I had to physically restrain her from making the bed each morning. That week passed by in a flash, the sea air and the wonderful beaches that seemed to stretch for miles with the Atlantic breakers pounding the shores made the pair of us think that we were in heaven. For once in our lives we did not have a care in the world and I felt that it was worth every penny to see how much Catherine benefited from the experience. Each evening after dinner we would go out for a walk along the Strand and on a few occasions we met old friends and went for a couple of drinks. Catherine did not normally drink so each night she was a little tipsy by the time we got into bed and after my problems in the past with alcohol I also drank very sparingly. But sadly our holiday was soon over and we reluctantly made our way back to the railway station and caught the train to Killarney.

On our arrival in Killarney much to Catherine's pleasure she was able to spend the rest of the day shopping for presents for our sons. That evening we were both very tired and exhausted after an enjoyable day so we made our way back to the station and caught the last train to Charleville.

When we arrived back in Springfort, we talked well into the night telling our sons how wonderful our holiday had been. Before going to bed to bed I promised Catherine that our first holiday together would not be our last, and in the next few months we started to make plans for the following year. The next holiday we decided would be to the city of Dublin because from Charleville station, we were now able to travel on the Cork to Dublin express which would get us into Dublin in five hours.

Before planning our Dublin holiday Catherine and I decided to go racing. Horses have always been a passion of mine and it had been a lifetime ambition to actually go to watch them as a spectator. I was not to be disappointed as the thrill of seeing them up close reminded me of when I had my first job working at the Sir Wrixon-Becher stables. Both Catherine and I agreed that although the flat races were enjoyable, the real excitement was watching the horses over the jumps. My enthusiasm for horse racing was obviously more enjoyable when I managed to back a couple of winners. Both of us that autumn thought that this was the beginning of our ambition to visit and enjoy the many places of interest in Ireland now that we had our new found freedom.

That Christmas free from the daily worry of running the farm, we spent our days visiting old friends and family, little knowing this would be our last ever Christmas together. Since my childhood as I have previously said I always enjoyed the Christmas festivities and although my parents were always poor my mother had always tried her best to make the feast of Christmas the special event of our year, even when times were hard and food was scarce, which was more often than not. Catherine and I had tried to carry on this tradition throughout our married life. We always attended early Mass on Christmas Day and afterwards rushed back to Springfort to prepare the dinner for our neighbours and friends especially the poor lonely souls who lived on their own. In the past it had been a struggle, but this year for once we were able to put a feast on the table fit for a king. Everyone who came that year agreed with me when I praised my wife for the wonderful meal she had prepared.

During the evening musicians arrived and the party was soon in full swing, I was even persuaded by my wife to dance and surprised everyone including myself as I danced a Kerry reel. Eventually our friends departed and Catherine and I were both glad to get to bed as we were obviously very tired after a very long day. But for some reason we found it very hard to get to sleep that night so Catherine began to speculate about how long it would be before our two sons found themselves wives and settled down. This subject was her main worry because like all mothers the world over she fretted that her two boys would never find the right girl.

The next morning we all woke bleary eyed and after breakfast set out for Charleville, for the annual hurling match. This year the opponents were Ballyhay a team with a fearsome reputation for foul play. On hearing that the challengers were from Ballyhay, hundreds of eager hurlers had arrived in town many of whom had travelled many miles to participate. Some of them it was later reported had even come from as far a field as the town of Limerick such was the reputation of the opposition. In that time before the advent of properly organised matches, each team could consist of at least one hundred players and this year was no exception, with over two hundred participating. The match traditionally started at the Parish boundary in front of large crowds of eager onlookers who were always sure to shout plenty of words of advice, or in most cases abuse at the players.

Catherine and I watched as the ball was thrown high into the air at a spot called High Pike, this signalled the start the match. Before the ball had even hit the ground a huge roar went up from the local spectators all shouting, "All for Home" which was the traditional war cry of the Charleville supporters. The object of the game was to endeavour to carry the ball to a predetermined spot in the adjacent parish. From the onset of the match Ballyhay were on the offensive as play continued through meadows flooded by the recent heavy rains the water in some places was over a foot deep. But this problem and various other obstacles had to be negotiated before the game reached the river Awbeg. On reaching the river bank a furious melee developed in the midst of which we could see our two boys hacking and kicking for all their worth. But it was not to be Charleville's day and though our team fought gallantly against the odds, they gradually tired and eventually had to concede defeat. Fortunately for everyone concerned there were no serious injuries that year, but in years gone bye it was not uncommon for participants to end up in the infirmary with all sorts of nasty injuries. After the match Catherine and I decided to return home, leaving our sons in town to enjoy the rest of the evening with their team mates and it was way past midnight when our two very weary sons finally arrived home.

With the arrival of the New Year of eighteen seventy-four, we had every reason to be extremely optimistic for the future and to our immense pleasure William told us that he had met a young lady at the Charleville Fair from the local village of Tullilease, named Mary Egan. Obviously my wife Catherine was overjoyed at hearing the news, but I cautioned her optimism by saying that it was too soon to get excited.

During the next few days William acted like a love sick puppy and wandered around the farm in a permanent daze. Both Catherine and I knew the reason for his strange behaviour but kept our thoughts to ourselves. It was obvious to us that he was wondering how he should proceed with his wooing of Mary. After days of indecision he finally plucked up courage and without telling us he headed for the Egan family home. The next day after being constantly grilled by his mother he finally told us what had happened the previous evening. On his arrival at Tullilease, the first person he met was Mary's father John Egan, who asked him in a stern voice what he wanted. William throwing caution to the wind replied that he had come to ask permission to take his daughter Mary to the dance in Charleville on the following Saturday. Mr Egan who later recalled that he was very amused at our sons request and questioned him closely about his background. His attitude was all a charade, because it would appear that his daughter had also been acting strangely and both he and his wife had also realised that she was in love. After his initial rudeness John Egan brought William into the house to meet his family, unfortunately Mary was out in the fields but her brother rushed out to find her. On seeing each other again William told us they were both tongue tied and very embarrassed with

Mary's parents making all the conversation. But when eventually Mr Egan told his daughter that William had asked permission to take her to the dance she begged her father to agree. Her prayers were answered as both her parents gave their consent to her request.

During the next couple of months it seemed that all the work on the farm was being undertaken by our other son James, as William was spending more and more time with Mary and her family at Tullilease. On the weekend before Shrove Tuesday he informed us that he was going to propose to Mary, at Shrove time. We thought this was a little premature as we had not yet even met his future wife. But at William's insistence we gave him our blessing as Shrove time was still traditionally the time for couples to get engaged. On hearing the news Catherine insisted on going to town with him to buy a new suit, as she was anxious that he was well turned out when he proposed to Mary.

On the following Tuesday after breakfast we all wished him luck as he left on his mission to Tullilease. At the time I wondered who was more nervous William or his mother but all I do know is that I was glad when that day was over because Catherine became more and more stressed worrying about the outcome. There was to be no going to bed for any of us that night until William returned. Hours went by with Catherine staring endlessly out of the window and all the while praying for good news. She should not have worried because when William eventually arrived home he told us he was now the happiest man in Ireland, everything had gone well and he had been welcomed into the Egan family.

As was traditional we now had to arrange for Mary and the Egan family to visit Springfort for the most important part of the betrothal procedure, this was the inspection of our farm by the father of bride. This ancient ritual had to be carried out before he gave his full consent to the marriage.

The days leading up to the visit by the Egan's were a nightmare for both me and my son James as each time we tried to disappear we were captured and another job was found for us by either William or Catherine. Morning, noon and night there was a brush thrust into our hand and everything that moved was scrubbed and everything that did not move was painted. By the day of the Egan's visit, Springfort was fit for the Pope himself to come and say the Stations. Catherine sent the three us off to early mass that morning so that she could make her final preparations, her last words to us was not to hang around chatting when the mass finished. So with William nagging us, we were not able to stay for the usual Sunday morning gossip as we were made to rush back home. The waiting was unbearable, but at last we heard the sound of the Egan's horse and trap coming up the lane and William ran down to greet them. They say that first impressions are normally right and on meeting my future daughter in law, I must say that I agree. Because when Mary stepped down from the trap that morning; I realised why my son was so captivated, for although still very young she was extremely attractive and her smile would break anyone's heart.

Later when we chatted together it was soon apparent that she was no ones fool, fortunately this observation was to be proven correct on numerous occasions in the future. After William made the introductions we all sat down for dinner and much to everyone's pleasure at the end of the meal I gave a short speech in which I spoke of the joy we both felt that our son had proposed to their beautiful daughter Mary and we hoped and prayed that the young couple would be happy together in the future. In conclusion I said that Mr and Mrs Egan would always be welcome at Springfort. Later I explained to John Egan that I had recently handed over the management of the farm to my sons. In the circumstances I thought it was only right for William to show his future father-in-law around Springfort in order for him to explain how their new ideas had produced the improvements he would see on his inspection.

For the first time in my life I had to keep a low profile, because Catherine had told me not to interfere and let our son show Mr Egan around the farm. This was very hard for me to do, but deep down I knew she was right. On returning from the inspection, I could tell that Mary's father was very impressed in all that he had seen and for the rest of the day he did not stop asking questions regarding our farming methods. Before he left he expressed the hope that with our help, he could carry out some of the improvements on his farm in Tullilease and so we made arrangements for us to visit them on the following Sunday. After they departed Catherine, who by now was completely exhausted complemented William on his choice and I totally endorsed her feelings. James who had spent most of the day in the background was also very complimentary about his future sister in law.

Now that William was about to get married, we knew that it was time for us to make improvements to the accommodation of our house. It was obvious that an extension would be needed and so with the help of one of my cousin who was a builder in Churchtown, we installed an extra room in the loft which was for James and another room was added onto the side of the house for the newlyweds. With these additions completed William invited Mary and her mother to view the alterations we had made. It was very obvious to us that they were both impressed but Catherine insisted that the future bride should choose her own furnishings for the bedroom. This suggestion was readily accepted and in the following weeks the three women met in town and purchased the necessary furniture and fittings.

The final procedure before the marriage could take place was arranging the dowry; this was the only part of the marriage contract that I always dreaded. I had many discussions with my wife about this matter because we were both aware that the Egan's could ill afford to settle a large dowry on their daughter. My main concern was to avoid embarrassing our son's future in-laws and settle this delicate matter amicably. The only way out of the problem we eventually decided, was for me to meet John Egan in Charleville and discuss the problem over a drink. This meeting confirmed my opinion of the Egan family, they were honest and hard working and like us they had only wanted the best for their children. The matter in hand was soon sorted amicably and we both had an enjoyable evening and before parting we shook hands promising to meet again after the wedding.

With the problem of the dowry now behind us, we started to make preparations for the forthcoming wedding. But once again in my life tragedy struck, because just as I thought that we could now relax and enjoy the last years of our lives together my wife was about to be taken from me. During the whole of our married life, I cannot recall Catherine ever having a day's illness, even in terrible famine years when the fever was rife throughout the country. But all this was to change dramatically when we were caught in a violent storm as we returned from mass on a Sunday morning in late May. On arriving home Catherine although soaked to the skin insisted on feeding the chickens and looking for some eggs for my breakfast. To my eternal regret I went off into the fields instead of making her change into some dry clothes. Sadly by the time she got back to the house with the eggs she was shaking violently with the fever. By this time my son James had arrived home from mass and he was shocked to see how ill his Mother was. In his panic he ran out into the fields looking for me. Fortunately I was walking back to the house when I saw him rushing towards me and from his demeanour I immediately knew that something dreadful had occurred, On reaching the house I quickly realised the reason for his concerns because I found Catherine sitting hunched up by the fire shaking violently with the fever and to my horror she was still dressed in her soaking wet clothes.

James, to his great credit realised that a doctor was needed and so he rushed off to Charlevile to get Doctor Morrissey.

While I waited for James to return I knew my first priority was to keep Catherine warm and try to get her to take a hot drink. But everything I tried to give her she refused, so in desperation I brought a load of turf into the house and soon had a roaring fire going. The heat from the blaze quickly increased the temperature of the room and gradually Catherine's body stopped shaking and she fell asleep. Fortunately James had found Doctor Morrissey at home and the good doctor saddled his horse and was with us at Springfort within the hour. By the time he reached us my wife's condition had rapidly deteriorated and her breathing had become very erratic. After a thorough examination the doctor confirmed that she had pneumonia and his advice was that if there was no improvement by the morning we should take her to the Infirmary in Kilmallock. Worryingly by the time William returned from visiting Mary at Tullilease that evening, Catherine's condition had deteriorated even further and by now she was having terrible trouble with her breathing. Thankfully the doctor had given me a letter of introduction to the Matron of the Infirmary and so it was decided that we must somehow get her to Kilmallock.

The next morning William left before dawn and went into Charleville to hire a suitable vehicle to take his mother to the Infirmary. Fortunately Catherine had a good nights sleep and I even managed to get her to sip a little of the medicine the doctor had prescribed and by the time William arrived back with the hired carriage she had even managed to eat a little food. The saddest thing for me were the tears that ran down my wife's face as we left Springfort on that fateful morning, it was as if she had a premonition that she would never return.

Before leaving we decided that it was better if William stayed at home and that James should accompany me to Kilmallock. The journey was a nightmare for Catherine, as it seemed we hit every bump on that badly rutted road but fortunately when we arrived at the Infirmary I was immediately taken to the Matrons office. After introducing myself I produced the letter of introduction from Doctor Morrissey and explained my wife's condition. On reading the doctors letter she immediately rang a bell to summon help and within minutes Catherine was surrounded by nurses. The nurses gently lifted her onto a stretcher and carried her into the hospital where they carefully laid her into bed. Before I could thank the Matron and her staff for their kindness, I was quietly but firmly told to leave and not return until that evening. The Matron stressed that after the long journey my wife was exhausted and now needed to rest. That evening she was sound asleep when I returned so realising that she must rest I caught a train back to Charleville.

The next morning after packing a bag with a change of clothes, I returned to Kilmallock as I intended to stay there until Catherine was well enough to return home. In the afternoon when I returned to the Infirmary she was sitting up in the bed waiting to greet me. I was overjoyed at seeing her looking so well and could not hold back the tears of relief. The visiting hour was soon over and as I left Catherine said she would like to see William and Mary as she was anxious to find out how the wedding plans were progressing. Fortunately much to her pleasure the young couple came to see her the next day.

By the end of May as Catherine's health began to improve I started to make arrangements for her homecoming. A week later with my preparations complete, I arranged an appointment to see the Matron to ask if Catherine was now well enough to return home. I began by expressing my grateful thanks for the wonderful care and attention that they had given her during her stay in hospital. We then discussed how long it would be before she was allowed home; the Matron stated that in her opinion Catherine should be strong enough to leave the following week. She suggested that if I could afford it I should take her to convalesce at a seaside resort. On hearing this advice I mentioned that we had been to Ballybunion the previous summer for a holiday. The Matron thought that this was the ideal resort to take her as the fresh sea air and walks on the beach were the tonic she needed before the busy harvest period began. After hearing this great news, I could not wait for visiting time to tell Catherine what the Matron proposed. Obviously she was delighted at the prospect of leaving the Infirmary and going to Ballybunion, but she confessed she would really prefer to go straight back home to Springfort. Sadly it was not to be because at the end of May, her condition suddenly deteriorated and she was once again having great trouble with her breathing.

At the beginning of June when I arrived at the Infirmary for my daily visit something wonderful occurred. As I was about to enter my wife's room a nurse stopped me, this was very unusual, but she said my wife wanted to be alone for a couple of minutes because she had a special visitor. As I sat outside her room and waited I racked my brain trying to think who this person could be, knowing that it must be someone special. Eventually the nurse came out and told me that I could now go into the room; on entering there sitting beside the bed was a very smartly dressed young man. At first I did not recognise the visitor but as I approached the bed he jumped up and threw his arms around me. The surprise I felt when I realised it was our son Michael, who after receiving my telegraph message, had immediately booked a passage and sailed on the first available ship from New York.

His arrival at her bedside was obviously a tremendous fillip for his mother and for the next few days her condition showed some signs of improvement, but on the evening of the fourth of June her breathing became laboured and her condition quickly deteriorated. The hospital doctor was called but he sadly informed us that she was slipping away and he advised us to call the priest to say the Last Rites. By this time James had arrived with William and so together with Michael, her entire family were all present when the priest arrived. It was as though I was having a terrible dream, my wife who had been the mainstay of all our lives was passing away in front of us and we could not do anything to help her, God knows what I would have done without my sons support during that long and tortuous night, but fortunately we were all there when Catherine quietly passed away.

That morning the three of us caught the first train back to Charleville, but before we left Kilmallock, Michael [who had automatically assumed control of the situation] went back to the Infirmary and told them that he would return as soon as possible to make the necessary arrangements for the removal of the body. He told me later that my welfare was his first priority as he knew how devastated I was and how alone I would feel. On arriving back at the farm I immediately went out into the fields and started work. Over the years I have always found that keeping busy has helped me through the bad periods in my life. Knowing this my three sons kept their distance and left me alone to do my grieving. As I have said my eldest son Michael had assumed control and on our return to Springfort he immediately started to make all the necessary arrangements. This was to prove crucial, as the farm work had obviously been neglected over the past couple of months. With Michael taking care of the preparations to return his mother's body back to Springfort, my other sons could concentrate on this work.

When the news spread that Catherine had died, people started arriving at the house. Family, friends, neighbours all came to pay their respects and offer their help. William's future bride Mary and her family were the first to arrive and they immediately began to help us prepare for the wake. I had often heard said that you know whom your true friends are when problems arise; well I now know that at that sad time in my life I could count my friends in their hundreds.

Obviously the first thing Michael had to arrange was the removal of the body from the Infirmary back to the farm. With this in mind a carriage was hired and Michael and James returned to the hospital to carry out this sad task. On their return journey from Killmallock many people came out of their houses as they passed to say a prayer for the deceased while others followed the carriage, as was tradition. Many who followed walked in solemn procession all the way to our farm and as a mark of respect curtains were drawn at every house and cabin it passed. By the time it reached Springfort the procession was thought to be over five hundred strong. Then on reaching the farm the coffin was immediately carried into the house by my sons and their friends. With the help of our neighbours, together with the Egan family we had already prepared the house in readiness for the wake. Tradition now dictated that we provide sufficient food, alcohol and tobacco for all who came to pay their last respects, so William had undertaken this task and journeyed into town with orders to buy the required provisions. I told him that he must not spare my purse, as I knew that Catherine's popularity in our parish would attract huge crowds to her wake.

On being carried into the house the coffin had been placed on the table in the middle of the room. As each mourner arrived they entered the house and then knelt beside the coffin to say a prayer for the repose of the soul of the deceased. Then one by one they came over to offer their condolences to the family, everyone young and old who came that day expressed their sadness at our great loss. For many of her old friends it was obviously a very emotional occasion and on seeing her lying in the coffin they broke down and had to be led away in tears by their husbands. The whole day was a terrible ordeal for me and I prayed it would soon be over. But it was not to be, as more and more people arrived many having travelled miles to pay their last respects.

During the evening I eventually managed to leave the house and in the farmyard I found there were tables of food laid out for the throngs of mourners. In the midst of the crowd rushing around making sure that everyone had their fill was my future daughter-in-law Mary. At that moment the sight of her seemingly having the situation in full control lifted my spirits as it was plainly obvious that she was a very capable young lady. On catching sight of me Mary immediately rushed over to ask about my wellbeing, in reply I said that although it was a difficult time for me the help and support I was receiving from her and my sons was helping me to cope. Also I expressed my grateful thanks for all her help and kindness, but she explained that she was now part of the family and it was her duty to help me on this very sad occasion. She then made me sit down and brought me a plate of food and insisted that I eat. Feeling better after the meal I spent the rest of that long evening meeting and thanking people for their thoughts and prayers, but it was not until the early hours of the morning that everyone left and we were at last able to get some sleep.

I rose early the next morning and found that my three sons were already clearing up the debris from the night before. Once this work was completed William and James left to go to the cemetery at Dromina to dig their mother's grave. Michael stayed behind with me to greet people as they arrived and by the time the Parish Priest came, the house and yard was again packed with hundreds of mourners from our parish and beyond. What surprised me was the number of my old work colleagues from my construction days who came to pay their respects, many of whom I had not seen for years. But once again I was staggered at how much my wife Catherine was loved and respected by all that had known her.

When my two sons returned from the cemetery there were calls from the assembled crowd for silence and then the Priest said Requiem Mass. At the end of the mass, Michael, at my request spoke about his mother's life and the terrible times she had lived through. But he said even in those dark days when food was scarce and many were starving she could always be relied upon for help and subsidence. At the end of his eulogy he repeated the words of Father Cullen our Parish Priest, who had said "that sadly Charleville would never see her like again;" this last remark was greeted with a roar of approval.

At the end of the service the coffin now started its final journey to the cemetery at Dromina. Relays of bearers were assembled and with military precision the coffin was carried on the shoulders of relatives and friends. It was always considered a great honour to be asked by the relatives to be a bearer and obviously on this occasion there was no shortage of volunteers. As the procession moved off, hundreds followed some walking others on horseback and many riding in carriages. Such was the multitude that followed the coffin on its way that it was reported in the local newspaper that hardly a shop or business was open as everybody was attending the funeral. For me the burial was the most traumatic event of that long day. I had thought that the wake was unbearable but nothing can compare with the sense of helplessness and utter despair I felt as the coffin wife was laid to rest in the grave. It was at this moment that I realised that I would never again see her happy smiling face in this world. Unfortunately that thought was to haunt me for many years.

After the funeral we slowly made our way back to Springfort and for the first time in my life I can honestly say I now felt my age, my whole body was weary and I was so grateful when a friend offered me a lift in his carriage. On arriving home our neighbours and friends had cleared and tidied the house and again laid out tables laden with food for the returning mourners. That evening I sat and chatted with my son Michael, because since his return from America we had not had an opportunity to talk. Sadly he was returning to New York the next morning so we obviously had much to discuss in the few hours that remained. In our conversation I was delighted to hear how happy he was in America and how much he was missing his family.

CHAPTER ELEVEN

Before leaving Springfort that morning James and William had quickly shown their brother Michael around the farm and had pointed out the many alterations they had made in the past few years. On our walk to the station I was pleased that Michael talked enthusiastically to me about the improvements his brothers had made and told me he hoped I would write each autumn after the harvest with news of the progress we were making. All too soon we were at the station where some of Michael's old friends were gathered to see him off on his long journey, their banter and leg pulling reminded me of years gone by and somehow helped our parting. As the train pulled out of the station I can now confess that my emotions finally got the better of me and I broke down and cried. Michael had been a tower of strength during the past days and with his affable nature and natural good humour, had greatly helped the three us somehow survive the great loss we had suffered.

I felt totally devastated now he was gone and it seemed as if another great part of my life had departed for ever. It was at that moment that I finally felt the loss of Catherine, this feeling left me inconsolable and deeply depressed. My two remaining sons were obviously very distressed to see me in this condition, but I urged them to return to the farm as I felt I needed to be alone.

I sat for hours on the platform that morning wondering how I was going to cope with life in the future. Eventually I decided to seek advice and guidance from Father Cullen our parish priest. When I arrived at the church I lit a candle and said a prayer for the repose of the soul of Catherine and as I was about to go into the Presbytery, Father Cullen came into the church accompanied by a colleague who I straightaway recognised as Archbishop Croke of Cashel. Thomas William Croke and his family had been associated with our parish of Charleville for many years. I had actually known him many years before when as a curate he had visited us at Springfort on many occasions.

Before Father Cullen could speak, the Archbishop realising who I was immediately expressed his condolences at my sad loss... This kind gentle man informed Father Cullen that as a young man he had made regular visits to our farm for the music and dancing that we then had on Saturday nights. On explaining to them the reason for my visit, they invited me to join them in the Presbytery for a cup of tea.

At first I declined but as they both insisted, I relented and followed them into the house. Fortunately both men instinctively knew the reason for my visit to the church that afternoon and sat and listened intently as I unburdened my thoughts and worries to them. Tears were running down my face by the time I had finished speaking about the wonderful life we had shared together. The Archbishop after hearing about my sense of loss and the feeling of hopelessness suggested that as it was such a beautiful afternoon we should take a walk in the garden. I thought that this was a wonderful idea, but questioned if he had time as I knew he was a very busy man. He said on the contrary, he was visiting Charleville that day to discuss with Father Cullen and various other individuals the way forward for a new radical organisation that he was proposing. On our walk the Archbishop explained that it was his hope and aspiration that Ireland could regain its cultural heritage. With this in mind he said he envisaged that an Athletic Association should be founded. His vision for this Association was that the national games of Hurling and Gaelic football would have playing fields in every town in Ireland. He went on to explain that unless this was achieved the English sports of Soccer and Rugby would soon proliferate and our national games would die out. During our conversation he kept stressing the need for people in the local communities to get actively involved and he thought that with all my connections in the Charleville area I would be an ideal candidate.

As I listened to him I was extremely impressed by the tremendous enthusiasm he had for the project and I could not stop myself from being swept along by his visionary ideas. His underlying message was that although Ireland could not at this time obtain our national identity politically, we could retain and enhance our national sporting and cultural heritage by the playing of our own home grown games. Interestingly his other radical proposal was the revival of the Gaelic language. Since the Famine, I knew that sadly there had been a rapid decline in the speaking of our native language and I agreed that this problem also had to be addressed. On parting I gave him a solemn promise that I would give my help and support in the founding of the Charleville branch of the Gaelic Athletic Association, a promise that I have endeavoured to keep. Our conversation that afternoon somehow gave me a real sense of purpose to my life, which I now realise, was exactly what I needed.

When I arrived home both William and James were very worried about me, James, had been out looking for me for hours and the only place he had not visited was the church. They told me that they were very distressed by my unusual behaviour that morning and my long absence from the house. But I explained that I had needed some time on my own for reflection. My whole life I said had changed during the past few months and when Michael boarded the train that morning, I was suddenly overwhelmed with grief and remorse. Previously I had either their Mother or my Brother Owen to offer help and guidance when times were hard, but now both had departed [God rest their souls]. It was this realisation that had left me feeling depressed and lonely. Both William and James were totally shocked and upset at my explanation and begged me to pull myself together, both saying that they still needed my experience and help if they were to run the farm successfully. They then asked me where I had been until this late hour. When I explained I had gone to the church and had a chance meeting with Archbishop Croke who I knew personally, as he had been a curate in the parish in years gone by. They were both extremely impressed when they heard that Archbishop and Father Cullen had listened in silence to my outpouring of grief and how they had both comforted me with their words of sympathy. Archbishop Croke, had I said, kindly promised that he would say a mass for the repose of their dear mother's soul at Cashel Cathedral.

I then went on to tell them about the Archbishop's ambition that one day there would be a playing field in every town and village in Ireland where the national games of Hurling and Gaelic football would be played. It was also his dream that these centres would help start a revival of the Gaelic language and culture. This conversation with Archbishop Croke had I explained lifted my spirits, as he had made me promise to help in the founding such a club in Charleville. On hearing my story, both sons agreed that this was exactly what I needed and they both promised to help me in any way possible. After mass on the following Sunday, I was chatting to my old cronies when the curate came up and said that the Parish Priest would like to speak to us. At this meeting he told us about the Archbishops idea of for the founding of an association to promote the playing of Gaelic Sports in Ireland. With Archbishops suggestion in mind he said that we should form a committee in the Charleville area. My old friend John Nolan and I volunteered and it was agreed that there should be a meeting once a month in the Presbytery with the ultimate aim of founding a club in Charleville. The first priority of our committee was to find a suitable site and raise sufficient funds for the project. But all this was to be wishful thinking, because over the next ten years the political and financial situation once again deteriorated and as you will see the major preoccupation for all of us was again focused on keeping a roof over our heads and food in our stomachs.

During that summer we were very busy with the harvest, the weather that year was exceptional and we made the most of our good fortune working from dawn to dusk until all the crops were gathered. Fortunately being so busy had helped me as I was usually too tired to dwell on my great loss. When most of our harvesting was finished at Springfort, William went off to the Egan's at Tullilease to help his future in laws. His assistance was really appreciated by John Egan, as both of his boys had recently emigrated to America. My sons were very pleased with the prices they received for the cattle they sold that year at the October market and so they were in good form when they returned.

For the first time in years I did not go with them because after working hard on the harvest my advancing years were now catching up with me. I now longed for the quieter winter months when I could retreat to the reading room in Charleville and catch up with the latest news.

That first Christmas without Catherine was obviously a very sad time for me, because in previous years we had always visited family and friends together. But with the coming of the New Year my spirits were lifted as we made the final preparations for William and Mary's wedding

That January we all went to the Charleville Fair to get rigged out for the occasion. In those times, the women from Coals Quay, in Cork City, were renowned for the selling of very good second hand clothes. The following verse was written by a local poet named Tommy Power to celebrate this annual occurrence and is titled.

The Cork Women's Corner, at Charleville Fair:

> *On the day I was born twenty years ago now*
> *My father from Charleville brought home a cow,*
> *For the baby was big, fat an' han'some as well,*
> *An' he roared mile murdher I often heard tell.*
> *All the neighbours examined the parcel he brought,*
> *While he proudly explained how he haggled an' fought*
> *Buying up clothes for the christenin' an' lots more to spare*
> *At the Cork Women's Corner at Charleville Fair.*
> *'Tis there you can buy the best clothes second-hand,*

Once worn by ladies an' lords of the land.
Silks an' satins the finest that ever were seen
That once may have draped the proud form of a queen;
The quilts made of flannel or best eiderdown
An' the blankets the best ever sold in the town.
Faith! There's no such good value to be found anywhere
But the Cork Women's Corner at Charleville Fair.

Ev'ry day that passed by fat an' bigger I grew,
All because I had nothing at all else to do;
An' in spite of my size, still no problem arose
About shirts, boots or socks or the shape of my clothes.
For my father one day ev'ry month went to town
An' always he brought me a good knock-me-down
Of the pick of the market for good wear-an'-tear
From the Cork Women's Corner at Charleville Fair.

Time passed an' I came on to man's proud estate,
An' my clothes were the finest an' most up-to-date;
An' the girls looked sideways an' soon they began
To think an' to say, "He's a lovely young man,"
An' he's sensible, too, for he buys all his clothes
From the hat on his head to the boots 'round his toes
From the finest selection to be found anywhere
At the Cork Women's Corner at Charleville Fair.

Now the greatest event in the course of my life
Will be soon coming off – I'll be taking a wife,
An' I'll want a new outfit an' a swell one at that,
A suit of blue serge an' a swanky soft hat.
Then I an' my sweetheart together will go
To buy wreathes an' veils an' a lovely trousseau,
White shoes and silk stockings at our wedding to wear
At the Cork Women's Corner at Charleville Fair.

On reaching town that morning we all quickly realised that without Catherine to guide us, we did not have any idea how we should proceed. It was I knew going to be a long day in town before we purchased what we all hoped would be suitable to wear on the big day. Obviously William was in need of a new suit and he was very anxious that the material he liked would please his future wife. At my suggestion he went to Tullilease the next day to show a sample of the cloth to Mary that he had chosen. On his return we were much relieved when he told us that Mary was very happy with his choice, also she was impressed that he was having a new suit especially made by a tailor in Charleville for the occassion. Fortunately for us Mrs Egan had now taken charge of all the wedding arrangements and because she was a very formidable lady, we soon learned that it was best to leave everything in her capable hands. This was to prove a sensible decision, as William, and Mary's wedding turned out to be a great success.

During the weeks preceding the wedding I managed to make myself as scarce as possible by spending every hour in the reading room in town while the house was decorated from top to bottom in readiness for the arrival of my daughter-in-law. The boys were grateful that I was not around, but that did not stop them ribbing me and they jokingly asking me if I had found a new lady friend. I had learned from past experience that when it came to house decorating the best thing for me to do was to disappear from view. With all these activities taking place the wedding was soon upon us and I was constantly being told that on the big day, I was not do one of my disappearing acts; I was also warned that I must be on my best behaviour. This was obviously said in jest as both my sons, especially William, were now becoming nervous. Unfortunately, during the week before the wedding we received a letter of apology from Michael in New York. The letter informed us that one of his children was very sick and in the circumstances he would not be returning home for the wedding. This was a great disappointment, but we all understood and I immediately arranged for a Mass to be said for the recovery of my granddaughter.

With all the wedding preparations completed, we were fortunate because the day of the wedding, [the eleventh of May eighteen seventy-five] dawned bright and sunny and also very warm for the time of the year. That morning we were all up very early and by nine o'clock all the farm work was completed. After breakfast relatives and friends began to arrive and it was with much cheering and laughter that we set out on our journey to Tullilease Chapel. I counted a total of fifteen carriages packed with merry makers following us that morning and typically it was not long before the alcohol was being freely distributed. By the time we reached the Chapel I could sense that William was becoming very nervous, but when Mary arrived looking so young and radiant he soon relaxed and quickly became his usual confident self. That morning I could not help thinking how proud Catherine would have been to see her sons on this wonderful day, James who was obviously the best man stood at the alter by his brothers side. The small church was packed, with many of the congregation having to stand, but thankfully the priest shortened the service because the heat in the chapel had quickly become unbearable.

After the ceremony everyone made their way to the Egan's farm and as we approached the house some of William's friends rode towards us on horseback. These boisterous young men all carried a bottle of spirits which they had procured for this special occasion and you can imagine it was not long before these bottles were being passed around for the guest's consumption. On reaching the house I was amazed to see the wonderful spread of food that was laid out for the wedding feast, Mrs Egan had I thought made a banquet fit for the Queen of England.

Very soon crowds of people arrived, tables had been laid for them in the barn and the farmyard, but as guests of honour we sat in the farm house with the young married couple and the Egan family and enjoyed the sumptuous food that had been prepared for us. When the meal was finished I plucked up courage and gave a little speech thanking Mr and Mrs Egan for their wonderful hospitality and then called for everyone to toast Mary and William and wish them a long and happy marriage. As I sat down the guests gave three cheers for the young couple and then it was James's turn to speak, he started of by saying how much his mother had longed for this day, and he was certain she was looking down on us. He then went on to welcome Mary into the Casey family and then to roars of approval he said how beautiful she looked on this her special day. Mary, on hearing these kind words started to blush with embarrassment, but William assured her that he totally agreed with his brothers sentiments.

After the speeches the tables were quickly rearranged and the music began, James, as best man traditionally started the dancing and the musicians like the drinking was soon in full flow. For me the highlight of that day was seeing William leading Mary out onto the dance floor, the young couple was obviously very much in love and the happiness on their faces was a joy to see. The rest of the day passed in a blur, dance proceeded dance, and then we were entertained by some great singing, many of the singers giving us renditions of the old traditional ballads that I had not heard for many years. During the evening the musicians, at the request of my sons, played a couple of step dances and they prevailed upon me to show everyone the Kerry dances my mother had taught me when I was a child. Although I was to suffer greatly for the next week, my efforts were greatly appreciated by all of the guests and my sons said they were very surprised how good I danced, but my whole body was to ache for days after.

Later William and Mary left the party and were driven to Charleville station as they were catching a train to Ballybunion for a week's holiday. Their carriage was accompanied to the station by many of their young friends, all on horse-back and as you can imagine it was quite a send off. After their departure, the party was soon back in full swing, but by this time I was feeling very tired after the long day. Unfortunately one last important matter had still to be settled, this was the payment of the dowry. For this reason John Egan asked to speak to me alone in private. It was with a great deal of embarrassment that I accepted the agreed sum of one hundred pounds; because I knew that he could ill afford it. But before I departed I thanked him for his hospitality and assured him that we could always be counted on if he needed help in the future.

On completion of this very delicate matter, I went in search of James, who was as usual surrounded by a crowd of young ladies. By now he was very intoxicated and everyone was calling for him to do his party-piece, this was him dancing the horn pipe on a sixteen-pipe keg of porter. The keg was rolled into the centre of the farm yard and then he called for the musicians to play the tune. Immediately he heard the music he leapt on to the barrel and to everyone's amazement danced the horn pipe for a full five minutes. By the end his whole body was perspiring from his efforts, but he finished to thunderous applause from the admiring audience.

I now wanted us to leave for Charleville, but James would not listen to me and it was dawn by the time we eventually left for home.

It was to take me many days to get over the excesses of the wedding, but I somehow managed to drag my tired body around the farm the following week, until the newlyweds arrived back from their holiday. After their week in Ballybunion, both Mary and William looked wonderfully well and said they were now looking forward to their life together. Unfortunately as I now know, that due to many unforeseen occurrences this would to be the only holiday they would ever spend together. But from a purely selfish motive I found it was wonderful to have a woman around the farm again, because since the death of my wife the house had lost its homely atmosphere. Mary would soon get us three men organised and what a joy it was for all of us to once again have a freshly cooked meal each evening. Within weeks this young slip of a girl had all of us in fear of her, the house was spotless and God help anyone who was untidy. But we all soon learned to do what we were told and we greatly appreciated the improvements she made.

It was obvious to everyone that the young couple were very much in love and devoted to one another. Consequently it was no surprise to me when in autumn of that year; Mary announced that she was going to have a baby. This was cause for great celebrations and obviously we invited Mary's family to Springfort to join us, because this would also be their first grandchild.

Thankfully the harvest was again a success after all our hard work during summer. William and James's policy of improving our livestock by purchasing better stock was now beginning to reap dividends, as the local dealers quickly became aware of the quality of our cattle. Also it was about this time that at Mary's insistence we started to produce and sell dairy products and obviously this also increased our income. Her idea was eventually to prove a great success because in later years when Charleville opened one of the first Co-operative Creameries in Ireland, we were one of the farms in our area to join this revolutionary organization.

After the annual October Fair, I now had time to return to catch up with the latest political news. My main source of information was as always the reading room in town, where I could be normally found especially when the weather was bad. But that autumn passed very quickly and soon it was Christmas time again. That year Mary's, youthful enthusiasm helped us all enjoy the festivities. In the past the house had always been decorated from top to bottom, in readiness for the most important festival in our Christian year. Mary was determined to surpass everything we had achieved in previous years. [In the event she surpassed herself,] because when I arrived home from visiting some old friends on Christmas Eve, I was astounded to find the farm was illuminated by hundreds of candles with freshly picked holly adorning the entrance to the house. The next morning we as usual attended early mass and on returning home the house was soon full with William and Mary's, young friends that had been invited to share our Christmas feast. Later that morning much to my surprise and pleasure Mary's family arrived carrying presents for all of us. So although I missed Catherine, the joy and fun we had on that special day helped me to forget about my sad loss for a few hours.

It was early in the New Year that my son James began to get very restless and argumentative. Although he would not admit it I knew what was on his mind, William, his brother was now married and starting a family and he began to realise that it was time for him to leave and make his own way in the world. This worried me because the thought of him emigrating like millions of other Irishmen including his brother Michael filled my heart with a terrible foreboding. At the end of January he started to disappear for day's on end, he was then coming home worse for wear from the drink and when confronted became extremely violent. My concern was that he was now mixing with a bad crowd in town, so I decided to take it upon myself to confront him. As you may recall I had nearly lost my wife and family by acting in a similar fashion and so I was determined to ensure my son realised the perils that he faced. With this in mind I was waiting at the door when he finally arrived home at the end of February after three days of heavy drinking. At first many angry words were spoken which we later both regretted, but the next day when he sobered up he was very contrite and apologised. I must say that fortunately he did heed my words as he has never to my knowledge ever been inebriated since that day.

But my joy was short lived because; a couple of weeks later he informed us that he would leave Springfort in the spring to seek work. This decision obviously upset both William and Mary, but he solemnly promised us that whatever happened in the future he would never under any circumstance leave Ireland. This promise he made with a willing heart because he realised how much he meant to both me and his brother. After the decision was made, James soon became his old self again, but in May after we had finished sowing our crops he left us and went off in search of work. We all knew that we had lost a great worker and our loss would surely be someone else's gain. It was then no surprise when in late June I received a letter from him which informed us that he had found work in Coolmine, a village near the town of Michelson. The tenant farmer who had employed him was in declining health he wrote, and his two sons had recently emigrated so he was now looking for someone to manage his farm.

In late July he wrote another letter informing us how happy he was in Coolmine and that he would like me to go and visit him as soon as possible. On reading his letter William urged me to go the next day, because from the tone of the letter he knew that James had something on his mind. So early the next morning I caught the train to Mitcheltown, changing at Mallow.

When I left the railway station, I followed James's directions and soon found my way to the Roche's farm. On my arrival I was very impressed by the hospitality I received, Mr Roche who like me, had recently become a widower was as James had written a very sick man. But he made a great effort to make me welcome and could not praise James enough for all his hard work. As we sat chatting James came rushing into the house to greet me, he was followed by a very young attractive girl who he introduced as Anna. On meeting Anna I could now see why my son was so happy to be here in Coolmine. After the introductions the only subject they both wanted to discuss was my daughter in law Mary's health and when was the baby expected? I informed them that all was well and that we hoped to have good news before the month was out.

While we sat talking about the prospects for that year's harvest and the latest farm prices, Anna was busy preparing our lunch. After the meal I was taken on a tour of the farm and was very impressed by what I saw. They had about twenty five acres of prime land, but Mr Roche confessed that since his wife had died he had lost some of his desire and the farm had become somewhat neglected. Then sadly he had become seriously ill, this illness had left him very tired and weak and so the arrival of my son was a godsend. During the evening as we sat there talking, Anna went off and made a bed up for me, as they all insisted that I stay the night. As the evening wore on it was obvious that James and Anna were very tired from their exertions of the day and so they both went to bed leaving the two of us to talk.

Now that we were alone the sole topic of our conversation was the obvious attraction that James and Anna had for each other. Michael Roche was he said secretly hoping that this mutual attraction might eventually lead to a proposal of marriage. I assured him that it was very clear from what I had witnessed today that the two young people had fallen in love and I predicted that my son's future was here in Coolmine. On hearing my prediction, Michael struggled out of his chair and from a cupboard produced a bottle of whisky and although I very rarely drank, obviously on this occasion I could not refuse. As we sat chatting that night we both quickly realised that we had a lot in common and so it was very late when we eventually retired to bed.

The next morning, after breakfast James accompanied me back to the station. As we walked along he told me that this was the happiest time of his life.

In reply I confessed that I had come to try and persuade him to return home, but this idea was stupid, as I could see that his life was now here in Coolmine. In past years James had always sought my advice and this day was no exception because before we parted that morning he asked me about my impression of Anna. I told him that if he wanted my advice it would be to strike while the iron was hot, as I was sure that there must be a queue of young men hoping to make her acquaintance. Also I divulged that Mr Roche, had also expressed the hope that a match could be made.

My words of advice and encouragement he greatly appreciated and from the look on his face, I knew that I had made the right decision in not standing in his way, but before parting he made me promise to return within the month, because although he was very happy, he still greatly missed all of us at Springfort.

When I arrived back home, both Mary and William were waiting impatiently for news. It was evident they said, that as I had stayed the night in Coolmine, they knew that my visit must have been a success. I started off by saying that my original reason for going to see James was to try and persuade him to return to home with me to Springfort. But on reaching my destination, I had quickly realised that he was very happy working on Michael Roche's farm and when I saw my son together with the farmer's daughter Anna it was obvious that they were both in love. I then told them about my conversations with Mr Roche who also realised the situation and would give his blessing to them if they wanted to marry. Both William and Mary were delighted by the news and expressed the hope that they could soon visit Coolmine but as the birth of their baby was imminent that was obviously impossible.

By now Mary was becoming increasingly tired and with the hot weather we were having that summer, we all prayed that the baby would soon arrive. Fortunately our prayers were answered because after a short confinement a baby boy was born on the twelfth of July, eighteen seventy-six. The happy couple named their first son Edmund; he would be the first of the many children Mary produced. The day after the baby was born I wrote to James in Coolmine and Michael in New York informing them of our good news. In my letter to Michael, I also told him that I hoped it would not be long before his brother James married. In the letter I explained that after the death of his mother James had become very restless and much to my displeasure had left Springfort, to find work. I went on to tell him about my visit to the Roche's farm in Coolmine and how welcome they had made me. It was I explained that after I met Anna Roche, the farmer's daughter, it became obvious why his brother would soon be married.

Thankfully Mary was soon up and about and she was very pleased when James brought Anna to Springfort to see baby Edmund. It was a wonderful day for me, to once again see my two sons laughing and joking together and both the young girls beginning a friendship that has endured to this day. As usual, knowing that my presence was not required, I quickly disappeared and spent the afternoon in the reading room in Charleville catching up with the latest political news. By the time I got back to Springfort, James and Anna had left because they were worried about Mr Roche. The poor mans health had deteriorated and he now spent most of his days in bed. But their visit had proved a great success and Mary told us that Anna was hoping that James would propose to her.

The months of August and September were as always the busiest time of our farm year and in the absence of James we were obliged to take on a farm hand to help us out that summer. We were fortunate that the hay we had cut for the winter feed was soon dry in the warm sunshine and on the day we hauled it home and built a large haystack in our farmyard, many of our friends and neighbours came from far and wide to help. At the end of that long day we all trooped back to the house where the usual feast had been prepared for the hungry workers. Later although weary, the music began and the traditional party ensued.

After mass on a Sunday at the beginning of harvest time we would decide whose farm was the first to be helped. Then during the following week's weather permitting we would all go to help each other until everyone's harvest was gathered in. Those golden days with everybody working together as a community were the essence of life in rural Ireland. The banter and good humour helped us forget our struggles of past years and gave us all renewed hope for the future.

In late September with most of the harvesting finished, we all decided to visit James at Coolmine. He had been urging us to go and see them for some time and in his letters had also mentioned how sick Mr Roche was. On the journey Mary said how nice it was to get away from the farm and how much she was looking forward to meeting Anna again. We were not disappointed by the reception we received because James and Anna, were waiting at Mitchelstown station for us and transported us back to their farm. When we arrived we were surprised that Michael Roche came out to greet us, but I was greatly shocked to see how much his health had deteriorated since the last time we had met. But he made a big effort to make us welcome and he was especially pleased to see my grandson Edmund as he told us he had always loved children around the house.

While he was playing with the baby, I noticed that James had become very agitated and was waiting for the girls to finish preparing the dinner. As they brought in the meal they were both giggling like two young school girls. It was obvious that something was about to occur and I was not in the least surprised when James stood up and announced that he had waited for both families to be together before he asked Mr Roche's permission to marry his lovely daughter. Michael Roche rose from his chair with some difficulty and with tears running down his face, said how proud he would be to have James as a son in law and that he had prayed this would to happen before he died. At the end his speech he sat down and William; proposed a toast to the happy couple on that very special occasion. All through the meal Anna and Mary sat and discussed the forthcoming wedding, while the four of us talked about the weather and other farm topics.

After dinner Michael Roche who was by now totally exhausted retired to bed leaving the three of us to have a stroll around his farm. Both William and I were very impressed by what we saw on our tour and eventually I returned to the farmhouse and left my two sons discussing the improvements that could be made and how to implement them. Later that evening as we sat and ate supper, it was agreed that we should stay the night and leave early next morning. The hospitality we received at Coolmine was wonderful and has remained so until this day, Michael Roche, as I previously said was a very sick man, but the news of the forthcoming marriage seemed to give him a new lease of life and to his enormous pleasure he managed to live long enough to witness the birth of his first grandchild.

It was nearly twelve o' clock the next morning when we eventually got to Mitchestown station and by now William was anxious to get back to Springfort, but as you can imagine with a wedding to plan and the obvious need for it to be at an early date nothing in the world was going to get in the way of the two planners. William and I had decided that we would go back home and Mary would stay with the baby for a few days to start making preparations for the wedding. On our train journey back to Charleville we both whole heartedly agreed that James had made the right decision, as it was now time he settled down. On our return to Springfort we both noticed how quiet and empty the house seemed without Mary and Edmund. Surprisingly they did not return home for another a week, by which time William, was getting extremely anxious. When she finally arrived home she explained that the reason for the delay was that both she and Anna had wasted no time, as all the arrangements for the wedding were now complete. Her visit to Coolmine had obviously been a great success and was to be repeated annually for many years. Whilst in Coolmine she had also taken the opportunity to ask Anna and James, to be sponsors at Edmunds Baptism, which was to take place at the parish church in Charleville at the beginning of October. This service unfortunately was to be very upsetting for me, because I would have loved for my dear wife Catherine to have been there to see her first grandchild baptised.

In contrast to Williams and Mary's wedding at Coolmine was a very quiet affair. Because of the distance we had to travel unfortunately only a few members of our family could afford the fare to Mitchestown, but for the ones that did come there was great excitement as it was their first ever train journey. On our arrival in Mitchelstown we made our way to the church where we found James waiting for us. He looked very smart in his new suit and with his brother William as best man, they waited nervously for the arrival of the bride. Soon the church began to fill and then Anna arrived with her father and her brother Thomas who had returned from America especially for the wedding. The bride was absolutely radiant and the presence of her brother at the ceremony made the day extra special.

After the church service we all adjourned to the local hotel for the wedding feast. At the end of the meal I felt compelled to speak, I said that in just over a year I had lost my wife and my two sons had married. Fortunately for me the marriages of my sons and the subsequent birth of Edmund had helped me to somehow get over the loss of my wife Catherine. I went on to say, that I know that she is looking down on us today and giving all of us her blessing. In closing I said I wanted to especially thank Anna's brother Thomas for making the long and arduous journey back from America to be with us on this wonderful day, as I knew how much his visit had meant to both his father and sister. Before we left for home that evening, I managed to have a long conversation with Anna's brother about life in New York City, as I was very interested to find out more about the area my son Michael had just moved in to. Thomas was very impressed when I told him that my son had recently received promotion in the New York Police Department, and was now a sergeant. When I mentioned that he had recently purchased a house in Staten Island, he gave a whistle in amazement saying that it was a very desirable area.

That evening the young couple went off to Killarney for a couple of days. While Thomas Roche stayed onto run the farm until they returned, he also wanted to spend some time with his sick and ailing father. After the excitement of the wedding, we soon found that Christmas was again rapidly approaching. Mary wrote to Anna and James inviting them and Michael Roche to spend the festivities with us and much to our pleasure they accepted our invitation. As I recall the house was full to bursting that year as Mary's family also came from Tullilease to see their grandson on his first Christmas. That the afternoon John Egan, Michael Roche, [who's health had improved] and myself decided to have a walk around the farm and as usual the main topic of conversation was farm prices and the eternal wish for good weather in the coming year, but we all agreed that it was great news for the three us that our youngsters were married and settled at last. Because it gave the three of us great pleasure, to see our next generation taking on the responsibility of running our farms.

CHAPTER TWELVE

In February eighteen seventy seven, I was pleasantly surprised to receive a letter from my cousin James Stephens. He was still in exile in Paris, but for once in his life he did not complain about being penniless. Instead, this time he wrote to tell me the wonderful story of the freeing of Irish patriots from the convict settlement in Fremantle, Western Australia, which had been orchestrated by the Irish Republican Brotherhood of New York.   [The organiser of the expedition was John Devoy, one of James' old companions in arms. After the failed rising in eighteen sixty-five, Devoy you might recall, was one of the leading conspirators who had arranged Stephens' sensational escape from Richmond Jail, Dublin. John Devoy was born at Kill County Kildare in eighteen forty-two and as a young boy he had witnessed the full horror of the Famine years. Without doubt this catastrophe had left him with a burning desire to overthrow the Tyranny that he thought had stood by and watched the Irish people die in their thousands. From a young age he felt he required military experience and with this in mind he travelled to France and joined the French Foreign Legion and saw action in Algeria. On his return to Ireland he joined the Fenian Movement and in eighteen sixty-five James Stephens appointed him as Chief Organiser for recruitment of British soldiers into the Fenian Party. After helping Stephens escape he went on the run, but was ultimately captured and sentenced to fifteen years penal servitude.

He was to spend five terrible years in prison during which time he was always a thorn in the side of the authorities and so they were glad for him to be sent into exile in America. On his arrival there he was treated like a hero and he received an Address of Welcome from the House of Representatives in Washington. Devoy then became a journalist for The New York Herald and also quickly became very active in the Clan Na Gael the Irish American organisation dedicated to Ireland becoming a Republic. He was eventually to rise to leader of the Clan and under his Leadership it was to become the most effective Irish Republican Organisation in America. This quietly spoken man with piercing blue eyes was later described by *The Times* of London as 'the most dangerous enemy this country has had since Wolfe Tone', a description he considered the highest possible compliment.]

My curiosity had been first aroused in September eighteen seventy-six, when rumours started to surface in Ireland that a major escape of Fenian prisoners had taken place from the penal colony of Western Australia. Obviously the British Government and the authorities in Dublin Castle tried to suppress the story, but still the rumours persisted. So it was with great interest that I read the full account of the dramatic escape, as told by John Devoy in the following letter he sent to James Stephens.

My Dear James,

Please accept my apologise for not writing sooner, but you will understand why I felt compelled to write to you at this time when you read the following account of the heroic rescue of our friends and compatriots. Unfortunately I have been extremely busy, but I feel you should read my first hand account which will undoubtedly raise your spirits.

"In June eighteen seventy-three, I was most distressed when I received a letter from an old friend and fellow Fenian named James Wilson, James you might recall had helped in your escape from Richmond Jail Dublin. He was subsequently arrested some time later and was then transported for his Fenian activities. For the past ten years he and other patriots have had to endure the brutal punishments that were inflicted daily in the penal prisons of Western Australia.

The underlying message in his communication was that the long years of harsh treatment had taken its toll on the Fenian prisoners. As a result, many had given up all hope of freedom; while other poor souls had passed away. He and his fellow prisoners he wrote were alive but were all ailing. Wilson went on to stress that he himself expected death in the near future. He then told me at length of how he had nursed a fellow inmate an old acquaintance of ours John Keating in his final hours before he died from a broken heart. His letter ended on a deeply disturbing note: if nothing was done to help us we shall surely die.

As I read his heart-wrenching story, I tried to understand the terrible strain that these men were now under. They who had lost everything fighting for Irish freedom and were thousands of miles from home; they had no hope of rescue and were simply waiting for death.

But it was the last passage of Wilson's letter that was the most distressing, and I quote, "And what a death is staring us in the face, a death of a felon in a British dungeon and a grave amongst the British ruffians, it is a disgrace to have us in prison today, a little money judiciously expended would release everyman that is now in Western Australia." He went on to write the words that no Irishman will ever forget: "Now my dear friends remember that this is the Voice from the Tomb,

*think that we have been nearly nine years in this living Tomb, since our first arrest,
and it is impossible for mind and body to withstand the continuing strain that is
put upon us."*

On receiving this searing communication I was determined to act, and so at
the next Clan Na Gael meeting in Baltimore that July, I read the contents of James
Wilson's letter to a stunned audience of more than sixty delegates. At the end, I
beseeched them to throw their weight behind a rescue attempt, which I believed
should be made as soon as was possible. Some of those present had spent years in
British prisons, and they knew from their own terrible experiences what hell their
fellow Fenian comrades were now enduring. After much discussion, the Supreme
Council of the Clan recommended the setting up of a rescue committee. This decision
was only taken after much debate amongst the delegates, with some even querying
the authenticity of Wilson's letter. It was only when I produced the envelope with its
Western Australian postmark, that they were convinced that it was not a forgery. My
main worry now was that as more and more people heard about the possible escape
attempt, news of our plans would reach the ears of the British Government. We all
suspected that they had agents working against us in New York and other major
American cities.

Eventually an Australian Prisoners escape committee was set up. Its members
were James Reynolds, Doctor Wilson-Carroll and me. At the end of the Baltimore
conference I was approached by a gentleman named J.C.Talbot a merchant from
San Francisco. In our conversation Mr Talbot promised to raise funds for our
project on the American West Coast. He said there were many who sympathised
with the Irish cause in California and he was sure they would contribute when
they heard about the proposed rescue attempt. In the coming months Talbot
thankfully lived up to his promise. He was to prove invaluable to our cause; in fact,
without his help the whole project would have floundered. How ever the initial
subscriptions were very slow and I fretted that we would never receive sufficient
funds for the rescue attempt.

The committee's other main preoccupation at this time was whether to hire a
whaling ship to sail to Australia or would it be more practical to actually purchase
our own vessel. After much debate we decided that if sufficient funds became
available, I would seek the advice of Captain Henry C. Hathaway resident of the
town of New Bedford. An acquaintance informed me that Hathaway had been the
Captain of "The Gazelle" when it had carried out an audacious rescue from the
Western Australian penal settlement in an town of Banbury in eighteen sixty one.

234

When I arrived in New Bedford, I made enquires about the whereabouts of Captain Hathaway. On being informed that he was now the senior officer of the local police force, I was directed to the police headquarters. On my arrival there, I produced the letter of introduction that my colleague had furnished me with and was immediately shown into Hathaway's office. When I explained the reason for my visit I was pleasantly surprised at the tremendous enthusiasm that he had for our project. He was ultimately to prove a vital link in its success, because without his help and local knowledge we would never have made the contacts that were the main reason for our eventual success.

All this was in the distant future however. For now, Captain Hathaway being a former whaling skipper with an immense amount of experience was the ideal man to speak to about our preparations. I had told him our initial idea was to hire a ship, but he was firmly against this. He went on to explain that if the whaling was good on the voyage, the skipper would be tempted to keep hunting, as he could make much more money by catching a couple of large whales than we could ever afford pay him. But if we purchased and fitted out our own vessel and appointed a trustworthy Captain and the whaling was good, the voyage might pay for itself. The captain then could sail onto Australia and hopefully carry off the Fenian prisoners. Listening to his suggestion I immediately realized that he was right. At the end of our discussion I therefore thanked him for his sound advice and hurried back to New York, where I put his proposal to the escape committee. I also begged the Clan to raise the urgently required funds, as donations were still very slow.

During the following weeks I managed to persuade the rescue committee that Hathaway's suggestion was the only real alternative. With their endorsement I returned to New Bedford and once again met Captain Hathaway. On hearing that I now had the authority to purchase the required vessel, the Captain wasted no time in introducing me to another vital figure in our project: his personal friend, the dynamic John T. Richardson. It was on Mr Richardson's advice that we ultimately managed to purchase a suitable whaler. This was the ship that became immortalized under the name, "Catalpa".

But the preparations were agonizingly slow. More delays followed as we had to wait for the ice on the river to melt. Only then could our vessel be moved to a dry dock to be fitted out for its epic voyage. Expenses began to pile up. The fitting out of the ship was to prove enormously expensive and I was staggered at the final cost. In this the busiest time of my life, John Richardson's help, both financial and practical was invaluable. I know that I would not have been able to have co-ordinated the project without his help.

Over the next few months I spent every waking moment travelling to numerous towns and cities fund raising and after much effort I eventually managed to finance the fitting out of "The Catalpa." It was now that we had the greatest boost to our endeavour. With the help once more of John Richardson, we managed to obtain the services of his son in law, Captain George B. Anthony as skipper. It proved an inspired appointment as Anthony was to prove to be perhaps the only man alive who could have carried out this dangerous mission on our behalf, and as we shall see his choice of Sam Smith as first mate was also of great significance.

Unfortunately delay followed delay. By March of eighteen seventy-five, I still had grave doubts that "The Catalpa" would ever leave the port of New Bedford. It was thus a huge relief when she finally set sail on the twenty ninth of April eighteen seventy five. I and the other members of the committee dined on board with Captain Anthony and after wishing him God speed we disembarked onto our accompanying yacht and watched as the whaler gathered speed and headed out into the Atlantic.

At this time the skipper was the only person on the ship who knew the true purpose of the voyage. It was a secret he kept for many months, before informing his first mate, Sam Smith. According to the entry in the ship's journal, he invited Smith into his cabin and said, I quote, "I want to tell you before we get to Tenerife that "The Catalpa" has done all about the whaling she will do this fall." He then informed Smith that they were bound for the coast of Western Australia to liberate Fenian prisoners from British Jails. "The ship had been bought for that purpose and that purpose alone," Anthony revealed, "and you have been utterly deceived in the object of the journey. You have the right to be indignant." After a few minutes' deathly silence, Smith asked a few questions: "Then were we not going to sail to the River Platte, South America," "No certainly to Australia." Anthony replied. Then he tried to smooth any hurt feelings: saying, "God knows I need you, and I give you my word that I will stand by you as never a man stood by another," he declared. Much to his great pleasure, Smith replied: "Captain Anthony I will stick by you even if the ship burns and goes to hell of her jib boom."

Although the fitting out and financing of "The Catalpa" had been paramount, I had also agonised over the other aspect of our rescue plan. We knew that if our endeavour was to succeed, we must send separate agents under cover to Australia to prepare the groundwork in readiness for the escape of the prisoners. This was to be the most dangerous mission of all; because if the authorities had any inclination that an escape plan was being hatched they would increase security and arrest anyone they thought was behaving suspiciously.

For this perilous task I chose an old friend and colleague from my Fenian days in Dublin, his name was John J Breslin. John had been a prison guard in Richmond Jail, Dublin, in the eighteen sixties, and had shown tremendous courage in helping us with your sensational escape. He was to prove another inspired choice, for as we shall see his coolness under pressure would ultimately ensure the success of our project. The other agent we chose was recommended to me by Mr Talbot. His name was Captain Tom Desmond. A highly decorated Civil War veteran, Desmond was to be the unsung hero of the mission. As Breslin told me later, he could not praise Desmond enough; he was he said the ideal partner.

After many delays and a shortage of funds, Breslin and Desmond finally left San Francisco on the thirteenth of September eighteen seventy-five, to sail across the Pacific Ocean bound for Sydney Harbour Australia. For greater security, the two men travelled separately, Breslin had booked a cabin under the assumed name of James Collins and had given his occupation as a Californian gold speculator, whilst Desmond had to settle for a berth in steerage, under the pseudonym of James Johnson. On the long monotonous voyage across the Pacific both men did not communicate with each other.

It was imperative that they adopted a low profile and did not bring any undue attention onto themselves. Compared to the terrible suffering the crew of "The Catalpa" were experiencing during the many months crossing the Atlantic, their passage was dull but uneventful. After a leisurely passage they landed in Sydney Harbour and were soon introduced to the various Fenian groups that were very active in the town.

But Captain Anthony and the crew aboard "The Catalpa" were to spend fruitless months sailing in the Atlantic searching for whales. Unfortunately apart from hunting and killing a couple of small ones their voyage was proving a disaster. Eventually with their food and water stocks exhausted they were obliged to make for The Azores, a group of islands in the middle of the Atlantic Ocean. After docking six of Anthony's crew absconded and were never seen again. Obviously this further disaster put the whole mission in jeopardy but the ever resourceful Captain and his First Mate decided to leave port before any other sailors deserted. This decision meant that they would now have to ration food and water on the long voyage to their final destination. Also the partial failure of Captain Anthony's navigation instruments had caused them to sail hundreds of miles off course. It was only when they fortunately met another ship that the Captain could ascertain their position and luckily purchased some much needed supplies. These problems obviously delayed them and by now they were three months behind schedule.

As they neared Cape Town, Anthony agonised whether he should seek fresh supplies but decided that he could not take the risk of more desertions. This decision was to have a profound effect on the health of his crew during the remainder of their voyage to Australia, because by the time they reached their destination many of them were suffering from scurvy and other serious ailments.

Meanwhile after landing in Sydney, Breslin and Desmond managed to contact John Kelly and John Flood, who were highly active in the local Irish circles. These two influential Fenians introduced them to another very important figure in our story, a certain John King. King it seems had already set up his own rescue fund. This fund was his own idea and its ultimate object was to free the Fenian prisoners in Western Australia. King informed Breslin that he had spent the past seven years prospecting for gold in New Zealand and whilst there he had collected funds for his project from Irish sympathisers in the colony. On meeting Breslin, John King was immediately won over to our cause, especially when he heard that the Brotherhood in America had commissioned its own ship which was now sailing for Western Australia to make the rescue attempt. Without any hesitation King placed the funds he had available at Breslin's disposal. King also promised that he would bring any further funds that he collected directly to Western Australia. This money would eventually be crucial to the mission, because as usual with our organisation funds were always in short supply. After this meeting King immediately telegraphed one of his associates, a former Fenian prisoner now living in Queensland who he knew was also busy fund raising. He informed his friend that he was leaving Sydney immediately to rendezvous with him in his hometown of Brisbane. Later it transpired that the combined sum that John King and his fellow Fenian sympathiser managed to raise was the staggering sum of four thousand pounds in gold.

Tom Desmond who was kicking his heels decided that it was too dangerous for him too spend too long hanging around in Sydney, so he set out at once for Albany, Western Australia. As there were no direct sailings to Albany he had to travel from Sydney to Melbourne, and then had a long wait to catch a steamer to his destination in Western Australia. Once again Desmond was worried that his presence might be detected by the authorities so he went to ground until the steamer left port. By a strange coincidence Breslin travelled on the same ship as Desmond to Albany, *but once again they did not acknowledge each other. On his arrival in Albany the ever resourceful Desmond quickly realised that it would be more beneficial for the rescue attempt to base himself in the town of Perth. Perth was at that time a very small city with a population of seven thousand inhabitants, on the Swan River. As the only city in Western Australia it had recently been recognised as the state capital of Western Australia where the government now had its offices. Obviously because of Perth's larger population Desmond hoped that he could remain there undetected this was to prove a wise decision for the ultimate success of the mission. Fortunately once in Perth, Desmond managed to find work in the local carriage factory and by keeping a very low profile over the many months of waiting he did not attract any unwanted attention from the authorities.*

Whereas when Breslin arrived in Albany he at once boarded the steamer, "The Georgette" a steamer that carried the mail to the coastal towns along the coast of the colony that was also was to play a central role in the drama that was to unfold in the coming months. On board "The Georgette" Breslin saw for the first time the coastline from where he would endeavour to carry out his rescue attempt. After months of travelling he landed at his final destination the small town of Fremantle in November eighteen seventy-five.

As it was his first visit to the Southern Hemisphere, he was naively surprised to find he had arrived at the start of the Australian summer. Despite all the planning both financial and logistical he had not realised that the seasons were the opposite of what he was accustomed to in America., he was also to find the following months unbearably hot.

In Fremantle, Breslin was also surprised to find very pleasant lodgings at a local hotel called The Emerald Isle. This family run hotel was owned by an Irishman called Patrick Keating and his wife who were originally from Galway town. Breslin soon settled in and spent the first few days resting after his long arduous journey. At the time he thought that he would only have to wait a few weeks for "The Catalpa" to arrive; little realising that the whaler was still thousands of miles away and he still had many frustrating months to wait.

Desperate to avoid detection by the authorities, Breslin worked hard on developing his cover. When signing the hotel register he gave his occupation as a Californian land and minerals speculator. In his hotel room he had deliberately left letters lying around: one of which stated that he was the owner of mines in Nevada and another advised that one hundred thousand dollars had been deposited on his behalf in the Hollanders Bank in San Francisco.

The second letter confirmed that the other members of the syndicate are agreed in allowing you to be the sole judge whether to invest funds into Australian gold shares, timber, or grazing land. Breslin knew these letters would be read, and the rumours soon spread around the town about the rich Yankee. This news that he had the enormous sum of one hundred thousand dollars to invest in the small under populated colony of Western Australia, caused quiete a stir. Obviously the rumours had the desired effect, as no one was going to query his movements in the future and this enabled him to travel freely and without hindrance.

Breslin's decision to base himself in Fremantle quickly proved to be the correct one, for with its close proximity to the prison he could now plan his next move. He had began to attend mass at the local catholic church where he found the church full of prisoners dressed in their familiar canary yellow clothes. There, he soon befriended the local parish priest, Father Patrick McCabe. The idea to contact the priest had come from John O'Riley in Boston and once again, O'Riley had come up with an inspired idea because when Breslin divulged his real name, the priest was delighted to meet this Fenian hero, whose fame for freeing James Stephens from jail had reached this far-flung colony. When Breslin then revealed his real purpose, the priest immediately gave his full backing to the mission and promised to relay messages to the prisoners.

In this the first of their clandestine meetings, the priest told Breslin that the best prisoner to contact was a certain Will Foley, a former soldier who had a ticket of leave. This ticket meant that Foley was in essence a free man and could leave the colony providing he had clearance from the authorities.

At the first meeting between Breslin and Will Foley which had been arranged by McCabe, Breslin was immediately impressed by Foley, quickly realising that here was a man he could trust. In their conversation Breslin stressed that the utmost secrecy must be observed in this and all future meetings. Before they parted he handed Foley a note, stressing that it must only be given to James Wilson, the author of the Voice from the Tomb letter. Will Foley true to his word went directly to the prison stables, where Wilson was working, as a trusted convict. On handing him Breslin's note, Foley told him to read it and then destroy it immediately, Wilson on reading it, thought at first it was a hoax but on being assured by Foley that it was genuine read it again. The note said and I quote, "To James Wilson and all the rest, Greetings from those who have not forgotten and are close by. Destroy this letter for the sake of Old Erin, the Tomb is now ajar." In later years he was to explain, that he was certain when he first read the note that he was the victim of an elaborate hoax, but on reading it over and over again he realised that it was true, and did what he was ordered and ate it.

During the proceeding weeks Breslin had reconnoitred the local area and made his plans for the rescue. He soon realised that only prisoners with trustee status should be considered, as they were free to move about outside the prison during the daytime without too much supervision. With the coming of the New Year, Father McCabe decided to visit the various convict stations and depots in the out lying districts of the colony, saying mass and hearing the convict's confessions. For this task he needed a driver and he was able to persuade the prison Superintendent that James Wilson was an ideal choice. This arrangement allowed a clandestine meeting to take place between Breslin and Wilson; the rendezvous was deep in the bush, four miles from Fremantle. This meeting was the stuff of legends, for here were two men shaking hands for the first time, one of whom had travelled thousands of miles to rescue the other and the other man who had lost all hope of freedom, but both linked by a common cause, an Irish Republic.

After the greetings and handshakes, Breslin outlined his plan for the rescue, explaining to Wilson that he was hopeful that "The Catalpa" would soon arrive from America. At first the prisoner was very sceptical and said that the plan was unworkable, but when Breslin emphasised that the Clan had purchased its own whaling ship for the rescue and barring an accident he was certain it would arrive in the colony as he had every confidence in its skipper Captain Anthony. When he heard about the lengths that the Fenian Brotherhood of America had gone to after receiving his letter, he could not believe what he was hearing. During Breslins explanation Wilson's whole attitude completely changed as he realised that here was a man who was totally dedicated to freeing him and his fellow Fenians. At the end of this first meeting, Breslin read out the names of the Fenians who he hoped to rescue, but he insisted that all those named must be on their best behaviour and the utmost secrecy must always be observed. The names on the list were as follows Hogan the prisons printer, Cranston, who worked in the storehouse, Darraugh, who was a clerk in the office; Hassett who was the Superintendents gardener and lastly Harrington who worked at the docks, all these prisoners had trustee status and were unlikely to get into any trouble with the prison authorities. Finally it was agreed that the only way that contact should be made was through Father McCabe.

Unfortunately for the conspirators the planned rescue was still many months away and for long periods both prisoners and rescuers doubted if their plans would ever reach fruition. Whilst Breslin was laying plans for the arrival of the whaler, the *progress of "The Catalpa" was very slow and by January eighteen seventy-six, they were still sailing in the South Atlantic, thousands of miles from their final destination. During the next two months progress was still painfully slow, but Anthony's entry in the ships log dated tenth of March, noted that the wind had changed and the ship started at last to make good headway. By now they were running out of food and fresh water and so it was a very relieved Captain and crew that finally sighted the coast of Western Australia on the twenty seventh of March eighteen seventy-six. The following day they sailed into the harbour of Banbury and dropped anchor. On their arrival Captain Arnold immediately ordered a landing boat to be readied, it was soon lowered over the side and he went ashore. Once on land he reported to the Custom House as was required. Long hours of tedium followed as the officials went through the landing procedures, the Custom officers then stressed that he must give plenty of notice before he left Banbury. That evening after checking that there were no messages for him at the telegraph office, Anthony decided to go to the local hotel and enjoy a good meal, hoping that the "The Catalpa's" arrival in port might have alerted his fellow conspirators. But when no one approached him at the hotel he returned to his ship in a very despondent mood.*

Meanwhile Breslin after the long months of waiting was by now convinced that something untoward had happened to "The Catalpa" and in desperation sent a coded message to me in New York. In my reply I stated that to the best of my knowledge she was still on its way to Western Australia. On receiving my reply Breslin now finalised his preparations for the rescue, but by February of that fateful year his financial situation continued to deteriorate and by early March his position was becoming desperate and he wondered how long he could keep up the pretence of playing the rich Yankee. Fortunately his prayers were now answered, when on returning from a reconnaissance trip, he was informed by the proprietor of the Emerald Isle hotel that a visitor wanted to meet with him on urgent financial matters. That evening as he pondered who this mystery person might be, John King alias George Jones was directed to his room. On hearing a knock on his hotel door, it was a huge relief to Breslin to find that his visitor was in fact the ever reliable John King. After their initial greetings King undid his shirt to reveal his money belt, which contained the enormous sum of eight hundred pounds sterling. Obviously Breslin was delighted with this windfall because it ensured that he could now finance the rescue attempt.

Later that evening they sat and discussed the rescue plans, King then informed him that he had received an urgent message from the Clan in New York, telling him about Breslins dire financial situation and also they suggested that he should offer his assistance in forthcoming escape attempts. Both the money he had brought and the offer of help were gratefully accepted, as John King had shown himself to be a reliable and trustworthy agent during Breslin's stay in Australia. In the coming weeks two more of Kings fellow Fenian conspirators arrived in Fremantle, these were Michael Brennan and James Sugrue, both of whose assistance was to prove vital on the day of the rescue. By late March all of their preparations were complete and they all hoped and prayed that the whaler would soon make an appearance.

Over the coming days Breslin spent each morning anxiously scrutinising the ships bulletin boards at the docks hoping to see if "The Catalpa" had finally made port. After months of waiting it was an immense relief when he finally read that the whaler had arrived in Albany. Rushing back to his hotel room he composed a coded message and telegraphed it to me in New York informing me of the whaler's arrival in Australia. Obviously after all my trials and tribulations I could at last relax a little. Whilst at the telegraph office Breslin sent the following message, to Captain Anthony, Master Barque Catalpa, Banbury, "Have you any news from New Bedford and can you come to Fremantle?" The next morning Anthony had risen early and received Breslins message, he replied at once saying, "No news from New Bedford, shall not come to Fremantle," this message confirmed to Breslin, that the arrival of the whaler had not aroused any undue attention. Breslin then managed to get a note to the prisoner Wilson which said, "Our friend has reached port with greetings from Old Erin, he wishes you well and hopes you are always amenable to your warders he hopes to see you again soon."

That afternoon Breslin booked a seat on the stagecoach leaving for Albany the following morning, After a sleepless night he boarded the coach for the long dusty journey to meet his fellow conspirator, his only worry was how he would make contact with Captain Anthony without raising suspicion. By a strange coincidence Anthony was purchasing meat for the crew when the stagecoach from Fremantle pulled into the market square in Albany. On seeing Breslin step down from the coach, the butcher mentioned to the Captain that the gentleman who had just arrived from Fremantle was another Yankee and insisted on making the introductions. Obviously they now had the ideal cover, so after a brief conversation they arranged to have dinner that evening.

That evening under a starry Australian sky Anthony and Breslin dined together and bizarrely this was the first time that the two key figures in this epic mission had met. Over the meal Breslin outlined his plan for the rescue attempt; obviously both men knew the dire consequences of failure. If the plot failed and they were arrested they faced either summary execution or years in prison. They also both knew that the utmost secrecy must be maintained at all times, Anthony assured Breslin that most of his crew were not even aware of the real reason for their visit to Albany. Breslin then advised Anthony that after much deliberation he felt the ideal site from which the prisoners could be picked up and transported back to "The Catalpa," was along the coast at Rockingham Beach, a long stretch of sand, south, of Fremantle. In their discussions that evening they both decided to travel on the steamer "The Georgette," which was sailing the following morning back to Fremantle. Anthony was particularly keen on making this trip as he wanted to explore the coast line before committing himself to Breslins plan.

So the next morning they boarded the steamer and Breslin was pleasantly surprised to see how quickly Captain Anthony had introduced himself to the Master of "The Georgette," Captain Grady. The two men he observed were soon discussing the tides and currents along the coastline together, Breslin could actually see Anthony using the Captains binoculars to get a better view of Rockingham Beach. On their arrival at Victoria Quay Fremantle that afternoon, they were both horrified to see a British Man of War the gunboat H.M.S Conflict, tied up at the opposite end of the quay, worryingly they both realised that this could spell disaster for their enterprise because the naval ship was easily capable of outrunning the whaler. From the conversations they had with the crew of the gunboat they found out that it was due to sail to Perth in eight days time. Also they were informed that it had a complement of thirty sailors and possessed two guns. According to the sailors they talked to, there was still some doubt where they were heading after visiting Perth, some thought their destination was north to Darwin, whilst others said they were headed east to Adelaide. If it sailed North, Anthony advised Breslin, it would be the flank of "The Catalpa's" escape route and their rescue mission would have to be abandoned, but with any luck if its destination was South to Adelaide, this would leave the coast line of Western Australia clear of danger. They agreed that when "HMS Conflict" left Fremantle, Breslin would send a telegram to Anthony which would read, "Your friend N or S has gone home, when you sail." If the gunboat headed to Adelaide as they hoped, their prayers would be answered.

At this time they had no other option but to carry on with their preparations and so with this in mind they rode down to Rockingham, timing the journey at two hours twenty minutes. On their arrival Anthony was pleased to discover that Garden Island sheltered the long arc of Rockingham Beach from the open sea, this *he explained to Breslin would make the landing and disembarking easier. On the beach they discussed the arrangement for getting the escape party onto the whaler as no suitable boats were available to purchase or hire. After much discussion Anthony reluctantly agreed to use his own whaleboat to complete the rescue. He then promised Breslin that if the prisoners were delivered to the beach, Anthony himself would convey them to "The Catalpa" which would lay ten to sixteen miles out at sea. This distance he calculated would take at least five hours to row. With their plans now successfully completed Anthony enthusiastically marked the spot chosen for the rendezvous with two large driftwood logs that they hauled to the edge of the sand dunes. Now satisfied with their days work the two conspirators rode back to Fremantle to enjoy their dinner, and on the following morning Anthony boarded the stagecoach for the journey back to his ship in Bunbury.*

On Tuesday morning the eleventh of April during Holy Week, in eighteen seventy-six, Breslin woke to find the warship HMS Conflict, had gone from the wharf. Rushing along to the ships bulletin board he discovered it had sailed for Adelaide leaving their escape route open. Breslin quickly sent his coded telegram to Albany and as soon as Anthony received the news he ordered his boat over the side and went ashore to seek port clearance. This frustrating process was to lose him a whole day and by the time the paper work was completed it was too late to sail. The next morning Anthony sent the following message, "I sail today, Goodbye, answer if received", Anthony. On receiving the message in Fremantle, Breslin calculated that if "The Catalpa" had left that day, which was Wednesday, it would be off Rockingham beach by the Friday. Worryingly for their plans as it was Easter Week he knew that on Good Friday all government buildings in the colony would be closed meaning that all prisoners would be locked up in their cells. In desperation he sent off this urgent reply, "Friday being Good Friday I shall remain in Fremantle and start for York on Saturday morning. I wish you may strike oil, Collins." Fortunately for the mission Anthony went ashore before sailing and read Breslin's reply. Also whilst in town that day he found that everyone was speaking pessimistically about the weather forecast and the north westerly gales that were expected. Local seamen advised him not to leave the safety of the port until the storm had blown itself out.

The next afternoon Maundy Thursday, Breslin was delighted to receive the following reply from Anthony, "Yours received. Did not sail today. Winds ahead and rising. Sailing in the morning. Goodbye. Anthony." He now knew that "The Catalpa" would be off Rockingham on the Saturday morning and so he alerted

Tom Desmond who was still living in Perth. Desmond after months of waiting was at last ordered to set off at once for Fremantle in a hired trap, loaded with guns, ammunition and a change of clothing for the prisoners. Later that evening Breslin also managed to get messages to the prison warning them that the escape was now planned for Saturday. With all their plans finalised once again fate was against them, as by seven o'clock on that Thursday evening, "The Catalpa" was taking the brunt of a north westerly-storm. During the night she dragged her anchor and it was to take all of the Captain Anthony and his crew's expertise and strength to stop the whaler from running aground.

As dawn broke on that Good Friday morning the winds were still so ferocious that it was obvious that they would not be leaving Bunbury for Rockingham that day. It was not until the afternoon that they were finally able to launch the whaleboat, on this occasion Sam Smith went ashore. Frustratingly because it was Good Friday the telegraph office was shut. But Smith had over the previous days got to know the local telegrapher, Beatrice Warren and he managed to persuade her to send this message, "Can you advance more money if needed. Will telegraph you again in the morning."

Breslin had attended mass on Good Friday afternoon and on his way back to his hotel called in at the Fremantle telegraph office that was fortunately open, here he received Anthony's latest coded message which confirmed that there would be no "Catalpa" tomorrow. Somehow he managed once again to get the message to the now distraught prisoners that there would be no escape attempt on the Saturday. In this his final message he wrote that he would give a signal at mass on Easter Day if the attempt was going to take place on the Monday The signal was simple, he would put a finger by his nose and then draw it across his right cheek. Easter Saturday morning was again to see Breslin at the telegraph office; this luckily was for the last time. The final message that he received was the delightful confirmation which read, "I shall certainly sail today. Suppose you will leave for York on Monday morning, Goodbye." Now that he had final confirmation that "The Catalpa had set sail, he managed to alert all the participants in the rescue attempt confirming that it would definitely take place on Monday.

Meanwhile after leaving Albany at dawn, by noon on Easter Sunday, "The Catalpa" was laying offshore thirty miles south-west of the Rottenest lighthouse. On board the whaler Anthony was now preparing to go to Rockingham Beach in the whaleboat. For this dangerous mission he handpicked men he could trust. On completion of his preparations he cautioned Smith to keep "The Catalpa" twelve miles off the mainland, outside Australian territorial waters. He also said that if the water police approached, he was to inform them that the Captain had gone ashore to purchase a new anchor. In his final instruction he made Smith promise that if they did not return with the prisoners he was to go off on a normal whaling expedition and hopefully earn enough to cover the expense of the voyage. The ships whaleboat was then lowered over the side and the rescue party set a leg of mutton sail and they soon left their sister ship far behind.

The weather that afternoon was perfect for sailing and they soon found themselves at the southern end of Garden Island, off Rockingham. From there they surfed the breakers into the smooth waters of Rockingham Sound. With his telescope Anthony spotted his markers ashore and by eight thirty that evening, they were eating their meal of biscuit and cold ham, washed down with a tot of rum. After their meal, well fed and watered the crew stretched out and were all soon asleep in the grassy sand dunes not realising the dangers they were about to encounter the following day. That night Anthony was obviously the only one who found it hard to sleep. He lay there wondering what tomorrow would bring, he alone knowing the terrible consequences of failure.

The next day Easter Monday was by tradition 'Perth Regatta Day,' one of the largest social occasions in the calendar of the small colony of Western Australia and so everyone's attention was focused on this event. The only men who had their minds elsewhere were the Fenian prisoners and their desperate rescuers. Before five thirty that morning, the Irish Republican Brotherhood man John McCarthy set out from Fremantle on the Bunbury road, in his possession was a pair of heavy-duty wire cutters North of Fremantle on the road to Perth, Patrick Walsh similarly equipped was also on the move, their orders were to cut the telegraph wires. This action would greatly delay the government's response to the rescue on that fateful day. The two Irish Republican Brotherhood men on completing their task had orders to return to the Emerald Isle Hotel and then brazen it out as there was not enough room for them on "The Catalpa."

At seven thirty, Breslin, Desmond and the two other Irish Republican Brotherhood members, Michael Sugrue and Patrick Brennan were already on the road travelling South in three carriages. Once clear of the town they stopped and made their final preparations. On arming themselves with revolvers Breslin stressed they must only be used as a last resort. Then with a growing sense of excitement they drove on towards the prearranged rendezvous on the Rockingham road. On their arrival at

247

the meeting place, Desmond recalled later it was a beautiful autumn morning and as they sat and waited he said he was fascinated at seeing all the wonderful birds that lived in the Australian bush. All of sudden much to their immense satisfaction they saw the first three convicts approaching, Wilson, Cranston and the oldest prisoner Michael Harrington. When they spotted the carriages the prisoners ran towards them shouting with delight and jumped aboard Desmond's wagon. With these three men on board Desmond set out at once for Rockingham, Breslin could see them immediately start stripping off their penal clothes and throw them into the bush. The second group of escapees Darragh, Hassett and Hogan, now came into sight, waving their hands and shouting, the noise and commotion upsetting the horses, but Breslin firmly reined them in and they soon settled into a trot. The three prisoners now had to run behind the wagon and jump onboard. Once aboard they quickly grabbed at the waiting pile of civilian clothes and immediately began changing.

At nine o'clock that morning the ever reliable John King, who was designated to be the rearguard for the mission, mounted his horse and nonchalantly rode up Fremantle High Street heading north as though his destination was the town of Perth, but he suddenly veered around and headed south and rode through the towns back streets. Riding at a steady pace so as not to attract any undue attention he caught up with the carriages of Breslin and Desmond near the Rockingham Hotel and was able to tell them that thankfully there was no sign that the escape had been noticed and all was quiet. Greatly relieved at the news the whole party headed towards the rescue boat on the beach.

Meanwhile on the beach that morning Anthony and his crew were woken by noise of men working on the nearby jetty that belonged to the 'Rockingham Jarrah Timber Company.' Cursing his luck that there were men working on what he thought was a holiday in the colony, Anthony walked over to speak to one of them. In his conversation with the foreman, William Bell, he told him they were on their way to Fremantle to purchase an anchor, but Bell shook his head., he said, "I know the truth; you are deserters from a ship." Anthony ignored this accusation, but what was to worry him was when Bell told him that the stack of timber the men were working on was due to be picked up by the steamer "The Georgette" that morning. As they chatted, Bell advised Anthony to keep in close to Garden Island going out, as this would avoid a wedge of coral in mid-channel. The Captain thanked him for his advice, but the news that the steamer was on its way was of great concern to him as he knew that it could wreck all of their plans.

248

The first carriage to arrive on the beach was driven by Brennan and he soon spotted the crew of "The Catalpa." By now Bell was the only one left working on the timber wharf and Brennan immediately urged Anthony and then Breslin to shoot him. From what was later to occur that morning, in hindsight they all agreed that they should somehow have incapacitated Bell. The other carriages were now finding it very hard going because after the heavy rain of the previous day the sand had become very boggy and the wheels were sinking into the wet sand. But at last near the dunes the trees gave way to low bush and finally the prisoners could see the whaleboat that had come to their rescue. The convicts jumped out of the carriages and in their excitement they slapped the rumps of the horses who galloped madly off into the undergrowth. On seeing the Fenians rush towards them Anthony's crew drew their knives in fright, thinking it was the Custom and Exercise men. By then pandemonium had broken out and it was to take all of Captain Anthony's authoritativeness to restore order. Anthony said later that his priority that day was to get the whaleboat and the men off the beach, because he had already spotted the smoke from "The Georgette" on the horizon and he knew that its arrival at Rockingham would spell disaster for all of them.

In a final act of bravado Breslin, before boarding the rescue boat called for order and he withdrew from his pocket a sheet of paper and read the following statement "This is to certify that I have this day released from the clemency of Her Most Gracious Majesty, Victoria, Queen of Great Britain, six Irishmen condemned…for having been guilty of the atrocious and unpardonable crimes known to the unenlightened portion of mankind as "love of liberty" and "hatred of tyranny." For this act of 'Irish assurance" my birth and my blood being my full and sufficient warranty." At the end of his proclamation, he added "I've the honour and pleasure to bid you good-day. From all future acquaintance, excuse me, I pray." Breslin then wrapped the letter in sealskin and bound it to a piece of driftwood; he then ran up above the shoreline and with a shout of defiance pushed the long piece of wood into the sand. By now the whaleboat had been boarded in an orderly manner and the crew having pushed the crowded boat out into the surf, quickly jumped aboard and then began rowing. From his vantage point in the stern Anthony now saw Bell mount one of the horses and ride off to raise the alarm.

Within two hours Anthony could see armed police together with native trackers already on the beach. Back at the prison the alarm had been raised at nine-thirty that morning when it was found that the prisoner Hogan was missing. Immediately there was a check of all the other convicts and it was found that

249

a total of six were missing. From the veranda of the Port Hotel, McCarthy and Walsh said later that suddenly chaos in the town ensued, with police and warders rushing in all directions, but what greatly added to the panic was the realisation that all the telegraph wires were cut and the Governor could not be informed of the escape. In the midst of all the panic William Bell came galloping into town on one of the escapees horses, yelling and shouting to everyone he met that he had seen the escape taking place at Rockingham Beach. With this knowledge the police were sent straight there with orders to apprehend the prisoners and their rescuers.

Also about this time the head of the Water Police, Superintendent Stone, on hearing about the jail break and the involvement of "The Catalpa" endeavoured to telegraph the gunboat "HMS Conflict," in Albany, but the line was dead. By the time the telegraph was repaired, "The Conflict" had left Albany bound for Adelaide.

By noon on that fateful Monday, "The Catalpa" was sixteen miles offshore in calm seas, but during the afternoon the wind started to increase and white horses appeared. This was obviously going to make the task of spotting the whaleboat even more difficult. As darkness came on, Smith ordered lookouts to be posted in each of the ships topmasts and lanterns lashed to every mast as well as the bows. "I wanted;" he said later, "the ship to look like a floating city." At five o'clock that afternoon the men on the whaleboat briefly sighted "The Catalpa," but in the gathering gloom they soon lost all sight of her. Throughout that terrible night the storm increased and the heavy seas poured water over all those aboard the whaleboat. At times the seas nearly engulfed them, the convicts Hogan and Cranston were kept busy all night bailing water and then to increase their problems the mast snapped and everything, timber, rigging, sail and halyard were washed over the side and threatened to drag the boat down with it. Only quick thinking by the third mate saved them, he grabbed an axe and hacked off the shrouds and then managed to haul the tangled mass back on board. Luckily they then managed to reconstruct the debris into a jury mast. Anthony later confessed that he had his doubts that they would ever see their sister ship again. But towards dawn on the Tuesday morning thankfully the winds had began to moderate and when the sun eventually came up on that eventful day, all the men on the whaleboat cheered as they saw "The Catalpa" sailing towards them.

But to their horror smoke from the steamer was clearly visible and soon "The Georgette" was near enough for Anthony to have the sail taken down and he ordered then everyone to lie still in the bottom of the whaleboat. Fortunately the steamer passed them by and Anthony said later that he could plainly see *an officer on the bridge searching the shore of Garden Isle, obviously thinking that the whaleboat had foundered in the heavy seas. "The Georgette" now pulled alongside "The Catalpa" and Superintendent Stone of the Water Police announced his intention to come onboard and search for the missing convicts. In reply Sam Smith was said to have answered, "You try it and you'll be goddamned and sorry. What the hell did we lick the pants off you damn Britishers in eighteen twelve for? You don't own the goddamn ocean!" Smith was then seen to pick up a harpoon with the obvious intention of resisting any attempt at boarding.*

Captain Grady of "The Georgette" now informed Stone that the ships coal was running out and they must return to port and refuel. The Superintendent confident that due to the lack of wind "The Catalpa" would not be able to leave its station, agreed to return to Fremantle. Anthony on seeing the steamer sailing back to port immediately ordered the crew to start rowing again and rehoisted the jury mast. By now "The Catalpa" was barely visible, but Wilson found a red whaling flag and started waving it. On seeing the flag, Smith ordered the crew to hoist the ships topgallant sails and the whaler was soon running strongly towards the whaleboat. But a police cutter was also out searching for the escaped prisoner and on spotting the whaleboat endeavoured to cut it off before it reached the safety of its mother ship. On seeing the cutter heading for them, Anthony ordered all the men to arm themselves, he himself was as determined as the Fenians to resist any attempt at being arrested. But thankfully he could now see that "The Catalpa" was winning their desperate race for freedom.

When "The Georgette" arrived back in Fremantle, Walsh, McCarthy and Father McCabe were relieved to see that there were none of the escaped prisoners on board. But as soon as it docked, working parties immediately started to fill the ships coal bunkers. Meanwhile at sea that dramatic afternoon the Coxswain of the police cutter tried all he knew to catch the whaleboat before it reached "The Catalpa," but at two- thirty that afternoon, Anthony's badly damaged boat slammed alongside its mother ship and immediately the ships crew winched them aboard. It was later stated by both Captain Anthony and Sam Smith that the final distance between the two boats was less than two hundred yards. Once back onboard his ship the Captain embraced and complimented Sam Smith and then ordered the ship's steward to prepare the best dinner the ship could afford, the Fenian's were then able to sit down to have their first meal as free men in many years. But later Anthony would recall, that much to his distress there was no wind that night and "The Catalpa" did not move one inch from its station.

While this drama was taking place at sea, back in Fremantle, Governor Robinson ordered a nine pound field gun to be hauled on board "The Georgette", together with a large compliment of the Pensioner Guards and also a contingent of heavily armed policemen, this he said was to ensure the whaler was boarded and the prisoners and their rescuers were detained. But in a meeting he had with Superintendent Stone before "The Georgette" left port, they both agreed that if "The Catalpa" was outside Australian territorial waters it would be illegal to board her, the only way they could recapture the prisoners was by bluff and a show of strength. At first light on Wednesday morning, a very weary Captain Anthony climbed into the main topmast with his telescope and once again spotted the mast of "The Georgette." Ominously on this occasion the steamer headed towards "The Catalpa" flying a man of war and vice-admirals flag, Anthony knew that by flying these pennants the steamer really meant business. A south- east wind had began to blow but it was to slight to help the whaleboat escape and the steamer overhauled them with ease.

After hastily eating his breakfast Anthony order the Fenians below telling them that they could keep their firearms, but at all costs to keep out of sight. Too his crew he said. "If we are captured we will be imprisoned in the same jail as those brave souls we have rescued, I can assure you that the British authorities will show us no mercy and they will make us an example to stop any future rescue attempts. After speaking these words the men began to arm themselves, some with harpoon lancers and others with cutting spades that were normally used for slicing whale blubber. Sam Smith who was relishing the pending confrontation supervised the bringing up on deck of grindstones and spare spars all of which could be dropped on any boat that tried to board "The Catalpa." Also he ordered harpoon guns to be mounted on deck and a supply of brass cartridges made ready. This was only a show of defiance as the cannon on board the steamer could easily blow them out of the water.

Captain Grady on board "The Georgette" was concerned about the freshening wind and the help it would give the whaler, so he ran up a signal instructing "The Catalpa" to heave to and shorten sail. Obviously Anthony ignored both instructions. As "The Catalpa" did not comply, Superintendent Stone ordered a shot to be fired across the whaler's stern. The sound of the shot startled all on board and Breslin said later he thought this was the beginning of a deadly barrage but this fortunately did not happen. Anthony was to later confirm that the water from the cannon ball caused a splash as high as the ships mast head. After this dramatic event, "The Georgette" came alongside and the following conversation took place.

STONE, "I demand six escaped prisoners now on board this ship, in the name of the Governor of Western Australia....I know the men I want are on board, for the police saw them on board yesterday".

ANTHONY: "I have no prisoners on board."

STONE: "You have and I can see three of them."

ANTHONY. "I have no prisoners here. All are seamen belonging to the ship."

The wind was now threatening to produce a collision, so "The Georgette" was compelled to pull away from the whaler.

STONE, "I will give you fifteen minutes to consider what you do."

The tension was now unbearable on both ships, each Captain wondering what the outcome would be, at the end of the fifteen minutes, "The Georgette" again went alongside "The Catalpa" and Stone once again demanded the handover of the prisoners.

ANTHONY, "I have none on board."

STONE: "If you don't give them up, I will fire into you and sink you or disable you."

ANTHONY. "I don't care what you do, I'm on the high seas and that flag protects me."

"But if there were escaped convicts on board," said Stone, "your flag won't protect you in that."

ANTHONY: "Yes it will, or in felony either."

STONE: "Will you let me on board your ship to see for myself?"

ANTHONY: "You shan't board my ship."

STONE: "Then your government will be communicated with, and you must take the consequences."

ANTHONY: "All right."

There was then a further fifteen minutes wait, then someone called out to Anthony, from "The Georgette," that they had a telegram from the American government authorising the seizure of "The Catalpa". Anthony was to heave to. "I'll blow your masts out unless you do so." Once again Breslin expected "The Georgette" to open fire and disable the whaler, but once again this did not happen. By now both vessels were over eighteen miles off the coast, well outside Australian territorial waters.

As the wind increased, the British steamer could only watch as "The Catalpa's" sails filled and she headed offshore. "The Georgette" using both steam and sail followed the whaler for an hour, but as the wind became stronger "The Catalpa" started to draw ahead, Anthony then brought the prisoners on deck. "Boys, take a good look at her, probably you'll never see her again. "The Georgette" finally peeled away at nine- thirty on that dramatic morning, Captain Grady knowing that under international law his hands were tied.

That night another storm engulfed "The Catalpa," but by the Friday they were over four hundred miles away from the coast of Australia on their long journey back to New York. The journey was too be very acrimonious at times and lead too much rancour. It was only Anthony's strict discipline that somehow maintained the peace on board and both he and Sam Smith were very relieved when they finally docked in New York and the warring Fenian's disembarked. The last entry in "The Catalpa's" log book dated the eighteenth of August, eighteen seventy six, timed at one- thirty, read "Went to City wharf. Made her fast. So ends this pleasant voyage for Mr J.T. Richardson."

As soon as "The Catalpa" docked a very elated John Breslin went ashore and headed straight to the hotel ran by the famous Irish Republican Brotherhood man O'Donovan Rossa, in Chatham Square, New York. The Clan Na Gael organisation was totally unprepared and unfortunately I myself was in Philadelphia when I got the message from Dennis Rosa telling me that "The Catalpa" had docked in New York. Although very sick at this time I caught the first available train back to New York and drove straight to the Rossa Hotel. Much to my anger and frustration, when I at last managed to get the freed prisoners and their rescuers alone, I was immediately confronted by a barrage of complaints about my true and trusted friend John Breslin. This man who had given his whole life for our cause and who when asked had travelled thousands of miles to carry out the audacious rescue without a seconds hesitation. When I explained this fact to them there was silence as they reflected on my words then one by one they apologised and shook Breslin's hand.

By now it seemed every Irishman in the city was celebrating the return of "The Catalpa," huge crowds descended on the whaler and to meet and cheer the captain and his crew. I myself went down to the wharf where "The Catalpa" was docked and personally congratulate Captain Anthony. On meeting him again after his epic voyage, I could not believe it was the same person. When the whaler had started out on its long journey he had weighed one hundred and sixty pounds and his hair was jet black, but now he weighed only one hundred and twenty pounds and his hair was totally grey. As we talked in the privacy of his cabin I realised that his overriding wish was to return home to New Bedford as soon as possible. But we had other ideas and in New York that weekend Anthony presented the flag *of "The Catalpa" to the Clan and he then travelled down to Philadelphia where a great fete was held to honour him.*

When "The Catalpa" finally arrived back in its home port on the following Thursday, Anthony was greatly surprised to see huge crowds again waiting to greet him and also to hear a seventy-one gun salute fired in his honour, one gun for every state in the Union and one for every county in Ireland. The following evening John Boyle O'Reilly gave a speech to acclaim Anthony and his crew at Liberty Hall, New Bedford, "Anthony's self sacrifice and fidelity he said, as he took his life in his hands when he beached his whaleboat on the penal colony defying its fearful law, defying the gallows and the chain gang, in order to keep faith with the men who had placed their trust in him this is almost beyond belief in our selfish and commonplace time."

I have sent you this letter to inform you of the exploits of "The Catalpa" because it has galvanised every Irishman in America, with the result that donations have increased dramatically' and hopefully we shall be able to increase our support for those poor wretches that are now being evicted in Ireland during these troubled times.

God Bless You.

John Devoy.

When the full details of the escape of the Fenian prisoners from Western Australia was published in Ireland, later that year it enabled the Republican cause to regain credibility after the catastrophe's and disasters it had suffered in recent years. The rescue of the Fenians brought to the attention of the public the forced transportation of men and women from both Britain and Ireland and in the subsequent debate in the House of Commons that year the system was finally abandoned. Having had my dear brother Owen snatched from me and sent to Australia, I knew from personal experience the full horror that this iniquitous form of punishment has inflicted on its victims young and old, male and female.

CHAPTER THIRTEEN

Now with both my sons married, I had more time on my hands and my thoughts returned to my main interest, the current problems and politics of Ireland. For a brief period in the eighteen seventy's harvests had been exceptionally good and farm prices had gradually risen but unfortunately this brief period of relative prosperity was soon over. Let me now explain what happened. Evictions had again risen sharply in the years eighteen sixty to eighteen sixty-four, when on average there were two thousand a year. Then in eighteen sixty-five this number decreased and the figure dropped to eight hundred and thirty two, this trend was to continue until the end of that decade. This decrease in evictions was followed by a significant drop in emigration and the combination of the two was to lead to a feeling that Ireland was at last over its long nightmare. I have always thought that although eviction was terrible, the loss of all our young people caused a great deal of heartache both to them and the grieving family they left behind. For although when leaving they all promised to return, very few were ever to see the shores of Ireland again.

This improvement in the wellbeing of the Irish people was sadly not to last, as suddenly in the year of eighteen seventy-seven, farm prices began to drop and the weather we had that summer was atrocious with heavy rain and strong winds. This terrible weather obviously affected the harvest and at the same time cheap imported food was starting to flood into both England and Ireland. This was the result of the opening up of the vast corn growing areas in America and Canada, together with the development of efficient transport by both rail and fast steamships across the Atlantic. These imports forced the price of grain down to such a low figure that the Irish farmers could not compete. Month by month the price of grain continued to fall, inevitably this loss of income was ultimately to have dire consequences for the small tenant farmers. Unable now to obtain a sustainable price for their crops, once again they could not pay their rent and eviction loomed.

The wet summer and the resulting reduction in the potato crop to less than half of that of the previous year threatened the prospect of another famine and a return to the horrors of the not too distant past. All this was to lead to a doubling of evictions in eighteen seventy-eight, to the highest figure for ten years and by eighteen eighty this figure had doubled again. By now it was calculated fifty per cent of the population were living on private charity. Scenes reminiscent of the Great Famine were once again commonplace with evicted families flooding to the ports and leaving Ireland in their thousands. In the far west of the country the people's plight in some cases was the worst this century, with some nine-tenths of the population relying on charity to survive.

But politically Ireland was also changing, as we have seen Isaac Butt, to his great credit had began the process of uniting the Irish Members of Parliament into a cohesive party. This work was completed by the greatest Irish politician of this century, Charles Stewart Parnell. Parnell was an unlikely champion of the poor people of Ireland, born into the landed gentry with a country seat in Wicklow; he was also member of the Anglican Ascendancy. This man was to eventually mould the Irish Members of Parliament into the most unified party ever seen in Westminster and he was to keep the problems of Ireland at the forefront of business in the House of Commons until his untimely death. This time the poor starving Irish people were at last to have a powerful voice in both the House of Parliament in London and at home in Ireland and ultimately after much heartache, suffering and prolonged land agitation, William Gladstone the Prime Minister would eventually persuade his Liberal Party to pass legislation that would protect all tenant farmers from the thieving landowners and their henchmen. Parnell and his colleagues in Parliament for their part brought pressure to bear at every possible occasion in the struggle for long overdue improvements.

The Fenian Party now renamed The Irish Republican Brotherhood or IRB had after the removal of my cousin James Stephens from the leadership, elected as its new leader the uncompromising, deaf and almost blind Charles Kickham. During preceding years most of the IRB membership had been willing to cooperate with Isaac Butt; unfortunately they soon became disillusioned with this experiment. From this time until the present day the IRB compromise and have concentrated all their efforts on their ultimate goal of an Irish Republic. But this uncompromising stance by the leadership lead to a split in the party and John Biggar and John O'Conner Power, together with other influential IRB men, realised the absurdity of the situation and decided that to continue with their work in Parliament was their only viable option. This decision to remain as Members of Parliament would ultimately lead to them being expelled from IRB for what was perceived at the time as heresy. But with this split in the Fenian ranks came a feeling from the grass roots that they had to find ways of being more effective. I myself had sympathy with Biggar and O'Connor's ideas as the total membership of the organisation had fallen dramatically and the idea that the IRB could achieve their aim of an Irish Republic in the near future was obviously out of the question.

Although at this time their numbers were small, the actual influence of the Fenians on Irish politics in the preceding twenty five years was to be much greater in relation to its size. The reason for this anomaly was its close relationship with its counterpart namely the Clan Na Gael the powerful Irish Republican group in The United States. The Fenians in Ireland received substantial financial support and from time to time promises of arms to start another insurrection from their American brothers. Although at times very reluctantly, all Irish politicians had to take the IRB seriously, even Parnell at the height of his powers was to have secret discussions with John Devoy, now the chief executive of Clan Na Gael and other senior members of its executive on his various visits to America.

In the summer of eighteen seventy-seven, John Devoy sent his senior representative James J O'Kelly to France where he met Charles Kickham, James Stephens and other prominent exiled Irishmen in Paris. By a strange coincidence Charles Parnell was also in Paris at that time and was introduced to James O'Kelly, this chance meeting was to have far reaching consequences for both parties. Because in the course of the long discussions that took place, Parnell indicated that he was thinking of having some sort of political collaboration with the radical elements of the IRB At the conclusion of these meetings, O'Kelly rushed back to New York and immediately informed his boss John Devoy of Parnell's radical new proposals. Eventually after further meetings between the two groups, Devoy agreed to give Parnell the full backing of his American organisation. This historic agreement which became known as the New Departure was to lead to the extremist republicans calling a temporary halt to the aspiration of an Irish Republic. The aim of the accord was for a gradual approach of short-term objectives to be won at Westminster under the leadership of Mr.Parnell.

Unfortunately for most of the Irish population their priority was once again not political but survival as the situation in the rural areas was becoming desperate with worries that we would return to the catastrophic famine years of thirty years before. This fear was always uppermost in our minds, as anybody who had lived through those terrible times would never forget the pain and suffering the Irish had to endure. Although at this juncture Parnell and the Irish Members of Parliament were now a force to be reckoned with in Westminster, the age old problem of land reform and the benefit that security of tenure would bring was still only a dream. It was now at this the most critical period of the nineteenth century that Michael Davitt, the hero of the tenant farmers and the leading champion of Land Reform came to prominence.

Davitt as a young boy of five had witnessed his father and mother being evicted from their small holding in County Mayo during the Famine. Following their eviction they had emigrated to Lancashire, England, where because of the grinding poverty he was sent to work in a Cotton Mill. While working in the Mill, Davitt at the tender age of seven had lost an arm in a factory accident. As a young man he joined the Fenian Party and was involved in the abortive raid on Chester Castle. Subsequently as we have seen he was sentenced to fifteen years penal servitude in Dartmoor Prison. It was whilst in prison that he began to realise that most of the population had grown politically indifferent to the idea of an armed insurrection and the IRB needed to focus all its energies in a new direction. The change in policy he envisaged was to swing all the resources of the Fenians behind the problem that he had seen first hand as a boy; this idea was land agitation to obtain security of tenure for all tenant farmers and he was to subsequently spend the remainder of his life fighting to achieve this ambition.

On his release from prison after enduring many years of appalling treatment, this remarkable man toured the country explaining his ideas to his fellow Fenians and in December, eighteen seventy -seven, he met with Charles Parnell. This meeting was to prove crucial for both men as they agreed that in order to help the starving people of Ireland they must work together to solve the problem that had always bedevilled Ireland and that was Land Reform. After the meeting Davitt was later to remark to a friend "that he had just met an Englishman of the strongest type, moulded for an Irish purpose."

With Parnell and Davitt now both agreeing to work together and this coupled with the powerful backing of John Devoy and the Clan Na Gael in America, the British Government were now for the first time in history confronted by a united Irish movement. Meanwhile Davitt continued to expound his ideas and in a famous speech in Boston, USA in December, eighteen seventy- eight, he asked the audience a very relevant question, "Why is the average Irish farmer, not an active member of the Nationalist Party?" In his reply on behalf of the farmers he said, "If the Nationalists want me to believe and labour a little for independence they must show themselves willing to stand between me and the power that a single Englishman as a landlord wealds over me." This speech was reported in the Cork Examiner and many other Irish newspapers.

Sadly that winter the situation went from bad to worse and in eighteen seventy-nine, Davitt, who was now living back in his home county of Mayo saw at first hand that the situation on the land was nearing desperation. The agricultural crisis had deepened and once again the tenant farmers were unable to afford the rent because of the slump in farm prices and were threatened with the terrible sceptre that we all dreaded, eviction. Simultaneously with the fall in prices that year, the potato crop failed again and for many farmers their only thought now was to leave Ireland as the majority were now penniless and were facing starvation.

It was now very apparent to everyone that the Land Act, that was passed in eighteen seventy, was completely useless and not worth the paper it was written on. The effect on the landlord of having to pay compensation to the tenant for eviction was now totally irrelevant because under the clauses of the Act compensation only applied in cases of non payment of rent when it was deemed that the rent demand in question was exorbitant. By now the crisis was now so chronic in many counties of Ireland that the tenants could not even afford to pay their normal rent, let alone any increase.

It was at this time that I read with great interest about the drama unfolding on an estate in County Mayo, administered by an Irish Catholic priest named Canon Burke. On the estate the tenants made a stand and called a protest meeting at Irishtown, near Claremorris on the twentieth of April, eighteen seventy-nine. At this historic meeting that Michael Davitt organised, the tenants demanded a general reduction of rents and denounced as immoral the whole landlord system in Ireland. Fortunately due to the immense amount of interest that this protest received, Canon Burke quickly realised his error and immediately reduced his tenant's rents by twenty-five per-cent. The news of the tenant's victory at Claremorris set the pattern for land agitation across the country where similar conditions of hardship were now being experienced.

After the tenant's victory at Claremorris, Davitt now proceeded to extend the same principle on a national scale. When he organised a similar meeting at Westport, County Mayo, on the eighth of June, eighteen seventy-nine, he secured a promise from Mr Parnell that he would attend and give a speech in support of the beleaguered tenant farmers. In the week preceding the meeting, Parnell was put under intense pressure not to attend. But on a visit by Davitt's supporters to his hotel in Dublin, when asked would he attend? Parnell replied "Certainly! Why not? I have promised to be there and you can count on me to keep my promise.

At this meeting in Westport Charles Parnell set the tone of the whole subsequent Land League agitation.

"A fair rent," he declared, "Is a rent the tenant can reasonably afford to pay according to the times, but in bad times a tenant cannot be expected to pay as much as he did in good times... Now, what must we do in order to induce the landlords to see your position? You must show them that you intend to hold a firm grip of your homestead and lands. You must not allow yourselves to be dispossessed as your fathers were dispossessed in eighteen forty-seven... I hope... that on those properties where the rents are out of all proportion to the times a reduction may be made and that immediately. If not, you must help yourselves and the public opinion of the world will stand by you and support you in your struggle to defend your homesteads."

Subsequent events were to prove that he was as good as his word and on twenty first of October, eighteen seventy-nine, the National Land League of Ireland, was founded with Charles Stewart Parnell as its President. The Land League's objects were, to promote an organisation of the tenant farmers in order to bring about a general reduction in rents, protect those threatened with eviction and finally obtain "such reform in the laws relating to the land as will enable every tenant to become the owner of his holding by paying a fair rent for a limited number of years."

As I sat in the reading rooms in Charleville that year closely following these events, I sensed that something momentous was at last happening in Ireland, although it was not then immediately apparent. Starvation and large scale evictions was still affecting most of the country. Although most people's position now seemed hopeless, I felt that at last we had politicians who knew and understood our problems and were fighting to relieve the causes of our misery, Charles Parnell's tremendous commitment to our cause was to set the tone and give momentum to all the Land League agitation that followed.

Obviously there was much discussion both at Springfort and after mass on Sunday mornings regarding the aims and aspirations of Michael Davitt. At my son William's prompting I joined the Charleville branch of the Land League when it was inaugurated early in January, eighteen eighty. From its inception the Land League had received substantial American financial support with the backing of John Devoy and his powerful organisation Clan Na Gael. This support was a direct result of the Parnell, Davitt and Devoy's, New Departure agreement which over the coming years was to prove so vital in the success of the Land League agitation.

The tactics that the Land League would use to further their ends were revolutionary. Parnell, as we have seen had given his full backing to the Land League, but for political reasons he could not openly condone the use of violence. But once again the downward spiral of murder and intimidation became rampant as tenant farmers began to lose their homes and livelihoods. In a famous speech in Ennis in September, eighteen eighty, Mr Parnell proposed that "species of moral Coventry", as he called them, into which a proclaimed enemy of the Land League were to be placed by a rigid denial of all social or commercial contact on the part of his neighbours. This policy had been first advocated the year before as a Land League technique by John Dillon. Its endorsement by Irelands new Parliamentary leader in such graphic phrases, "About isolating such a man from his kind, as if he was a leper of old and showing him your detestation of the crime he has committed in bidding for a farm from which his neighbour had been evicted," gave us Irishmen a new firm spirit of self-respect with which to gird ourselves. During the next month this new technique was famously used against a man whose name will forever be identified with it the world over.

This man was the infamous "Captain Boycott," who was an evicting land agent at Lough Mask, in County Mayo; over fifty Orangemen were reported to have come from Ulster to help Boycott harvest his crops when no one else would touch them. In the following weeks these fifty men were to need seven thousand soldiers and militia to protect them, this figure was staggeringly one-sixth of the entire British military force in Ireland. Obviously this story was on everyone's lips and was to cause a sensation around the world. Boycotts crops were eventually harvested, but the cost was enormous and the campaign against him did not stop there, because when he went to Dublin on business, the hotelier refused to let him stay and so he had to return to England.

The popular power of the Land League was organised largely by the Nationalists and it spread rapidly throughout the country. Large demonstrations to secure reductions in rent were highly successful and many of the attempted evictions were physically prevented. Where eviction could not be prevented, victims were sheltered and supported while private charity kept the people fed. Many of the priests in rural

Ireland also worked tirelessly to try and alleviate the pain and suffering of their flock and Archbishop Croke proclaimed the Land League's principles of justice to the tenant to be moral and right. By the autumn of eighteen seventy-nine, parts of Ireland were it seemed no longer controlled by the Government, but by the Land League. Reductions in rent by up to fifty per cent in some cases had been forced on many landlords and where they had refused to yield to pressure or to their own moral promptings in face of the peasant's distress, it was often made physically impossible for them to carry out an eviction at all. The Irish correspondent of "The Times," described the Land League, as "a very distinct and potent government which is rapidly superseding the Imperial government."

With its problems in Ireland mounting by the day the Government in London, now once again led by William Gladstone in the winter of eighteen-eighty, resorted in its time honoured fashion, by introducing yet another Coercion Bill, in order they claimed to restore order. Parnell and his supporters fought this Coercion Bill in the House of Commons with all the persistence and ingenuity that their past experience had taught them. But the Bill was eventually passed and the suspension of Habaes- Corpus, [i.e. imprisonment without trial] was to lead to the arrest of prominent members of the Land League. This was then quickly followed by the suppression of the Land League itself. But to fill the void a new organisation called the Ladies League, with Charles Parnell's sister, as one of its senior members was then inaugurated.

On a personal level my one remaining aspiration was to purchase Springfort, I had always clung to this dream and was determined to somehow fulfil this ambition before I died. With this in mind I became a very active member of the local Land League Association, as I felt that with a leader of the calibre of Charles Parnell we could eventually achieve success.

Fortunately for us our long term strategy of concentrating our resources away from tillage into rearing livestock was vindicated, because the price of cattle had remained steady. Also William had carried on working hard to improve our herd and we were now reaping the rewards, as our cattle were always in demand on Market Day.

Our house was now becoming filled with children and in eighty-eighty, another boy was born and much to my pleasure he was named Patrick after his Grandfather. Then in eighteen eighty-one, another son John was born. With the house becoming crowded it was decided that a small cabin should be built for me. During the spring, of eighteen eighty-two, both William and I worked night and day to get my cabin finished and fortunately for us James came from Coolmine to give us a hand. When it was completed I thought that I might miss living in the house with all its noise and bustle.

But strangely this was not the case because once I had settled in I found that it was pleasurable for me to have somewhere to invite my old cronies and I could also now read my periodicals and newspapers in peace and quiet. The other benefit for me was that as the children grew up they usually came to visit me with their problems and ask for my advice. By now I was obviously not much use on the farm as all my years of toil had taken their toll. So it was decided that it was best for me to look after the children during the busiest times of the year, leaving Mary to help William on the farm.

Edmund the eldest was by this time over four years old and a real handful, he usually sought sanctuary with me as he was constantly in trouble with both his parents. When he was five it was time for him to attend school and with the recent opening of a new National School in Charleville, he was fortunate to be one of the first pupils to obtain a place there. At first he hated school because he was so used to being able have the run of the farm and I must confess he was allowed to do just as he pleased, therefore sitting doing school work was not at first to his liking and he found the first year very difficult. But he gradually settled down and by the time he was six he could not wait to return to see his friends after the long summer holidays.

In spite of the many problems that most of the population in Ireland were experiencing, we were very contended with our life at Springfort. During the summer of eighteen eighty-two, when I was on one of my occasional visits to see my son James and his wife Anna in Coolmine, they informed me of the great news that was Anna expecting a baby. This I told them was wonderful news and I could not wait to return to Springfort to tell Mary and William. The next morning I was up at the crack of dawn and managed to catch the first train back to Charleville, knowing that my son and his wife would be overjoyed when I told them the good news. I was not disappointed because on hearing that Anna was pregnant, Mary insisted that I return to Coolmine at once and she would accompany me. Obviously James and Anna were both surprised and delighted to see us and Mary soon began to give them advice about the forthcoming event. The next day the two girls went off to Mitchellstown to make the necessary purchases. Unfortunately Michael Roche's health had again deteriorated and sadly I had to sit by the poor mans bed for our chat.

On their return James was astounded at the amount of bags and boxes that the two girls returned home with. Thankfully for once all our cares were forgotten as the two young excited girls eagerly displayed to us the items they had purchased. The excitement and gaiety of that evening lifted all our hearts and even Anna's father joined in with the laughter and banter.

With harvest time approaching Mary insisted we returned home the next day, but before we left she made James promise to send for her when the baby was due. Four months later with Mary in attendance, Anna gave birth to a lovely baby daughter whom they named Catherine after my beloved wife; this obviously gave me immense pleasure. Unfortunately Anna had a difficult labour and because of this she was unable to have anymore children. Catherine was to grow up to be an exceptionally clever girl and would eventually become the first of my grandchildren living in Ireland to attend University.

That summer at harvest time, I went back to Coolmine to help James on his farm but I now knew that I was more of a hindrance than a help. It was always at harvest time that I realised how much I had slowed down, but I suppose that at the age of seventy-six, I was thankful for my continued good health, because one by one my old friends were sadly passing away. But James was as ever very kind to me and thanked me for my help; also he was always eternally grateful for my financial support when times were hard.

Politically the decade of the eighteen eighties was to be the most memorable in my life time. In the past few years you may recall the Land League had become all powerful and for a time had virtually ran the country, especially in rural Ireland. It had set up its own courts to hear tenant farmers complaints against landlords and their agents regarding high rents and other disputes. In the House of Commons in London, Mr Parnell and his colleagues had exploited the situation to the maximum, elevating the Irish question into the Parliament's chief preoccupation. But during this period Parnell was always very careful not to endorse the tactics of violence and intimidation that was associated with the Land League.

With all this happening the British press and the Tory opposition pressurised William Gladstone the Prime Minister, into introducing yet another Coercion Bill. At the same time as this Bill was passing through Parliament, Gladstone also introduced a new Land Act, this new legislation had at its core the three F's, firstly, fixture of tenure provided the rent was paid, secondly free sale of all tenants interests and improvements that he made to his holding during his tenancy, but thirdly and most importantly a fair rent. The act laid down that the ultimate definition of a fair rent would no longer be defined solely by the landlord or his agent, but by a Land Court, which would be under the jurisdiction of a government official especially appointed to adjudicate on land disputes. My personal thoughts were that if these proposals became law and they were strictly and fairly enforced, they would go a long way towards solving most of our current problems. In the coming weeks I scrutinised all the newspapers, wondering what would be Parnell's and the Land League's response to these far reaching proposals, which would actually become law in August, eighteen eighty-one. Mr Parnell, it would appear opposed this new legislation against the wishes of some of his colleagues in the House of Commons. But he was aware that whilst the Land League and the most strident of The Land Reformers amongst his Parliamentary Party, namely John Dillon, were opposed to this new legislation for not totally abolishing all landlords, this Act would be enacted whether they opposed it or not.

During this period and at the height of his power Charles Parnell had launched a newspaper called "United Ireland," with as its editor the former Fenian, Mr William O'Brien. This new publication aroused immense interest in Ireland and obviously it was also of great interest to me. In its articles and editors comments it was highly critical of the draconian Coercion Act that had seen the arrest of prominent Land Leaguers and the introduction once more of large numbers of soldiers and militia into towns and villages the length and breadth of the country. Once again tensions increased in Ireland and I wondered if my beloved country would ever be allowed to be free to follow its own course, or would it always be controlled by politicians that were totally indifferent to our problems.

By now both in speeches and articles in his United Ireland newspaper, Parnell's rhetoric was becoming increasingly militant against the new Land Act. In his speeches he constantly criticised Gladstone and the British Government, reminding them that his ultimate ambition was Home Rule for Ireland, adding that he would not rest until he achieved this goal. Under immense pressure from his party and the opposition, Gladstone acted and on October eighteen eighty-one, he ordered the arrest of Charles Parnell, William O'Brien and other prominent member's of the Land League. The prisoners were taken under heavy escort and lodged in Kilmainham Jail Dublin to await their trial.

These arrests aroused a sense of shock and horror all over Ireland that also reverberated around the world. But for Parnell himself he knew that the authorities had acted in panic and he was to use his arrest to his utmost advantage. This was adequately summed up in the following ballad that was sung at this time.

'Before this wrong of all wrongs of Ireland do grow pale,
For they've clapped the pride of Erin's isle into Kilmainham jail.

From their prison cells the prisoners jointly issued a call for a general strike against all payments of rent, once again the authorities over reacted, when on the twentieth of October eighteen eighty-one, the Land League was itself suppressed. With all these momentous events coming one after the other, the Irish people waited with baited breathe to see what would now occur. All through that long winter and into the spring rumours were rife about secret negotiation's being carried out between Mr Parnell and the government. Finally on May the second eighteen eighty-two, the prisoners were released.

It was later to be revealed that an understanding had been negotiated between Parnell and Gladstone; this agreement later became known as the Kilmainham Treaty. Under the terms of the Treaty it was agreed that in return for legislation to protect tenants with large arrears from eviction and the immediate repeal of the Coercion Act, together with the release of Parnell and his fellow prisoners, Parnell would call off the agitation on the land and cooperate in giving his backing to the new Land Act. It was further implied by Gladstone, that in return for Parnell's collaboration in the House of Commons with the Liberal Party and the continuation of their policy of "Justice for Ireland" which inevitability would include recognition as yet unspecified by Gladstone, of Ireland's aspiration to self- government.

The joy felt by the population at the release of Parnell and his fellow detainees was to prove short lived, as another tragic event in the long and troubled history of Ireland was about to unfold. The Chief Secretary for Ireland W.E. Forster had felt betrayed by Gladstone's decision to release Parnell and his fellow prisoner's and had resigned in protest. In his place Gladstone had nominated Lord Frederick Cavendish his nephew by marriage. This appointment when announced in the House of Commons was greeted by jeers and laughter. Cavendish was it seems a very likable person, but not thought of as strong enough to hold such a high position. One of the Irish Members of Parliament, Tim Healy said jokingly when the appointment was announced "We will tear him to pieces in a fortnight." sadly never was a truer word spoken in jest! Within the week Cavendish had been brutally murdered.

The dastardly deed was carried out at about half past seven on the evening of his arrival in Dublin. It was reported that he was found lying outside the Vice-Regal lodge in Phoenix Park hacked to death by assailants using twelve inch surgical knives. Tragically the body of the Under Secretary, Thomas Burke was also found nearby. These horrific murders shocked the nation and Charles Parnell's immediate reaction was one of despair and he briefly thought of resigning his position. Once again Gladstone had to appease English Public opinion by reintroducing Coercion but obviously Parnell and the Irish Party once again strongly opposed its reintroduction.

With the outlawing of the Land League, Parnell in October eighteen eighty-two, founded a new organisation called the Irish National League. The National League had as its slogan "Home Rule," for Ireland and it was to fight the General Election of eighteen eighty-five, with this as its main policy.

The election of eighteen eighty-five was the first one fought with the new enlarged electorate; this would enable many householders in the country the chance to vote for the first time in their lives. It was also the first election in Ireland that was fought mainly on the issue of Home Rule. Partly as a result of the enlargement of the electoral register, but mainly due to the personality and popularity of Charles Parnell, the Home Rulers emerged triumphant winning eighty five of the one hundred and three seats contested. This was to ultimately give the Irish Party the balance of power in the House of Commons when the new Parliament returned to Westminster.

When Parliament reconvened Gladstone quickly realised that the balance of power in the House of Commons was now held by the Irish Party and felt that now was the time to act and immediately introduced the long overdue Home Rule Bill. But far from the easy passage he had envisaged, this measure would split the Liberal Party. Because of this, on the second reading of the bill in June eighteen eighty-six, it was rejected by thirty votes, with ninety one of Gladstone's Liberal Party voting with the opposition. I must say that much to my surprise the mood in Ireland, immediately after this setback was one of optimism and the editor of the Cork Examiner wrote, "The progress of the cause of Irish Nationalism has suffered a check, but it has at the same time reached a point at which five years ago it would have been deemed simply impossible to reach within that period of time. The Irish question is now at the forefront of politics and the defeat last night cannot relegate it to a minor place." William Gladstone's defeat on his Home Rule Bill was to lead to the dissolution of Parliament and new elections. At this time there was still a feeling of great optimism in the country, unfortunately as I knew from past experience that if the Conservative Party won the new election all hope of major changes in Ireland were now doomed.

Once again due to appalling weather most of us tenant farmers suffered from a series of bad harvests and thoughts of Home Rule were unfortunately the last thing that we had on our minds. Farm prices for the first years of the eighteen eighties had steadily risen and the average tenant farmer had obviously benefited from these increases. From eighteen eighty-five, until the end of the decade the country once again descended into a deep depression. At markets all over Ireland the price of livestock and cereals fell dramatically in the autumn of eighteen eighty-five, this was due mainly to the cheap imports from America, but was also partly due to the banks being very reluctant to lend money to help. An added factor to our problems was to follow, as the year of eighteen eighty-seven, was the driest year anyone could ever recall. Once again rents went unpaid and again tenant farmers all over Ireland faced eviction and ruin.

Farmers now were being squeezed from all directions and many were unable to even pay the rents which had been fixed by the Land Act of eighteen eighty-one. But those unfortunates that were outside the operation of that Act were even worse off and evictions followed. Rumours that serious trouble was brewing had been circulating since the beginning of eighteen eighty-six. It was being said that tenant farmers on the estate of the Marquis of Claricarde were ready to fight any moves to evict them. But this predicted explosion of violent confrontation seems to have been avoided as long as there was a good prospect that the Home Rule would succeed in its passage through Parliament.

This was soon to change, because in the autumn of eighteen eighty-six, Charles Parnell and his Irish Party had tried valiantly to persuade the House of Commons to pass a Tenants Relief Bill, but this measure was rejected. With the knowledge that no help was forthcoming from the authorities, the situation in Ireland rapidly deteriorated. In October of that year the Nationalist newspaper United Ireland, carried a call to action under the banner "The Plan of Campaign" this article was written by the three men who devised the idea, namely John Dillon, William O'Brian and Timothy Harrington. "The Plan of Campaign," had as its main objective the collective bargaining on estates where a landowner refused to lower their rent demands voluntarily; as a consequence all his tenants were to combine to offer him reduced rents. If the landowner declined to accept this offer they would then not pay him any rent whatsoever, but instead contribute to what was to be known as the Estate Fund.

This fund would hold part of the monies that the tenants would have paid to the landowner if he had accepted what they interpreted as a fair rent. Furthermore the balance of the monies held would be used for maintenance and protection of the tenants who were almost certain to be evicted for implementing this radical policy. If the Estate Fund proved insufficient as most soon did the resources of the National League, backed by funds received from the Clan Na Gael in New York were to be mobilized. As for the Land Grabbers, for them there was as before the terrible threat of the boycott, this was to mean any farm where tenants had been unjustly evicted was to be strictly left alone and everyone who aided the evictors was to be completely shunned.

To the now desperate starving farmers and their families in the far south and west of Ireland, the advice contained in the Plan of Campaign and advocated in person at meetings in the distressed areas by Dillon and O'Brien was immediately seized upon. Although never a National Movement, its main area of influence was to be the counties of Tipperary, Limerick and Kerry, ultimately it would develop into a bitter and dangerous conflict. This in turn was to lead to the Government in London passing a crimes act that gave the authorities drastic new powers. Unhappily for me I would unwittingly witness these new draconian measures at first hand on a visit to Mitchelstown.

It was in late August eighteen eighty-seven, that I decided to make what was to be my last ever trip to see James and Anna in Coolmine. On my train journey that morning I could see for myself the effects the country was experiencing from the worst drought this century. My heart bled to see the parched fields and starving cattle, knowing that only heavy rain would alleviate the crisis we were all facing. On my arrival at Mitchelstown station James was there to greet me with his lovely daughter Catherine. At first I pretended that I had forgotten the bag of sweets that I knew she was expecting, but after seeing the terrible disappointment on her face, I searched in my pockets and much to her delight produced a large bag of her favourite humbugs.

On reaching their farmhouse I was greeted by Anna who had as usual prepared a hearty meal for me. For the next hour I discussed all the latest gossip at Michael Roche's bedside whilst James was out of the house taking care of the livestock, as due to the drought feed stuff was in short supply. That evening I played with my granddaughter until it was her bedtime, by this time I also felt weary from my long day. Before I went to bed we talked about the distressful state that the country was in and with the terrible drought we were experiencing James confessed that he would be pushed to find the rent that was due in October. We then talked about the falling prices at market and I could sense that they were all very worried for their future. As we sat there chatting, I was busy calculating how much they would require to carry them over the coming months. With these thoughts in mind I could not sleep that night agonising over how to help them in their predicament. Fortunately there was still a small amount of savings in my bank account and I hoped that it would be enough to help them through the coming winter.

The next morning over breakfast much to James and Anna's delight I told them that I still had enough savings in the bank to tied them over until their circumstances improved. Obviously my offer of help was gratefully received and I could see the anxiety lifting from their young faces. After discussing how much they would need, the conversation turned to what was happening locally. The largest landowner in the Mitchelstown area was Lady Kingston and it would appear from reports that she was not prepared to reduce the rent for her distressed tenants in that year of terrible hardship. In response a local farmer named John Mandeville had organised a rent strike on her estate. From all accounts tempers were now running high and the situation was getting out of control with threats and counter threats flying in all directions.

The local Member of Parliament and one of the prime movers of the "Plan of Campaign" that was sweeping Ireland at this time, was none other than the firebrand Mr William O'Brien! The previous week Mr O'Brien had come to Mitcheltown to express his support for the striking tenant farmers and had subsequently been arrested by the authorities on a charge of inciting tenants not to pay their rents. In the course of our discussion James told me that he felt that as usual the authorities were using excessive force in trying to suppress the threat of the "Plan of Campaign" movement. It was then he mentioned that the date for Mr O'Brien's trial had been set for the ninth of September. On hearing that the trial was imminent I decided that I would go to Mitchelstown on the day of the trial, but keep my intentions from James and Anna as I knew they would not approve.

The morning of that fateful September day was bright and sunny as I made my way from Coolmine to Mitchelstown. After an early breakfast. I explained to my son and his wife that I was going into town with the intention of withdrawing the money I had promised them. Before leaving I told them not to worry as I would not be back until late afternoon. As I neared Mitchelstown, the roads became crowded and the outcome of the trial was on everyone's lips, as it was very apparent that William O'Brien was a great favourite with the local people. On my arrival in the town I could feel the tension building, policemen and armed militia controlled every vantage point and the streets were full of tenant farmers and their supporters. As the time for the accused to be brought to the Courthouse approached, feelings amongst the waiting crowds began to run high and the overbearing attitude of the constabulary did not help the situation. All this was to ultimately lead to the terrible events that were to unfold in front of my very eyes. The tragedy that happened that morning would for ever be known as the "Mitcheltown Massacre" and the ferocity of the assault by the police on the unarmed protesters were to make headline news around the world.

'All that follows is what I personally witnessed." On the eventual arrival of Mr O'Brien and his co-defendants at the courthouse a terrific roar of support filled the air and the crowd surged forward to greet their heroes. What happened next has long been a subject of much heated debate. The police have always maintained that a volley of stones was thrown at them by the crowd and some of the constables even claimed that they had heard the sound of gun fire. But this has always been a matter of conjecture. From my vantage point all I can say is that during a brief speech given by John Dillon, Member of Parliament for East Mayo on behalf of Mr O'Brien that he gave on the steps of the court, I witnessed a few stones being thrown by some hot heads that were obviously drunk and not part of the protest. The police responded immediately by opening fire indiscrimately on the crowded town square. This caused immediate chaos, with the protesters running for cover in every direction, all trying to get away from the vicinity of the shooting. In minutes the square had emptied but tragically there were a number of casualties left lying in the town square. By now I had somehow found my way to the first storey window of a local shop that overlooked the unfolding drama. What occurred next I will never forget. A voice shouted at the policemen who were now reloading their rifles, the voice was that of Father Bartholomew McCarthy, the local curate, he told the police that he was about to help the injured and dying men and he would be showing a white flag. As he advanced towards the casualties the officer in charge ordered his men not to shoot, in minutes the priest was joined by a local doctor, but distressingly I saw the curate give the Last Rights to at least three of the innocent victims of this terrible outrage. Very soon the dead and injured were being carried to the local Infirmary. By this time I was in a state of shock and found that my whole body was shaking and tears of emotion were streaming down my face.'

Far in the distance I could see that a storm was brewing over the Galtee Mountains and very soon it struck Mitchelstown and within minutes the roads were awash as the rain lashed down. Fortunately by now all the casualties had been taken to the Infirmary, but it was a terrible sight to see the rain washing away the pools of blood from the recent carnage. After the storm had passed I somehow made my way to the local bank to withdraw the money I had promised James and Anna. With this transaction completed, I was soon back on the road to Coolmine, vowing that I would never return to Mitchelstown as long as I lived. The journey back to James's farm that day was endless as the recent storm had left the road in a terrible state. On my return Anna stared at me in disbelief as I told her about the terrible events I had witnessed that morning. When I finished she rushed out into the fields to find James. Soon they both returned with James scolding me for going into town on my own. When I told him about the happenings of that fateful day, he became very angry and it was to take all of Anna's powers of persuasion to stop him from doing something stupid as she knew from past experience that the authorities would flood the area with soldiers and militia to coerce the local people.

For the next couple of days I was in a state of shock and each night I had terrible nightmares. James insisted that because of my condition he forbade me to return home on my own, so in consequence he wrote an urgent letter to his brother in Springfort telling him that I had witnessed at first hand the "Mitcheltown Massacre" and this had traumatised me. On receipt of James's letter William caught the first train available bringing with him a collection of local newspapers all of which had headlines reporting on the tragic event I had witnessed. For me it was very comforting to see William and as usual when my sons and I got together the conversation carried on well into the night. It was to be nearly three o'clock in the morning before we eventually went to bed. The next morning I was very late rising and after eating my breakfast William and I said goodbye to James, Anna, Michael and my lovely granddaughter Catherine.

Sadly as I have said this was my last visit to the farm at Coolmine but I have never forgotten the wonderful welcome and hospitality that had greeted me on every occasion that I visited. My daughter-in-law Anna and I were always very close and would rib my son James mercilessly and although he pretended to be hurt he was obviously pleased that we got on so well.

On my arrival home Mary and my family and friends were surprised to hear my first hand account of the terrible events that had shocked and saddened the people of Ireland. Sadly although there was an enquiry that confirmed that the three farmers who had died and many of those wounded were completely innocent, as usual no one was ever bought to book for the indiscriminate killings. The official report that was eventually published stated that the mob attacked the police first with stones and then shots were fired and the police then returned fire in self defence. On reading this full official account of the tragedy, I went to see my Parish Priest Father Curran and explained what I had seen, he was very distressed and disturbed by my account and at his suggestion I wrote a letter to the authorities in Dublin Castle describing my eyewitness account of the Massacre. But as expected I have never had a reply to this correspondence and the whole enquiry was as usual a total sham.

Back in Springfort William and Mary were busily preparing our livestock for the most important event of our farming year, namely the October Fair, hoping against hope that prices would somehow improve as they had been very poor for most of the year. We had already decided that if our cattle did not fetch the required price we would return home with them and I would use my dwindling savings to buy winter feed. The long and exceptionally dry summer meant that the hay crop had been very sparse, so we were hoping and praying that we would find buyers for some our livestock. Fortunately these worries were unfounded, because after selling the cattle William still had sufficient money to buy all the supplies we needed and also pay the Land Agent our half yearly rent. Both William and Mary breathed a sigh of relief at their good fortune and before leaving town they purchased some small presents for the growing band of children that now inhabited Springfort.

Worryingly that autumn my health began to deteriorate and for the first time in my long life a doctor was called. After a thorough examination he explained that he felt that the trauma that I had recently witnessed had certainly affected me and said that the only cure for me was rest. For the remainder of that year I felt very tired and listless, but by the time spring arrived I began to feel like my old self again. Also to cheer me up the family had bought me a puppy and called it Patch. My new dog was to become a constant companion and we would go everywhere together. He even followed me to Mass each Sunday. By now the farmhouse was bursting at the seams, with a new baby appearing virtually every year. In eighteen eighty-eight, Mary had produced her seventh child which they named James. But with Mary now virtually confined to the house raising her young family, Edmund now twelve and Maureen aged ten were now a great help to their father on the farm.

With the price of livestock again falling at market that year, Mary suggested that we should try our hand at producing more dairy produce, as there was an increasing demand for milk and cheese. William wrote to his brother James, telling him what they were proposing to do and suggested that he came to Springfort with his family for a few days to discuss the idea. It was to prove an inspired decision. Because over the coming years, more and more of our income was to derive from dairy produce this helped us immensely because when the revolutionary Co-operative movement came to Charleville in eighteen ninety-one, we were one of the first farms in the area to become a member. At last we would have a steady monthly income and thankfully we were not now totally dependent on selling our livestock at market each year.

CHAPTER FOURTEEN

The radical change that William made from rearing and selling our life stock to concentrating solely on producing dairy produce was to prove a godsend for us; because as the children grew older they became more and more involved. This was especially so in Edmunds case, because by the time he left school at fourteen he was able to accomplish nearly every task on the farm. This was particularly useful because in eighteen-ninety there was a dramatic improvement in our financial situation when the first Cooperative Creamery finally opened in Charleville. Each farmer became a member of the Cooperative by purchasing shares in the enterprise. All participating members brought their milk into town each morning. The Creamery would then process that milk and we would then receive a monthly cheque in payment for the quantity of milk we had delivered. This was obviously a major financial improvement which was to ease William and Mary's anxieties in the future. In time, our locality would become famous all over Ireland and abroad for the quality of its dairy produce. The only drawback was that milk production was very labour intensive and so that Edmund and to a lesser extent his sister Maureen's help became increasingly important to us.

But this great change did give us a steady income that would ultimately enable us to take advantage of the Ashbourne Act. This legislation pushed through Parliament by Gladstone would eventually allow us to borrow enough capital to purchase Springfort.

In the spring of eighteen ninety, much to the delight of the children, William bought a little pony and a cart; this was to prove very useful for taking the milk churns to the Creamery each morning. As the oldest Edmund was entrusted with this important task and after much discussion the children named our pony Tinker. Tinker was their pride and joy and each day before he left for the Creamery he was groomed and fed better than any race horse in the county. But Sunday was the day they all looked forward to as they were allowed to take it in turns to have a ride in the cart on the journey to mass. Those few short years were a wonderful time for us all, freed at last from the threat of eviction as we could now borrow the required capital to buy the farm and we thought that at last our fortunes had finally changed, but as usual throughout my life our happiness was again to be short lived.

Unfortunately with the passing of the years I had become virtually housebound and now relied on my grandson Edmund to bring home the newspapers from town each morning. Sadly I will relate in this last chapter how Charles Parnell the one man who had achieved so much for us in his short political career was cast aside by his political opponents. The Irish political situation in the late eighteen eighties was a time of high drama that was mostly played out in the House of Commons in London. After the assassination of Lord Cavendish and Thomas Burke in Phoenix Park, Charles Parnell threatened to resign from the leadership of the Irish Party, but was persuaded to continue, by none other than William Gladstone. The controversy that was to dog Parnell for the rest of his life now came to the fore, firstly with the publication of a letter in The London Times, on the eighteenth of April eighteen eighty-seven, which was purported to have been written secretly by Charles Parnell to the Phoenix Park assassins, assuring them that his public denunciation of their actions was merely for show and had no real meaning. This letter obviously caused a sensation, but after a specially appointed Government Commission carried out an exhaustive investigation the letter was found to be a forgery.

The allegedly incriminating document which The Times had published was found to have been forged by a journalist named Richard Pigott who confessed under cross examination. Pigott subsequently fled from England and made his way to Madrid where he tragically committed suicide.

The failure to discredit Parnell and his associates by the London Newspapers resulted in a surge of popularity for the Leader and the Irish Party, both in Ireland and the rest of Great Britain. In the House of Commons he was now known as the uncrowned King of Ireland and for a few short months there was a renewed determination by the Gladstone government to finally push through a Home Rule Bill.

But the controversy that would ultimately ruin Charles Parnell's career and lead to his untimely death was about to engulf him. On the Christmas Eve eighteen eighty-nine, Captain William O'Shea a former Irish Member of Parliament and colleague of Parnell's, filed a petition for divorce against his wife Katharine citing Charles Parnell as the correspondent. During the preceding months before the trial began in November eighteen ninety, Parnell seems to have been confident that any revelations would do him no harm and all through that year he was to continually assure his friends and associates that the outcome would not affect his political career. Some of this confidence was based on the belief that O'Shea could be bought off and the sum mentioned was in the region of twenty thousand pounds. But crucially at the last minute neither Mrs O'Shea nor Parnell could lay their hands on the sum of money required.

The subsequent trial proved to be a complete disaster from which Parnell would never recover. Day after day the humiliating details of deception and lies emerged as Captain O'Shea gave his evidence to the court revealing in great detail how his wife and Parnell had deceived him. The false names they had used, the many changes of addresses, the whole undignified mess was paraded in front of the court and were sensationally reported daily in the newspapers. During the trial the story was on every ones lips and it was soon obvious to me that Parnell could never recover from the humiliation, after the court agreed with Captain O'Shea's version of events. Crucially neither Mrs O'Shea nor Charles Parnell ever contested a word of his damming account. It was no surprise to anyone who had followed the proceedings when O'Shea was granted a divorce by the court. Subsequently within months Parnell and Mrs O'Shea would marry.

Immediately after the result of the court case The Irish Parliamentary Party, to its great credit passed a vote of confidence in Parnell's leadership. But already storm clouds were gathering, William Gladstone by now the leader of the opposition, was himself under intense pressure from members of his party for supporting Parnell, wrote a letter to him begging him to resign for the sake of Home Rule. Parnell, on receiving the vote of confidence from his own party chose to ignore Gladstone's advice, but some of the Irish Members of Parliament were now beginning to have second thoughts about Parnell's leadership. Firstly from the threat of the Liberals, to abandon the alliance and secondly from the condemnation of Parnell by the hierarchy of the Catholic Church in Ireland.

Suddenly and dramatically support for his continued leadership began to ebb away. In a long damaging debate in the committee rooms of the House of Common in London, that began on the first of December eighteen ninety, the Irish Party, went back on its unanimous decision and voted forty-nine to twenty-nine against Parnell's continued leadership.

Tragically for Ireland as a result of this setback for Parnell, the Irish Parliamentary Party immediately split and in a succession of by-elections in Ireland fighting erupted between Parnellite and anti-Parnellite candidates. Making the long laborious journey from Brighton where he now lived with his wife, he campaigned week after week in support of his candidates in three separate by-elections, all of which he decisively lost. At one of them it was reported, he had lime thrown in his eyes that left him partially sighted. To his great credit he still fought on, thinking that in time the tide would undoubtedly turn in his favour. Then on Friday the twenty fifth of September eighteen ninety-one, he crossed over to Ireland for what was to prove to be the last time. Ironically on board the same steamer was my cousin James Stephens [returning from his many years in exile] and so by a strange coincidence, although they never met, these two true Irish patriots who had spent their lives striving for justice for Ireland were in close proximity to one another.

On the following Sunday, Parnell spoke at a meeting in pouring rain at a small town in County Galway, bare headed and with one of his arms crippled with rheumatism in a sling he was by now a shadow of his former self. By the time he finished his speech he was soaked to the skin, but tragically the change of clothes that had been packed for him had somehow gone astray and so he had to sit for many hours shivering in a wet suit. He then travelled back to Dublin, where he spent a few days resting before returning to England on Wednesday the thirtieth of September. As he boarded the steamer for his return journey he promised a friend that he would be back in Ireland on Saturday week. His prediction was to be only a few hours out because tragically he passed away in Brighton, on the tenth of October with his grieving wife Katherine by his bedside.

The following day his body arrived in Kingstown harbour and within the week he was interned in Glasnevin cemetery Dublin. The whole of Ireland remained in a state of shock for weeks afterwards, for although Charles Parnell had many faults he was a man who had given the poor a voice in the House of Commons and he had propelled the problems of Ireland to the forefront of politics in England. Although I personally had not agreed with many of his policies, I knew that Ireland would never see the likes of him again in my lifetime.

Unfortunately for me and my family the final and certainly the worst chapter in my long life was about to engulf us. Let me explain, by the beginning of the eighteen-nineties my life's ambition was seemingly at last going to be fulfilled, when William made our application to the authorities to obtain government funds for the purchase of Springfort. The Ashbourne Land Reform Act as I have already said had given tenant farmers the chance to buy their holdings from the land lords with funds borrowed from the Government at favourable interest rates. As a result after a long delay in the Act being implemented we were at last beginning to feel its impact in our part of Ireland, but now on the verge of achieving my lifetime ambition disaster struck. In February, eighteen-ninety, we had the worst snow storms of the century and for six whole weeks there were gale force easterly winds and driving snow. After the blizzards we were left with snow drifts that were over thirty feet high in places and with all of the streams and wells in our area frozen solid. During this terrible period our main priority was obviously the welfare of the livestock and William and his eldest son Edmund spent every waking minute working on building temporary shelters to house them. Also worryingly the feed we had stored for the winter was fast running out and with the roads now virtually impassable it was impossible to obtain fresh supplies.

It was now that I realised how useless I had become, because now when William needed me I was too old and powerless to help him. The heavy burden of responsibility fell completely on my son's shoulders, as he realised that we could easily lose our herd of cattle and everything we had worked for. He knew that we had to get through that terrible winter because it would be a total disaster if we lost everything now when we at last had the chance to purchase Springfort. William, to his immense credit slaved morning noon and night all through that terrible winter, arriving home each evening exhausted and soaked through to the skin. Both Mary and I urged him to slow down and think of his own wellbeing, but to no avail. By now we were both becoming desperately worried for his welfare and then tragically just as the weather started to improve he developed influenza. For a couple of days at the end of March he showed some improvement but on the second of April his condition rapidly deteriorated, with the identical symptoms that his mother had before her tragic death. On seeing my son with the terrible fever I was determined to take immediate action as I knew that every second mattered. The first priority was to call for the doctor, so Edmund, without any hesitation set out for town promising that he would return with Doctor Donnelly. As soon as Edmund had departed I instructed my other grandson Patrick and his sister Catherine to prepare the horse and trap. This time I was determined to get my son into the infirmary at Kilmallock without delay.

Unfortunately my assumption was soon to be proved correct, because within the hour the good doctor had arrived and examined my ailing son. After a very thorough examination, Doctor Donnelly gave the patient a strong dose of medicine and ordered us to urgently get him to hospital. By now Mary was in a state of shock at the realisation that her beloved husband's condition was now very serious. The poor girl's whole body was shaking with emotion, but against my advice she insisted on accompanying him to the Sisters of Mercy Infirmary in Kilmallock. Before they left I made Edmund promise that he would keep to the main roads, as it was essential that his father had as smooth journey as possible.

Once they had departed I realised that Mary should have stayed ay Springfort to look after her young family and it would have been better if I had travelled with William. But my worries were unfounded because Maureen my eldest granddaughter soon proved that she could cope in a crisis and took charge of the situation. Also Patrick realising that it was now his responsibility to do the essential farming jobs organised the younger children to help him. Under my supervision all of my grandchildren worked like Trojans for the following couple of days. That evening when all the children were asleep I sat down to write letters to my two other sons, because deep down I realised that William might not pull through. In my letters I urged both my boys to get to Kilmallock as soon as possible. James, I knew would travel to the hospital on receipt of my letter but I very much doubted if Michael would return from New York.

That that night I sat waiting for Edmunds return, as each hour passed my worries increased as I agonised over my son's illness. It was well past midnight when a very weary and bedraggled Edmund finally arrived home. On hearing the sound of voices Patrick came out from the bedroom as he was obviously aching to know the latest news. The poor boy was worn out and hungry from his long day as I made him a hot drink and a bite to eat, he told us that it was a long slow journey to the hospital but fortunately his father had slept most of the way. On reaching Killmallock Infirmary he and his mother were ushered into a room while his father was carried on a stretcher into the hospital and taken to a ward. After examination by the hospital doctor, his mother was told that the patient needed complete rest and that only close relatives would be allowed to visit. The Matron then politely asked them to leave as the patient was totally exhausted after the long journey. But before leaving for home, Edmund told us he went with his mother into town where she found a comfortable lodging house. That afternoon was the hardest part of the day as he was very reluctant to leave her alone in the town, but he realised he had to return home as quickly as possible as he knew I would want to know the latest news. After eating his supper I told him to get some sleep as we could discus our future plans in the morning.

Early next morning there was an urgent knocking on my door; this visitor was Joe Carroll an old friend of the family who had come to offer his help which was immediately accepted. News that William had been taken into the Infirmary had quickly spread and offers of help soon followed. In the circumstances I was profoundly grateful to our neighbours and friends, as it enabled us to organise visits to Killmallock and allowed Mary to spend as much time as possible with her husband. After receiving my letter in Coolmine, James and his wife Anna had rushed straight to the hospital and then came onto Springfort with the latest news. They informed me that William's condition was now stable and the nurses were hopeful that he was over the worst of his illness. Unfortunately their stay was very brief as they had left their daughter with neighbours for the day.

But before leaving they insisted on taking two of the children James and young Peggy back to Coolmine with them, a suggestion I readily agreed to. After my son and his wife left for home I decided that Patrick should travel to Killmallock and spend a few days with his mother and try to talk her into returning home. I knew from past experience how stressful her situation was and I also needed to speak to her about hiring someone to help us on the farm. My problem was that I was not now able to make the long journey to Killmallock and although I was not much use it was still best for me to organise the running of the farm. But luckily this problem was resolved when Mary's cousin Joseph Egan arrived to offer his help, Joe as we called him, was a young man in his early twenties at the time, immensely strong and always willing, he was the answer to all my prayers. I gratefully accepted his kind offer of help because there were a million and one jobs to be done now that the weather had at last improved. He would prove to be a tower of strength in our time of need. Nothing was ever too much trouble for Joe and with his help and tuition my elder grandsons will in time I am sure make excellent farmers.

After ten days in Killmallock much to my relief Mary and Patrick returned to Springfort, Mary was obviously completely drained, but still managed to cook us our first decent dinner in weeks. William's health had improved but the doctor was still worried that he would develop pneumonia as he was still very weak. That night before going to bed I insisted that we all prayed that William would quickly recover and that with 'Gods Will he would soon be restored to us'.

Once again in my long and troubled life, my hopes and prayers were dashed. On Friday the fifth of May, Mary and Edmund returned to the Infirmary taking with them Williams best suit of clothes, as we were all convinced he would be returning home with them. But the day dragged by with no sign of them and I was becoming extremely worried eventually I told Patrick, to drive the trap to the station as the last train from Kilmallock was due in Charleville at eight-thirty. Just as it was getting dark Patrick and Edmund, drove into the farm yard with their very distraught mother. The news they had was bad, William's condition had suddenly worsened and he was once again fighting for his life. Fearing the worst I advised Mary to return to the hospital the next morning, telling her that her place was now by her husband's side. Taking my advice, early the following day she packed her bag, this time vowing that she would not return to Springfort without her husband. This time she travelled alone, but during the following week Edmund and Patrick, took it in turns to visit the hospital, each time reporting that their father's condition showed no signs of improvement. By now my eldest granddaughter Maureen was begging me to allow her to go back to the hospital to see her father who she adored and so on the following Saturday, I relented. Before she left that morning she had managed to bake a special cake, as she was convinced that her father would be well enough to eat a slice of it.

That afternoon I was woken from my afternoon sleep by the arrival of a magnificent pony and trap. I was still half asleep when looked out of the window and to my great surprise I saw that our visitors were my son Michael with his wife Rachael. Stunned and surprised I was speechless as Michael, gave me a hug while urgently inquiring after William's health. By this time the children had rushed out to see who had come to visit. Edmund, the eldest was first to speak, telling his uncle how worried we all were for his father's health. Michael explained that on receipt of my letter he and his wife had caught the first available steamer from New York, in the hope that by the time they arrived in Ireland; William would have recovered his health and returned to Springfort. On hearing that his brother's condition had deteriorated he said that both he and Rachel would catch the evening train to Killmallock. Obviously with William so ill he was anxious to get to the hospital as soon as possible. As they pulled out of our yard, I felt sorry for my daughter-in-law Rachel who seemed completely bewildered by the turn of events. The poor women had travelled thousands of miles to meet us but before she could even say hello, she was had been whisked away.

Once they had departed I decided that it was imperative that my son James was made aware of his brother's return from America, so it was decided that

Patrick would be despatched to Coolmine, the next morning with the news. For the rest of us at Springfort, all we could do was to concentrate on the farm work and this is where young Joe and my grandson Edmund both proved invaluable. Most of the younger children were now attending school and under the supervision of Maureen, they would all rush off in the morning and return each afternoon to their allotted tasks. The only exception was the youngest Lillian, who was still too young to attend school and in her mothers absence followed me everywhere. In those troubled weeks, Lillian and I became very close friends. She is the most endearing child and her company at that time cheered me up when I became morose and grumpy.

But sadly there was to be no improvement in William's health and his condition deterioted with each day. Then early on the twentieth of May, a nurse from the infirmary called at Mary's lodgings and urged her to go quickly to her husband's bedside as she feared the end was near. Fortunately Michael, Rachel, James and his wife Anna were staying the night at a nearby hotel and on hearing that William's condition had considerably worsened, rushed to the hospital. Michael realised at once the seriousness of the situation and immediately sent for the local priest. On his arrival the priest gathered the family around the bed and sadly gave my son the Last Rites. The end came quickly and at the young age of forty William passed away; the only consolation for his beloved Mary was that in her hour of need she had his two brothers and their wives to comfort her.

Back in Springfort, we had prayed night and day that William would soon recover, not knowing of his tragic death. But all our hopes and prayers soon turned to despair, when on the following afternoon a carriage carrying William's body drove into the farmyard. On seeing the coffin my whole body began to shake and then I passed out with the shock. Both Michael and James thought for a moment that the terrible shock had killed me, but after a couple of hours rest, I recovered. The preparations for the funeral were our first priority but with James, Michael and their two wives helping, this was soon organised. Once again Michael as an experienced police officer automatically assumed control. Both James and I agreed that it was best if he made the necessary arrangements for the funeral, leaving us free to concentrate our efforts on managing the farm. It was in those few short days that I briefly got to know my new daughter-in-law Rachel. At first I could not understand her because of her American accent, but once I got used to this I found her to be a wonderful person who brightened up all of our lives at that sad time. Also Mary's mother on hearing the news of her son-in laws death rushed to be at her daughter's side, her presence was to also prove invaluable in our hour of need.

For me personally William's death was unbearable, for here was a young man in his prime with his future now seemingly secure, married to a young very intelligent hard working wife that adored him. Plus a family that were growing up who given time would I was sure be able to play a role in expanding and enlarging Springfort. Apart from my deep sorrow at losing my son I worried about poor Mary his devoted wife's health. With William dead her whole life now seemed meaningless and in the coming months she was to descend into a deep depression. But fortunately her vibrant young family would help her overcome this depression and by Christmas she had fortunately regained most of her old self esteem.

On the day of the funeral, hundreds arrived from all over the town land and we were very grateful to all our neighbours and friends who organised sufficient food to feed them. Also my sons had made sure there was sufficient tobacco and spirits available for the large throng that came to pay their last respects. On the morning of the funeral I did not feel well enough to attend the internment at the cemetery. Both Michael and James were very worried about my health and they thought it was best if I stayed at home and looked after the youngest children. In different circumstances it would have been wonderful for me to meet all our old friends and family, but all I wished for was this terrible day to end. Looking back now I know that all of the mourners that came realised the tremendous sense of loss we were feeling, because during the evening they gradually drifted away leaving us to mourn William as a family together.

On the following day both my sons and their wives started to make preparations to return home. James promised to help with the hay making later in the year; whilst his wife Anna told Mary she would bring their daughter for a couple of weeks in the summer holidays. Before they left Springfort I managed to have my first and only chat with Michael's wife Rachel. First of all I apologised and asked her forgiveness for the way she had been greeted by us. I then explained that when a stranger visited Ireland for the first time, especially my daughter-in-law, in different circumstances we would have thrown a big party and invited all of our family to meet her. Rachel was most upset by my outburst; in fact she said that she and Michael although devastated at William's death, hoped they had been of some small comfort to Mary at this most distressful time, I thanked her from the bottom of my heart for travelling so far to be with us.

As I sat and chatted with Rachel she told me about life in New York and how my grandchildren were now attending college. As I listened to her talking about the house they now owned and the social life they led., it seemed a million miles away from the very quiet life Michael had known on our small farm in rural Ireland. Deep down I was pleased that my son had met and married this attractive girl, because although she must have found our way life very backward compared to living in New York, I felt that in the short time she had spent with us at Springfort she had made herself at home. Before leaving, Rachel promised to write to me each month with regular reports of my American grandchildren's progress through college. This was a promise she would painstakingly keep, as I received a letter each month from her for the rest of my life. Little did she realise how much this correspondence was to mean to me, as I was immensely proud when I heard that her eldest son James had obtained a place at Washington University.

Obviously it was with great sadness that I said goodbye to Michael and Rachel, as we all knew that this was to be our final parting. Although he had now lived in America for many years, my love and admiration for Michael had never diminished and he will always remain a good son and more than that a great friend.

During the following summer we were inundated with offers of help and with Joe Egan working from dawn to dusk, Mary was very pleased with the results of our harvest. Luckily we were very fortunate that the weather that year was exceptionally good and we managed to save an abundance of hay for the following winter. That October on market day I made what was to be my last ever visit to Charleville. Now I decided was the right time to transfer the remainder of my savings at the bank into Mary's name. With this in mind I went to see the Bank Manager, who incedently I had known for many years. When I explained that with my advancing years I doubted if I would ever be able to make the journey into town again and in consequence I wished to transfer the balance of my account into my daughter-in-law's name he was very understanding and immediately amended the account according to my instructions.

With my urgent business now completed I went in search of my old cronies in their usual hostelry. Unfortunately as the years passed our numbers had gradually diminished, but it was still enjoyable to reminisce about old times with the old friends that still remained. When Mary was ready to go home she came to find me, obviously knowing where I would be. Our successful trip into town that day also seemed to cheer Mary and on our return journey to Springfort she did not stop telling me about all the local gossip. Over the coming months I urged her not to become a hermit but to go to town more often and meet up with her friends, thankfully she took my advice as these visits helped her get over her depression.

Although the children had lost their father, Mary decided that it was best for them if we carried on as normal at Christmas time. This was always a special time for all of us at Springfort and the children both young and old were all determined to keep up the tradition for their mother's sake. In the weeks before the festival, Maureen my eldest granddaughter regularly came to my room with her two younger sisters Peggy and Lillie and I taught them some of the old Gaelic songs that I learnt as a boy. At the same time the rest of my grandchildren worked hard practising their songs or dances that they were going to perform especially for their mother on Christmas Day.

As Christmas approached the excitement reached fever pitch and when on Christmas Eve a large parcel full of presents arrived from Michael and Rachel in New York the children would not go to sleep that night until their mother scolded them. The next morning they were all up very early pestering her to open the parcel from America. Eventually Mary relented and allowed them to find out what presents were in the parcel. Michael and Rachel had obviously given a lot of thought to the gifts they had sent, because all of the children both young and old were thrilled with what they had received. Maureen had been sent a lovely dress while the younger girls each received toy dolls that were dressed in the latest fashion. Both Edmund and Patrick received fountain pens, and John the youngest received a toy train. The generosity of their uncle and aunt that Christmas has been a topic of conversation until this day.

As I recall after mass that morning neighbours and friends began to arrive for the feast Mary had prepared. Although the proceedings were understandably sober at first the mood gradually changed when the alcohol began to flow. During the evening some of our guests produced their instruments and the music and dancing began. Later as was traditional each person present sang or recited their favourite song or poem. I sat and listened that evening to some wonderful singing, but when my three granddaughters sang the old Gaelic song that I had taught them the watching throng was silent until the last word and then everyone clapped and cheered. It had taken me a while to persuade her but finally Mary agreed to sing for us, after a very hesitant start it was thrilling to hear her beautiful voice again and the ballad she sang brought tears to everyone's eyes. Eventually when it was my turn to sing there was a call for silence and then to every one's pleasure I sang my favourite song "Dear Old Charleville" with words written by my old friend Thomas Reidy, now residing in the town of Boston, America.

You asked me for to sing a song
And to please you I will try,
I'll sing to you about a town
That is known to you and I,
Although three thousand miles away,
My heart it lies there still,
It's the place my eyes first saw the light,
It's the town of Charleville.

I loved that old familiar town,
It's the place that gave me birth,
The place I visit in my dreams,
To me it's first on earth.
Though the broad Atlantic may divide,
My heart goes back there still,
Amongst the friends I left behind,
In dear old Charleville.

When back to lovely Fortlands
We oft times used to stroll,
The boys and girls together
To the dear old 'Parasole',
We would pack our pockets up with crabs
Until each one had his fill,
Oh! They tasted sweet in those good old days
In dear old Charleville.

288

And back to lovely Stephen's Glen,
We oft time used to stray,
We would roll each other down the banks
To while away the day,
Those memories ever haunt my dreams,
Forget I never will,
Those boys and girls, friends of my youth,
In dear old Charleville.'

Farewell to you dear Charleville,
To your Turrets and Main Street,
Likewise Smith's Lane and Baker's Lane,
Where all true lovers meet,
To Saunder's Park, the New Line,
And the Walk down by the Mill.
Where my young days, those happy days.
Were spent in Charleville.

Farewell to Toberneena I would to see once more
And drink again from its crystal spring
As I did in days of yore.
Here's a health to you my dear old town,
Let tomorrow bring what will,
We will toast the friend we left behind
In dear old Charleville.

Here's a health to those who wish us well,
And to those who are far away,
The friends we love some lie at rest
Neath Ballysally, s clay;
Then here's to those we hope to meet,
To them to glasses fill,
In hopes we'll all return again
To dear old Charleville.

In winding up these simple lines,
I have one more word to say,
When my old frame its work has done
And my hair has turned to grey,
I hope the friends I leave behind,
When in death my heart is still,
Will place me with the friends I love
In dear old Charleville.

As I sat down the whole room erupted with applause and my three young granddaughters all came to tell me how well I had sung.

Gradually our guests departed thanking us for our kind hospitality. Obviously by now I was feeling very tired as it was well past midnight by the time I got to bed.

I also had two further reasons to enjoy my Christmas that year, firstly the Parish Priest Father Lillis, kindly came to the house to hear my confession and give me Holy Communion and the other surprise was a letter from my cousin and dear friend James Stephens, who was now at last living in comfort in a house near Dublin. In his letter he explained that he had only recently heard about my son's death and was sending us his belated condolences. But he then went on to complain about the present political situation, writing that although he had not agreed with some of Parnell's policies; tragically his death had led to the Irish Parliamentary Party splitting into small warring factions. He then went on to inform me that before he was allowed to return from exile the British Government had made him promise that he would never again become active in Irish politics. In the privacy of his correspondence to me, he still insisted that Ireland's freedom would never be achieved at the ballot box, but only by armed insurrection.

I immediately replied thanking him for his letter and wishing him very good health in the coming year. In closing I invited him to visit us again at Springfort if ever he was in our vicinity. In this letter I did not make any political comments, because unfortunately due to the traumatic events of the past year I had been unable to keep up to date with the latest news.

Fortunately the winter of nineteen ninety- one was a lot milder than the previous year and we had plenty of winter fodder for our growing herd of cattle. The summer when my grandson Patrick left school he came to ask my advice about his future. As we talked I realised that he was determined to work in the local horse breeding industry that was now beginning to flourish. On hearing what he had in mind I wrote to Jack Flannery, the owner of stables at Carrigeen near Churchtown. Jack's father was an old friend of mine from our days on the Dublin-Cork railway construction and I was confident that he would employ my grandson. My confidence was justified because within days I had received a reply offering my grandson employment. Obviously Mary was mortified at him leaving but she came to realise in time that it was best for him to learn a trade which would stand him in good stead for the future. After leaving us it was a month before he returned, but subsequently he came home each weekend. Every Saturday evening he would regale us with stories about the horses and the races the stable had won.

The Jack Flannery stables were now acquiring a reputation because of the many successes their horses were having and Patrick was obviously very proud of this.

With life at Springfort beginning to return to normal I now had time to catch up with the political situation. William Gladstone who was now an old man in his eighties introduced his second Home Rule Bill, to Parliament in the spring of eighteen ninety-one. This legislation was to have the backing of the now fractious Irish Parliamentary Party, but was totally opposed by the increasing number of Irish Unionists. The second Home Rule Bill was to eventually occupy more parliamentary time than any other bill this century, a total of eighty-two days were spent in debate. In the final vote in the House of Commons on the second of September, the Government had a majority in favour of thirty votes. Every one knew that unfortunately the House of Lords would reject it, which they did after only four night's debate in the early hours of the morning on the ninth of September by four hundred and nineteen votes to forty-one.

On hearing this result my thoughts returned to James Stephens and his chilling prediction that Ireland must have an armed insurrection to obtain its freedom. Sadly after this humiliating failure William Gladstone retired, a man who for all his faults, had been the only British Prime Minister in my lifetime who had tried to understand Ireland and its problems and had in many ways tried to alleviate them, he will be sadly missed.

Within months the ruling Liberal Party with Lord Rosebery now the Prime Minister called a General Election in which the Conservative Party won an overwhelming victory. This result was a disaster for the Home Rulers, as the Conservative's were totally opposed to any measures that would allow Ireland to have control of its own affairs. In Ireland the deep split in the Irish Parliamentary party now became abundantly clear when the election meetings were held by the various candidates.

There was tremendous local interest in the election in our constituency of North East Cork, when Michael Davitt announced his candidacy. Mr Davitt as you may recall had been a life long supporter of the poor and down trodden of Ireland and so for me he was an ideal candidate. But when it was announced in January eighteen ninety-three, that he would be speaking at an election meeting in Charleville, his Unionist opponents vowed to cause trouble. Unfortunately they were true to their word and the following account of what happened was reported in every newspaper throughout Ireland.

'When it was announced that Michael Davitt was going to Charleville to canvas support for the forthcoming election his Unionist opponents had promised to disrupt the meeting. In anticipation of trouble, fifty Royal Irish Constabulary officers, commanded by District Inspector Shee were drafted into the town to keep order. Large numbers of Nationalists flooded into the town; there they were met by equal numbers of Unionists hell bent on causing trouble.'

The meeting did not start on time, as Davitt had been delayed in Kilmallock, but at four o'clock that afternoon a telegram was received instructing the meeting to commence as Mr Davitt's arrival was imminent. Two wagonettes were drawn up in front of the Imperial Hotel on Main Street to form a makeshift platform. Father Lillis the local Parish Priest and a number of other dignitaries climbed onto the stage to start the meeting. As soon as they started to speak they were drowned out by the babble of noise from their opponents, the noise was so great that it was impossible for any of the speakers to be heard. Reluctantly it was decided to suspend the meeting until the arrival of Mr Davitt.

Each faction it was reported, had now armed itself with large sticks and pockets full of stones and rocks and was trying to get to close quarters, but they were being kept apart by the cordon of police. Eventually one of the Unionists jumped onto the platform where he was immediately set upon. These actions lead to a free for all. Many people were hurt as stones were thrown and sticks were used by the fighting mob. Father Lillis and other committee members were still sitting on the stage when a fusillade of rocks and other missiles was thrown at them. A crowd collected around Father Lillis for his safety. Unfortunately by now there were many casualties and splashes of blood could be seen all over the pavement.

By now men blood-smeared and with gashes on their heads and faces, were to be seen amongst the swaying mass of yelling and excited mob. Women and children had not been spared and many had received injuries before they succeeded in taking shelter. The "Davitt" procession was now coming into town, on board the first wagon was the Kilmallock fife and drum band, resplendent in their green and gold uniforms, the sides of their wagon were painted white on which was green lettering with the slogan "Unity in Strength". In the next brake were Mr Davit and his friends. Behind them were hundreds of supporters in various types of vehicles and on foot.

On arrival at Chapel Street the band struck up a martial air. In the next instant there was a rush from the Main Street and the laneway leading from Gorman's Square led by a mob carrying pocketfuls of stones, which they directed at the band and wagons. Davitt, it was said could be heard saying "This is terrible. Pull your hats down and turn up the collars of your coats." Davitt himself was then struck in the eye with a stone. At the top of Chapel Street he turned his brake towards The Turrets. "Where are you going?" shouted Davitt. "Drive down there" he said. Pointing towards the wagonettes outside the Imperial Hotel. "Oh, we'll be killed there sir," said the driver. "Never mind," said Davitt, "drive back."

Davitt escaped uninjured during another fusillade of rocks and stones. A suggestion to open the meeting at another part of town was met with a refusal from Davitt. The police eventually cordoned off the aggressive mob from the meeting, but beyond this protective measure they took no further action in quelling the disturbing element, although odd stones were still dropping in the vicinity of the wagonettes.

When the chairman John R Daly, addressed the meeting there were continuous interruptions. He appealed to the police to direct their attention to the stone-throwers at the opposite side of the street. "The object of this meeting", he said "is to dispel the idea that the Nationalists were going to pull down the flag and march behind the local standard-bearer of the Union, that product of fraud and corruption by which the country is being deprived of her legislative freedom."

On a proposal by Mr O'Connor, seconded by Mr Binchy a resolution was passed declaring their unalterable attachment to Irish National principles and that their belief that professions of a Unionist candidate in favour of any of these principles are illusionary and valueless, while he continues to support a government that refuses legislation in pursuance of them.

As Mr Davitt rose to speak there was tremendous cheering. The Unionist's attempted to drown the acclamation with jeers and shouts. Davitt directed his opening sentences to the unruly mob. "Fellow country-men," he said, "there are fifty or sixty rowdies disgracing Charleville and injuring the slender chances of their candidate Mr Sanders. I have been in Charleville too often to misunderstand the meaning of this rowdy conducting; it is not by blackguardism that Mr Sanders will get in at the election."

"I remember the Parnell Commission in London," he continued. "Robert Massey Dawson Sanders was a witness with Piggott and Le Carron against Mr Parnell. That is the man who comes impudently forward and now asks for your support. There was not before the Commission a more malignant witness or enemy of the Nationalists cause than this the same Mr Sanders. Do not fellow countrymen; sully the record of Charleville by electing this miserable land grabber and evictor as your Member of Parliament."

Davitt then took his listeners back over fifty years, when they had in their parish of Charleville a young curate who was "Resolute clear-sighted, patriotic and brave." "I refer," said Davitt "to Dr Croke". "Long before the Land League" he advocated "Land for the People." "Surely you who are proud of that chapter in Charlevilles history will not disgrace the name of Croke by voting for the name of Sanders."

This reference to Sanders was received by his Unionist supporters with much jeering and interruptions. "Never mind those miserable, drunken slaves," said Davitt rebukingly. "I spent three-quarters of my life trying to emancipate them, but you may as well be trying to train a jackass to behave himself in a drawing room as to expect decency or good behaviour from anyone who can support Sanders, or who is willing to sell his loyalty for a pot of porter."

"God save Ireland from ignorance and drunkenness and rowdyism of that character. On voting day, the Irish Party expects, the Irish Race will expect that you will not disgrace Ireland by returning Sanders." With these words the meeting ended but the newspapers reported that the police were kept busy for the rest of the evening with fights and skirmishes in different parts of the town.

Later that week, my cousin Jack Casey (the proprietor and editor of The Charleville Courier], came to visit me. We discussed these terrible events he had witnessed and also the intimidation and violence against the Nationalist candidates and their supporters that was now occurring all over Ireland. It was particularly bad in Ulster with the re-emergence of the Orange Order under the leadership of Edward Saunderson. With the prospect that Ireland might get Home Rule, Saunderson, and his ally Randolph Churchill, had during the preceding six years inflamed public opinion in Ulster. Churchill had made a particularly inflammatory speech in London in the late eighteen-eighties, when he declared that England could not leave the Protestants of Ireland in the lurch and that hundreds and thousands of English hearts- "aye and English hands" would stand with them. He then went onto make this arrogant statement, "The Protestants of Ireland," he declared, "on such an occasion as this and in a national crisis as this, are the only nation which is known to the English people."

Ominously Churchill was to follow this speech with further threats culminating with a reassurance to Unionists in Belfast, when he vowed that in the dark hour there will not be wanting to you those of position and influence in England who are willing to cast their lot with you-whatever it may be. "Ulster," he declared "would fight, and Ulster would be right". In Ulster there was at this time reports of enrolments of Orange volunteers between the ages of eighteen and sixty and of drilling with and without weapons. I then told Jack about James Stephens's prediction that Ireland's freedom could only be achieved by armed insurrection and unfortunately we both agreed that he was right.

Before he left the topic of our conversation changed and we talked about the great success that the local Charleville hurling team were having that year. The main reason for the team's improvement he told me was due to the arrival of Joseph Connelly and Thomas Harrington two young teachers from Dublin. These young men had galvanised the team by their enthusiasm and leadership and it was hoped that the team could win the Cork Championship in the near future.

The Gaelic Athletic Association itself had gradually increased its membership and by eighteen-ninety, most areas in Ireland had their own teams. These were mainly confined to towns, with each town having both a football and hurling team. In the last three years the growth of Gaelic sport has been tremendous, initially there had been many problems regarding who could participate, but thankfully these had been resolved. The main reason for the growth in interest I felt was the idea of having an Inter County Championship, with an All Ireland Final. This tournament soon became a major talking point throughout Ireland. The inter-county rivalry especially when Cork played Kerry was intense and the outcome of each match would be discussed for many weeks before and after.

But before Jack left that evening we talked about a series of articles that the school teacher Thomas Harrington had written for his newspaper The Charleville Courier. Jack told me that he had commissioned young Mr Harrington to interview any surviving veterans still living in North Cork who had taken up arms against the government forces during the aborted risings of eighteen forty-seven and eighteen sixty-seven, as he thought that their reminiscences should be recorded for posterity. He had then went onto say that he had suggested to Tom Harrington that I would be an ideal candidate to interview for his researches. On hearing this I shook my head and protested that I had never been actively involved in an armed insurrection.

Jack replied by saying that everyone knew that neither I nor any of my family had ever been active members of Fenians, but it was rumoured that we had harboured prominent rebels whilst they were on the run after the failed rising in eighteen forty-seven. It was also an open secret that one of these fugitives was my cousin James Stephens the founder and first chief of the Fenian Brotherhood, who was at that time the most wanted man in Ireland. My first instinct was to completely deny any suggestion that I had ever helped hunted fugitives and told Jack not to waste Tom Harrington's time coming to see me. My mind was in turmoil after Jack left that evening wondering what I should do. Fortunately my son James came to see me and I told him what Jack Casey had proposed. He had no hesitation in telling me that I must take this opportunity to tell my story as I had witnessed first hand many of the momentous events during my long life. After listening to his advice I realised that he was right and did not object when he went to call on Tom Harrington on my behalf.

Within days Tom came to see me and I was immediately impressed by his courteous manner. Over the coming weeks I relaxed in his company and he let me reminiscence for hours about the old days. He was also very interested in my surviving journals and I agreed to let him use them for the article he was writing. But the strain of losing my son was affecting my health and I was now struggling to rise from the bed each morning. Luckily Tom was a very caring person and with his help my health improved and he managed to finish his article. When his brief account of my life appeared in The Charleville Courier, my cousin Jack Casey was pleasantly surprised at the amount of interest it received and at his urging Tom began to write a series of articles on me. In consequence after asking my permission he decided to write a book which "God Willing" I will live long enough to read.

Lightning Source UK Ltd.
Milton Keynes UK
UKOW06f0913170415

249830UK00001B/13/P